"*A Strategic Understanding of UN Economic Sanctions* takes aid from multiple disciplines to offer a novel assessment of a form of international coercion whose actual harms are often overshadowed by its assumed potential benefits. This study steps out of the noisy debates against or in favor of economic sanctions as an effective tool to punish or edify the deviator and invites a reconsideration of the fundamental premises of such debates. Success or failure of what is often only one step behind military confrontation, the author suggests, is a multi-faceted political phenomenon that cannot be well captured through parsimonious ideas of punishment or correction."

—Hengameh Saberi, *York University*

"This book is an insightful and lucid analysis and evaluation of the role of sanctions in international politics. This is an important read and essential resource for scholars and policy makers interested in the effectiveness of sanctions as a policy tool to bring about change in the behavior of states."

—Muna Ndulo, *Cornell University*

A Strategic Understanding of UN Economic Sanctions

Economic sanctions are increasingly used as a legal, nonmilitary technique of combating abusers of international peace. However it remains unclear how the success or failure of these sanctions is measured. This book examines the seldom-explored United Nations' economic sanctions deliberation process and exposes systematic problems in the measurement of the success or failure of these sanctions. Centering on the key concepts of "peace and security," the author brings the reader's attention to the discrepancies that exist in the process of decision-making, implementation, and evaluation of UN-imposed economic sanctions. She engages international law and development methods to provide proof for the lack of consensus in measures of success and failure, which in turn suggests that sanction implementation on a uniform domestic front are unattainable. This thorough analysis concludes with suggestions for improving the sanctions process, only to clear the path for negating them as a whole and suggest alternative noncoercive measures for mitigating conflict situations and threats to peace and security.

Golnoosh Hakimdavar holds a Ph.D. from the Università degli Studi di Torino, Faculty of Law, Italy, has completed her LL.M. at Cornell Law School and her MBA from Chapman University. Aside from industry experience she has held a number of joint academic appointments, including as visiting scholar at Cornell Law School. Her research focuses on international law and development.

Routledge Advances in International Relations and Global Politics

For a full list of titles in this series, please visit www.routledge.com

79 **World-Regional Social Policy and Global Governance**
New Research and Policy Agendas in Africa, Asia, Europe and Latin America
Edited by Bob Deacon, Maria Cristina Macovei, Luk Van Langenhove and Nicola Yeates

80 **International Relations Theory and Philosophy**
Interpretive Dialogues
Edited by Cerwyn Moore and Chris Farrands

81 **Superpower Rivalry and Conflict**
The Long Shadow of the Cold War on the Twenty-first Century
Edited by Chandra Chari

82 **Coping and Conformity in World Politics**
Hugh C. Dyer

83 **Defining and Defying Organized Crime**
Discourse, Perception and Reality
Edited by Felia Allum, Francesca Longo, Daniela Irrera and Panos A. Kostakos

84 **Federalism in Asia**
India, Pakistan and Malaysia
Harihar Bhattacharyya

85 **The World Bank and HIV/AIDS**
Setting a Global Agenda
Sophie Harman

86 **The "War on Terror" and the Growth of Executive Power?**
A Comparative Analysis
Edited by John E. Owens and Riccardo Pelizzo

87 **The Contested Politics of Mobility**
Borderzones and Irregularity
Edited by Vicki Squires

88 **Human Security, Law and the Prevention of Terrorism**
Andrej Zwitter

89 **Multilayered Migration Governance**
The Promise of Partnership
Edited by Rahel Kunz, Sandra Lavenex and Marion Panizzon

90 **Role Theory in International Relations**
Approaches and Analyses
Edited by Sebastian Harnisch, Cornelia Frank & Hanns W. Maull

91 **Issue Salience in International Relations**
Edited by Kai Oppermann and Henrike Viehrig

92 **Corporate Risk and National Security Redefined**
Karen Lund Petersen

93 **Interrogating Democracy in World Politics**
Edited by Joe Hoover, Meera Sabaratnam and Laust Schouenborg

94 **Globalizing Resistance Against War**
Theories of Resistance and the New Anti-War Movement
Tiina Seppälä

95 **The Politics of Self-Determination**
Beyond the Decolonisation Process
Kristina Roepstorff

96 **Sovereignty and the Responsibility to Protect**
The Power of Norms and the Norms of the Powerful
Theresa Reinold

97 **Anglo-American Relations**
Contemporary Perspectives
Edited by Alan P. Dobson and Steve Marsh

98 **The Emerging Politics of Antarctica**
Edited by Anne-Marie Brady

99 **Genocide, Ethnonationalism, and the United Nations**
Exploring the Causes of Mass Killing Since 1945
Hannibal Travis

100 **Caribbean Sovereignty, Development and Democracy in an Age of Globalization**
Edited by Linden Lewis

101 **Rethinking Foreign Policy**
Edited by Fredrik Bynander and Stefano Guzzini

102 **The Promise and Perils of Transnationalization**
NGO Activism and the Socialization of Women's Human Rights in Egypt and Iran
Benjamin Stachursky

103 **Peacebuilding and International Administration**
The Cases of Bosnia and Herzegovina and Kosovo
Niels van Willigen

104 **The Politics of the Globalization of Law**
Getting from Rights to Justice
Edited by Alison Brysk

105 **The Arctic in International Politics**
Coming in from the Cold
Peter Hough

106 **The Scourge of Genocide**
Essays on Reflection
Adam Jones

107 **Understanding Transatlantic Relations**
Whither the West?
Serena Simoni

108 **India in South Asia**
Domestic Identity Politics and Foreign Policy from Nehru to the BJP
Sinderpal Singh

109 **A Strategic Understanding of UN Economic Sanctions**
International Relations, Law and Development
Golnoosh Hakimdavar

A Strategic Understanding of UN Economic Sanctions

International Relations, Law, and Development

Golnoosh Hakimdavar

NEW YORK AND LONDON

First published 2014
by Routledge
711 Third Avenue, New York, NY 10017

Simultaneously published in the UK
by Routledge
2 Park Square, Milton Park, Abingdon, Oxfordshire OX14 4RN

First issued in paperback 2015

Routledge is an imprint of the Taylor & Francis Group, an informa business

Library of Congress Cataloging-in-Publication Data

Hakimdavar, Golnoosh.
A strategic understanding of UN economic sanctions : international relations, law, and development / Golnoosh Hakimdavar.
pages cm. — (Routledge advances in international relations and global politics)
1. United Nations—Sanctions. 2. Sanctions (International law)
3. Economic sanctions. 4. International relations. I. Title. II. Title: Strategic understanding of United Nations economic sanctions.
KZ6373.H35 2013
341.5'82—dc23
2013005210

ISBN: 978-1-138-94469-5 (pbk)
ISBN: 978-0-415-53822-0 (hbk)

Typeset in Sabon
by Apex CoVantage, LLC

Contents

Illustrations

FIGURES

TABLES

Acknowledgments

Writing this book was made possible by invaluable support and encouragement of colleagues and several institutions. Above all others I would like to thank Prof. Gianmaria Ajani for his continuous guidance and confidence in my work since I began this project in 2007. The faculty and staff of Cornell Law School deserve special mention as I was fortunate to call Cornell home while I completed my dissertation, which later became the basis for this book. Special gratitude must be paid to my professors at Cornell, Robert Hockett and Muna Ndulo for taking the time, whether it was in the halls of Myron Taylor or over the telephone to help me shape my arguments. I would also like to thank Prof. Mitch Lasser whose criticism on the first drafts of this book and his friendship gave me the guidance and strength to follow through with this project. An immeasurable thanks to Dean Charles Cramton, Larry Bush, and Dawne Peacock for their institutional support. Special thanks are also due to my colleagues at CLEI and fellow J.S.D. candidates at Cornell, whose encouragement helped me through the most difficult days of this project. Thank you Toby Goldbach and Cynthia Farid for putting up with my endless emails and text messages as I worked on this book. Thank you to my friends in beautiful Settignano, Italy who provided the calm and quiet I needed while finishing parts of this manuscript. I am also grateful to Hannah Rogers for her careful reading of this book, as I have gone through revisions.

Grateful thanks to my mother for her continuous love and support, my father for his tolerance in moments of confusion, and my sister who is my idol. Of course all responsibility for the final outcome of this work, including any errors, remains mine and mine alone.

1 Introduction

> Not unlike the sorcerers of primitive ages, [great humanitarians] attempt to exorcise social evils by the indefatigable repetition of magic formulae. As the League of Nations was a failure, let us have another League. As the first and second Peace Conferences of the Hague did not succeed, let us have a third one. As arbitration never settled a political conflict which otherwise would have let to war, let us have more arbitration.
>
> —Hans Morgenthau, *Positivism, Functionalism & Int'l Law* (1940)

> Somewhere deep down, even the most dedicated human rights professional knows that what can seem urgent and noble is often also tawdry and voyeuristic. *Our ethics seems impractical, sentimental, inauthentic.* [. . .] Our pragmatism stains our piety.
>
> —David Kennedy, *The Rights of Spring* (2009)

After a decade of sanctions that killed over one million Iraqis, the economic sanctions on Iraq came to a partial end on May 22, 2003, two months after a military attack on the country. The outrage that was left after the sanctions led to extensive inquiry into the use of sanctions as a coercive measure. The consensus reached was that the Iraqi sanctions were not effective and that there was need for a new, more advanced type of sanctions that would not harm the population. Thus, politicians and academics began to introduce a new magic formula, "targeted sanctions," as a new method of dealing with threats to peace. This new form of sanctions targeted the ruling elite and minimized the effect on the general population.

Not long after the end of the Iraqi sanctions, targeted sanctions were imposed on Iran because of Iran's alleged quest towards development of nuclear weapons. However, the disguise of targeted sanctions has slowly begun to smear away as sanctions on Iran have strengthened. In March 2008, the United Nations Security Council (UNSC) imposed Resolution 1803 monitoring the activities of Iranian banks and adding restrictions on trade, an act which was the first step in moving sanctions back in the same direction as the comprehensive Iraqi sanctions. The idea of targeted sanctions is to sanction terrorists or the ruling elite by freezing their assets, travel, and sales of military equipment. As strength of this set of targeted sanctions has increased because of continuous threats to international peace, the sanctions have damaged the Iranian economy to the point that the population is devastated on all sides. United Nations (UN) sanctions imposed on Iran in 2010 were designed to minimize possible transactions that would go through Iranian banks and freeze the funds and assets of the Islamic Republic shipping lines. These sanctions were imposed in conjunction with a bilateral set of sanctions by the United States of America (US) and the European Union (EU), and sanctioned the Iranian central bank. The combination of these sanctions means that Iran can no longer use Society for Worldwide Interbank Financial Telecommunication (SWIFT) to handle their banking transactions. Consequently, transactions cannot occur in and out of the country.[1] The set of increased sanctions on the financial structure of Iran have led to the collapse of the currency. In 2012, *The Guardian* newspaper reported that the Iranian Rial had lost seventy-five percent of its currency in one year, leading to soaring prices for staples such as milk, bread, rice, and vegetables.[2] This form of extreme domestic economic struggle provides evidence that the Iranian targeted sanctions regime is following in the same footsteps as the Iraqi sanctions of the 1990s. The biggest problem with the growth of these sanctions is that the population is left with no real option; their energy depleted by their daily routine to feed themselves, they are left accepting their reality and finding means of dealing with their new fate. The difficulties that have resulted from the Iranian sanctions are so similar and horrifying to the Iraqi sanctions that some policy analysts have questioned whether an airstrike on the country would be less harmful than the long-term impact of current sanctions.[3] Unfortunately, power politics and the narrow national interests of the five permanent members of the Security Council overshadow the concern for improving the ability of the UN system to implement and design effective sanctions.[4]

Though economic sanctions seem to be a sound foreign policy tool, which carries a tacit intention that the frustrated population will rise up against their regime to bring them to compliance with the demands of the UN, the reality is much different. The impact of sanctions on the everyday life of the population creates a societal division. The society realizes that basic necessities of life are not available for common use. Those more fortunate have family and friends smuggle in cancer medicine, vitamins, and other medical supplies and equipment, while the less fortunate and the larger segment of the population are quieted by government propaganda. This not only divides the population, it creates a world of *them* and *us*. *Them*, are the sanction imposers, who, the local native government is able to tactfully convince the population, are the source of all of the social and economic problems of the state. *Us*, are the followers of the native government, who will protect this deceived population no matter how strong the external force of sanctions.

A young population that grows up living under economic sanctions looks at the world and the society around it through a crude lens of economic sanction, targets, and senders, which carry the constant questions of power struggles in international relations. Power differences defined by examples such as the US and China's "upbeat" outlook for "unprecedented measures" for United Nations driven sanctions on North Korea and on the other hand North Korea's belligerent retaliation.[5] These external power conflicts and looming sanctions work as tacit stimuli to increase the internal societal gap of target states as they alienate the population from the world, creating internal political and economic elite.

In the 2000's as sanctions resurface as the best foreign policy tool, with the same rigor as the early 1990's and the beginning of the Iraqi sanctions, I began my inquiry into this topic. In the past decade, there has been a great deal of important and innovative work on the effectiveness of sanctions and their political, societal, and legal influence in particular with respect to the ten years of sanctions on Iraq. The attempts made by this book are to showcase these works and introduce a more methodical approach to the presentation of sanctions in the disciplines of international relations, law, and development. Through this approach I attempt to answer questions beyond the effectiveness of sanctions but more directed to the determination of success. Success, which can be measured through a spectrum of perspectives, will be discussed in this book from the two sides of, *them* and *us*.

1.1 SANCTIONS STUDY AND THE CURRENT PARADIGM

In the past seven years, economic sanctions have generated ever increasing scholarly and policy interests. This is in part due to the proliferation of sanctions schemes since the collapse of the USSR, end of the Cold War, and the increased tracking of the negative effects of sanctions, which are documented more aggressively with the use of new technologies. Whereas before, documenting effects on civilian populations meant extensive fieldwork, data collection, and analysis, new technologies—such as satellite imagery, and improved public health statistics—have made measurements of "human effects" possible. Improved statistical methods have helped analysts determine some of the effects of given sanctions schemes on infant mortality rates, decreases in gross domestic product (GDP) per capita, and lower literacy rates. In the international, humanitarian, and human rights community, these advances are welcomed as they provide Nongovernmental Organizations (NGOs) and advocates with a more tangible cause-effect analysis, which they can then use to lobby policymakers. Thus, the role of the NGOs has proven to be crucial in bringing the negative causes of sanctions to the forefront of the sanctions debate. In fact, NGOs were instrumental in reporting the negative consequences of Iraqi sanctions to the United Nations Security Council (UNSC) members during the late 1990's and early 2000's. Notwithstanding this information, however, the management of the Iraqi sanctions or mismanagement of these sanctions resulted in extensive inquiries into the use of funds and manner in which food was distributed to the population.

Despite the outcry from the human rights community and progressive organizations, sanctions remain a potent tool in our policy-makers' political imaginations. The threat of sanctions or strengthening of existing sanctions has been escalating in the past years as the world has begun a battle against terrorism. As I have made changes to this book, the sanctions threat has been so constant that I found myself continually making additional revisions to chapters of this book, while the main underlying problems with sanctions and inquiries that I have raised here remain out of spotlight. The US, a UN member with the greatest influence and most interest in sanctions, has continued to push for increased economic sanctions. Since 2008, US Secretary of State, Hillary Clinton, has threatened not one but several nations with economic sanctions. The extent of these sanctions was evident from the rhetoric surrounding Assistant Secretary of State of Defense and Research Philip Goldberg's comments after his visit to Asia. The Associated Press reported in 2009 that, "Philip Goldberg, who had just returned from Asia, told reporters after meeting privately with the Security Council committee monitoring the implementation of sanctions against North Korea that there is 'a very strong commitment' not just by China and the US but by all 192 UN member states to enforce the '*unprecedented measures*.'"[6] On August 2, 2009, *The New York Times* reported that the Obama administration was contemplating a new round of sanctions against Iran for failure to comply with demands regarding its nuclear program.[7] Additionally in 2009, days after the first threat of Iranian sanctions, Secretary of State Hillary Clinton threatened Eritrea with economic sanctions for allegedly aiding Somalian opposition fighters.[8] Granted, the sanctions conversation has gone both ways. At the same time that America threatened new rounds of sanctions against Iran or North Korea, sensible policymakers also made inroads towards easing existing sanctions schemes, such as the sanctions against Syria[9] and Sudan.[10]

Although, it is easier to see the negative impact of sanctions, their use as a sensible foreign policy tool if applied correctly must not be overlooked. In this book I provide an evaluation of sanctions, exposing practical shortcoming of sanctions regimes. I proceed with the assumptions that a more directed, controlled, and procedural sanctions process, can apply the same technologies which are used in exposing negative effect of sanctions, which could lead to their more successful use in practice. Though unilateral sanctions remain important in the political atmosphere, this is primarily a book about an understanding of political affairs surrounding UN economic sanctions and how international law and domestic law coincide in maneuvering through sanctions. Given the prominence of this issue on the world political stage, much has been written on the humanitarian, economic, and legal facets of various sanctions regimes. This book attempts to break new ground by proposing a theoretical method of looking at sanctions—rooted in part in case analysis (historical and current) from a legal and economic perspective—through which particular trade sanctions schemes may be shown as economically inefficient and contradictory to the economic interests of the proponent of the given sanctions regime, as well as the global economy.

1.2 TYRANNY OF SANCTION EVOLUTION

The statement of UN Secretary General Ban Ki-moon on April 30, 2007 identifies the key challenges posed before the UN in crafting and implementing sanctions regimes. His comments bear repeating,

> Sanctions should include *carrots along with sticks*—not only threats, but inducements to elicit compliance. The target must understand what actions it is expected to take. And partial or full compliance should be met by reciprocal steps from the Council, such as easing or lifting sanctions as appropriate.
>
> There is ample evidence that sanctions have enormous potential to contribute to the maintenance of international peace and security when used not as an end in themselves, but in support of a holistic conflict resolution approach that includes prevention, mediation, peacekeeping, and peacebuilding. We should welcome the evolution of sanctions that has taken place: *where once they were an often blunt and unfocused instrument, today they have become a more precise tool.* Their increased use attests to their growing power. *Our challenge is to ensure their credibility and legitimacy in the eyes of the world as unassailable.* Only by our combined efforts can we hope to realize the full promise of sanctions in the interest of global peace and security.[11]

We can extrapolate the following theses and underlying assumptions from this summary and the detailed report of the UN Security Council Working Group on General Issues of Sanctions:

1. *Sanctions work*—they remain effective foreign policy tools;
2. Current sanctions schemes are "*precise tools*";
3. UN continues to *increase* the use of sanctions;
4. UN is working to boost *credibility/legitimacy* of sanctions.

These four theses are set as the analytical basis used to establish trends in the process of imposing, implementation, and removal of sanctions. Analyzing and unraveling each of these assumptions, particularly in the language of credibility is essential for the policy makers and students of economic sanctions.

When we look at the actual implementation of sanctions we begin to see patterns of failure, which touch upon broader issues of power and politics. The current dominant paradigm admits shortcomings in its approach and practical implementation of sanctions. But these shortcomings are seen as minor faults, which can be "fine-tuned," ironed out, and resolved by simply developing more precise targeting techniques.[12] John Bolton, the US representative to the UN referred to this need for invigorated efforts to "fine tune" sanctions several times as he responded to questions posed by a US Senate investigation committee inquiring about the Iraqi sanctions administration and the Oil-for-Food program.[13] Bolton's comments centered on oversight and accountability, as he criticized the UN's administration of these sanctions, and elaborated on the lack of current functional oversight in the administration of sanctions.[14] Similar discussion about administration of Oil-for-Food and more broadly the Iraqi sanctions were further intensified after the humanitarian impact of ten years of comprehensive UN sanctions against Iraq became clear and led to the creation of *targeted* sanctions. While it is true that more precise targeting eliminates many of the grave externalities of sanctions, I challenge the assumption that sanctions will become effective foreign policy tools once this is accomplished and suggest that without resolving the major underlying theoretical and institutional problems of sanctions, no sanction scheme can be effective. Fixed within the sanctions process is the need for clear implementation of any sanctions regime. However, as we will discuss in the following pages, the implementation process remains unclear and ad hoc.

1.3 IRAQI SANCTIONS AND PAUL CONLON PAPERS

Since the formation of the UN, no sanctions regime has been more far reaching than the Iraqi sanctions. For this book, I have relied on a series of papers and documents currently held at the University of Iowa. These declassified documents and material from the Iraqi Sanctions Committee were Dr. Paul Conlon's personal collection of primary materials from when he served as the former deputy secretary of the Iraq Sanctions Committee.[15] The Iraqi sanctions were the most comprehensive in the history of UN-imposed sanctions. Although ten years have passed since the sanctions were removed after a military attack on the country, which overthrew Saddam Hussein's government, the results and side effects of the sanctions are slowly surfacing. The scandals of the Oil-for-Food program only became known and investigated after the US military attack on Iraq in 2003 and the removal of sanctions. The scope of these scandals that led to the resignation of several UN officials and wide criticism of UN became evident in 2005. Thus, though ten years have passed, these sanctions are still relevant if not crucial to the study of sanctions. To learn from the mismanagement of these sanctions would help restore a form of trust in the UN. At the outset the lessons learned from Iraqi sanction's impact on the population and their effectiveness seemed to be plentiful, unfortunately, however any lessons learned appear to have been short-lived as threats of comprehensive sanctions on Iran are now more prevalent than ever. The continued US request for China's and Russia's cooperation with respect to furthering UN sanctions on Iran is to strengthen sanctions to the same extent as comprehensive sanctions.[16] Keeping in mind that Iraqi sanctions ended with a costly military attack on the country, further inquiry into the Iraqi sanctions would assist policy makers in their future sanction decisions. The result of this inquiry would hopefully limit future excessive harm through sanctions and give policymakers a distinct process to follow. In doing this, I have also relied on primary material, which also include UNSC and UNGA resolutions and Charter, and the work of current scholars as my secondary source.

Dr. Paul Conlon, whose papers, communications, and comments I rely on, was originally a lecturer and researcher at various Swedish and German universities and later an analyst and consultant in the oil industry. From 1988 to 1995, he worked for the United Nations, originally for the Centre against Apartheid, later for the sanctions branch of the Security Council. From 1990 to 1995, he held various posts within the UNSC Sanctions Committee for Iraq. After his separation from the UN, Dr. Conlon deposited his personal papers, including his manuscript and notes for his book *United Nations Sanctions Management: A Case Study of the Iraq Sanctions Committee 1990–1994* with the University of Iowa.[17]

In an interview with a former UN official I was asked of the importance of the Iraqi sanctions for my research and the use of documents provided by an academic who was not the chair of the Iraqi sanctions committee but merely a *mid-level official*. This question from the outset came across somewhat uneasy for me. Why would there be so little value given to the work of those who are actually on the field and are directly observing the consequences of sanctions? A midranking official would have been at the center of communication and the correspondence that he had would have been directly relevant to the implementation of sanctions. In fact the importance of Dr. Conlon's book, position, and the papers is highly valuable in that it is much less biased and less formulated with a political agenda than higher ranked individuals. Such papers in their raw form provide us with an understanding of the sanctions committee that would not be possible through the interviews of high-ranking officials representing their country's political position. It should be noted that the skepticism that was voiced against use of these materials opens room for questioning the value given to the work done by UN employees. Considering that UN mismanagement is not a new topic to international political literature, it may be even necessary for the UN officials to pay more attention to the work of academics who are actively working with the sanctions committees. In effect, for the purpose of establishing a working framework for sanctions implementation, the work of those who are implementing the sanctions, academics who dedicate their research to this topic and NGOs would provide a clear, unbiased method for evaluating and exposing institutional problems within the UN and sanction implementation process.

1.3.1 Crossing Disciplines: Law, International Relations, and Development

The sanctions discourse presents a triangular connection between state relations, domestic law in administration of sanctions, and the sanctioned society. From one side, sanctions are a result of statutes, rules, treaties, and international legal customs, while on the other side they represent influential power and policy tools that are enforced by institutional means and have a direct impact on the society where they are enforced.

Initiating this discussion with international law, the study of economic sanction particularly international UN sanctions cannot be limited to one social science discipline as sanction theory and practice is in essence a multidisciplinary study. It would be limiting not to examine the legal complexities of implementing international sanctions on a domestic front, while the influence of international relations and power conflicts rises to the sanctions; surface, particularly since the discretionary enforcement powers of UN member states remains evident throughout the sanction process. I have tried to pull from law and development, political science, and international relations literature and theories to provide a more comprehensive picture of sanctions and the sanction process. I do hope that the cross of disciplines and the integrated approaches used are of value to specialists in each field.

International law method commonly refers to the "conceptual apparatus or framework—a theory of international law—to the concrete problems faced in the international community."[18] Method here refers to a systematic framework for understanding international economic sanctions by accepting the rules and treaties that govern economic sanctions. Thus to arrive at this framework, we must begin by the analysis of the governing treaties, customs, and relevant cases—the so-called "hard rules" of international law.[19] In this book as a foundational matter, statutes, rules, and policymaker's statements should be interpreted at face value. This is the classic positivist perspective, which observes law as "a unified system of rules that, according to most variants, emanate from state will."[20] Therefore, there is a reciprocal relationship between the state will and the formation of international rules. Even though it derives authority from formal sources, positivism maintains a normative and prescriptive function. Positivist scholars, practitioners, and judges can rely on universal expressions of state consent (treaty law) *and* their own vision of what international law should be to increasingly guide policy, so long as their vision finds "sufficient expression in legal form."[21]

The above formulation of international law has led, quite correctly, to charges of indeterminacy.[22] In the context of sanctions, indeterminacy is highly pronounced. The concept of sanctions lies at the center of the debate concerning the existence of international law (*i.e.*, issues of enforcement, supranational bodies, *etc.*). "However, as important as it may be, the concept remains legally indeterminate: both common practice and commentators describe some consequences of the violations of international law as sanctionism but they are not designated by that name in any text considered authoritative in terms of general international law."[23] If states, in order to impose their "vision of what international law should be" only have to ground their vision in "sufficient expression in legal form," then states can successfully advance contradictory positions (depending on their foreign policy objectives) because legal form is malleable—thorough analysts can back up any position with reasonable legal argument.[24] Though critical scholars such as David Kennedy and Martti Koskenniemi see indeterminacy as internal to the law itself: "The legal argument, inexorably, and quite predictably, allow[s] the defense of whatever position while simultaneously being constrained by a rigorously formal language."[25] It is within this language of international law and the UN that the contradictions of international law, are particularly evident in the sanctions discourse. Returning to Kofi Annan's statement earlier, why for instance, if there is, in the words of UN Secretary General, "ample evidence that sanctions do have an enormous potential to contribute to the maintenance of international peace and security"[26] is the UN challenged "*to ensure their credibility and legitimacy in the eyes of the world as unassailable*"? In other words, does not the fact that UN seeks to convince the world of the legitimacy of sanctions attest to the fact that they are not credible foreign policy tools? Critical legal studies open up these tautologies, emancipating us from blind adherence to formal legal rules, and an uncritical assumption of policymakers' good intentions. In the words of Martti Koskenniemi,

> None of this is to say that lawyers are, or should become, manipulative cynics—apart from the sense that *it is a crucial part of professional competence for the lawyer to be able to construct her argument so as to make it credible to her targeted audience*. Outside the relationship between the argument and the context, however, there was no external "method," no "theory" that could have proven the correctness of one's reasoning, the standpoint that one was called upon to take as part of one's professional practice.[27]

Does the UN have credibility/legitimacy before the world community, states, and individuals in imposing sanctions? If not, to what extent is the UN's attempt to project credibility a mask for a deeper theoretical/ideological instability? Is the UN system—and its underlying notions of international law—guilty of silencing voices of communities, stakeholders, and informal indigenous understandings about the world and global relations? Does the "formal predictability and substantive indeterminacy" of legal form operate to disadvantage minorities and weaken states who are often unrepresented in the methodological debates or purposely disenfranchised in international institution building? Social theorists like Roberto Unger view law "[a]s the result of the resolution of social conflicts and not some deduction from universal principles that rational people accept."[28] Whether based on class, property rights, or simply the defects of human nature, conflict exists; power conflicts between powerful firms, institutions, and states are an everyday feature of the contemporary global order. Thus the sanctions debate must provide an understanding of the interplay between power, politics, and legal institutions. The study of the complex patterns of what Koskenniemi calls "*status quo* legitimation," is key to understanding why sanctions are imposed against Third World states along geographic lines all too often resembling former colonial maps.[29]

These two approaches mentioned above, positivism and critical legal studies, straggle in the two extremes of the contemporary legal understanding of the sanctions paradigm. This pattern only presents one side of the sanctions equation, the complex implementation processes which states and institutions take in sanctions deliberations still remains unexplored. This is where international law and international relations correspond—particularly realism and new institutionalist theories of international law, which posit that political realities motivate and constrain state behavior. I am indebted to the work of Kenneth Abbott for this strain of analysis.[30] Likewise, my understanding of international law and institutions has been influenced by the new approaches to international law, such as TWAIL—Third World approaches to international law, popularized by Antony Anghie, Nathaniel Berman, and B.S. Chimni. This approach forms my analysis with respect to the power discrepancies in sanctions deliberations.

Each approach is a way of looking at international law, the UN, and economic sanctions, and understanding what they are and what they should be. Nevertheless, it is vitally important to examine the "big questions" of international law in discussing sanctions; indeed, it is impossible not to. In the words of recognized United Nations scholar and professor of international law at the Graduate Institute of International Studies in Geneva, Vera Gowlland-Debbas,

> As international lawyers know, the concept of sanctions lies at the heart of fundamental debates on the nature and function of international law. Sanctions are of course linked to the general problem of compliance inherent in the prescriptive nature of any legal order.[31]

The practice of sanctions raises even broader questions than compliance. Much like the *practice* of death penalty in the US, where as reported by Amnesty International states execute disproportionate number of defendants for killing white victims[32], raises questions much deeper than simply the issue of morality or efficacy of the death penalty as a deterrent. The practice of UN sanctions forces us to look at the possibly racist, discriminatory, or at the least unreflective way Western ethics and law operate to perpetuate longstanding patterns of colonial exploitation.

The above approaches shed important light on the purpose and function of the analytical method used here. They allow us to answer why the analysis of multilateral sanctions regimes is important and how the UN's reform of the sanctions apparatus and institutional logic could benefit institutions and societies. It is then important to take concrete analytical conclusions and ultimately turn them into normative policy recommendations, which suffer less from the defects, in the existing framework. "Method," metaphorically speaking, is window wash, allowing us to pierce through the stained glass of the way things are—obfuscated by custom, formalism, tradition—and to suggest original solutions.

Ultimately I am using this interdisciplinary approach to reach a policy proposal for the sanctioning bodies. The legal ramification of sanctions in international law is accounted for to ensure that policy proposals are actually in line with economic sanctions. In order to analyze the practical consequences of sanctions, it is necessary to diverse sanction case studies. Case studies allow not only for the analysis of the underlying reasons for the imposition of sanctions in a given case but also answer questions about specific Security Council decision-making processes and the domestic implementation of sanctions.

Thus, this book will fundamentally focus on the Security Council's activities, decision-making process, and the resulting resolutions that lead to economic sanctions. Although Security Council resolutions can vary in their scope, the focus of this book is on measures that are directed at minimizing threats to peace and other preventative tools against acts of aggression between states, in particular economic sanctions. The complexity of economic sanctions as a preventive tool is that they are deployed by the Security Council but are enforced independently by each member state. Additionally, although sanctions were intended to be preventive measures, they have evolved into coercive weapons of foreign policy or techniques for control of state behavior. Indeed, sanctions have been shown to be a driving force in what has become known as modern "economic warfare."[33] In the past thirty years the effectiveness of economic sanctions as a foreign policy tool has been questioned in numerous scholarly and policy works including UN documents. The question of effectiveness itself is multidimensional as it can be looked at through different lenses. Is effectiveness determined by the extent of economic loss that is inflicted on a sanctioned country or is it determined by a change to the country's policy? Or, are we able to quantify the effects of particular sanctions schemes on third parties? There is no question that economic sanctions are a form of foreign policy, but has the current practice of imposing and enforcing sanctions given us the data needed to determine effectiveness?

In other words, to what extent do we need to modernize/humanize our dominant theories of international law to reflect the negative consequences of economic sanctions? How do we reconcile the sovereign rights of nations to impose unilateral sanctions (trade embargos) with those nations' respective international responsibilities, such as those found in the UN Charter and in various other international treaties and emerging customs?

Overall, methods of sanction deployment, and their actual implementation remain the subject of continued attention among international relations and international law scholars. If as the late Harold Lasswell, a prime mover in the "behavioral revolution" and late professor of political science at University of Chicago[34] defines, politics is an adversarial process of decisions about distribution of value, then will the power complex continue to dominate the sanctions process.[35] Thus an effective sanction is only achieved when another state is controlled through power. Following this logic, the role of an international institution is diluted in intrastate power struggles, whether economic or military. However, by virtue, the role of the UN as an international institution armed with all of its member states is to create a balance by diminishing the power differences between states. In order to bring the struggles of the conflict between a member-empowered institution and the multitude of member state objectives to the forefront of the sanctions discussion, it is necessary to look at the process not the anticipated result of sanctions or their effectiveness. To direct our attention to the role of the UN in the sanctions process, and away from the adversarial result, I try to focus less on answering the question of effectiveness. Instead, I attempt to refocus our attention on the implementation problems that arise when an international organization is charged with unifying member states that have their own political and economic objectives. Focusing on how the institution's goals influence domestic policy changes and increased economic pressure on all parties involved would inevitably decrease discontent and at times retaliation.

1.4 CHAPTER LAYOUT

1.4.1 Understanding the Sanctions Convention

Although the past twenty years can be recalled as two decades of sanctions, where media attention, political discussions, and legal implementations of sanctions have become a focal point of interest, there still seems to be little consensus on the specific classification and meaning of sanctions. In order to grasp a better understanding of sanctions we need to evaluate them not with a result-driven lens but by searching through the parts to find trends, discrepancies, and ambiguities in the processes of UN-imposed sanctions. In the words of John Bolton there are three areas where the UN is lacking: responsiveness, transparency, and effectiveness.[36] The problem does not begin with the UN administration of the sanctions, but with the sanction itself. How can the UN effectively implement a nontransparent process that requires responsiveness of all member states with separate political agendas?

In order to proceed and even evaluate the above questions it is important that we set a uniform understanding of economic sanctions. Although this book is centered on UN economic sanctions, the extent of unilateral sanctions (particularly US sanctions) needs to be recognized. The second chapter of this book sets the basic definitions to be used throughout this book. Since UN sanctions are in essence the result of political decisions of member states, looking at multilateral and unilateral sanctions side-by-side creates continuity in the foundation of UN sanctions. Chapter two outlines the core arguments advanced by the proponents of sanctions in favor of sanctions as an economic foreign policy tool. The distinction between sanctions as a foreign policy tool or in David Baldwin's words, economic statecraft, and sanctions as a means to an end sets the basis for what is explained in the following chapters. This distinction defines whether the possible political agenda of the imposing states is the driver of sanction, if sanctions are imposed for lack of better options or lack of military or financial resources. To see the spread between the underlying reasons for sanctions we must also answer the questions of what are sanctions in theory and how do they work in practice? Do UN member states succumb to the pressure of more powerful states in imposing sanctions on neighboring countries? In proposing a sanction decision does identity or status of the state matter?

If we look at the law and policy literature, we can confidently begin by stating that there exists blatant *ambiguity* in the policy discourse concerning sanctions.[37] This is both a problem of form (terminology) as well as function (substantive decisions). Decisions are made to sanction a country, but comprehensive economic analyses are either neglected, or purposely withheld from the policy-makers' purview.[38] When used to promote an unarticulated foreign policy agenda, altogether different perspectives arise as well. Without a logical and systematic method for estimating the net economic impact of sanctions, policy-makers are left to their own devices, resorting to decision-making based on faulty and/or incomplete information, factors of political expediency, and like bias. Thus it is their political agenda based on incomplete information that leads their decisions. This political process in practice is further complicated when the sanction imposers are multilateral, not through the UN structure but through blocks of individual states such as the EU. The EU's mandate to impose trade sanctions would impact each EU member state separately and at a different level. A systemic comparative analysis of US sanctions legislation and EU sanctions legislation and legal cases will be conducted to provide a uniform understanding of sanctions. Such an understanding is necessarily historical as it studies the effects of former sanctions schemes and the evolution of sanctions theory more generally over the course of the last fifty years, particularly with the end of the Cold War. Drawing on a comparative law and economics methodology,[39] this book will analyze the legal issue of trade sanctions (through the prism of both public international law and domestic legislation). Moreover, in effort to adequately evaluate the politicized dimensions of economic or trade sanctions on a given country, we will look at economic sanctions through a broader critical law and development discourse.[40] Chapter four will cover most of this analytical-descriptive work and a set structure for addressing implementation of sanctions will be proposed.

1.4.2 Legality and a Uniform Approach to Sanctions

The sanctions discussion is extensive and varied. Though there are general understandings about what economic sanctions are and the UN Charter's articles relevant to imposing sanctions, there are definitional issues that must be addressed to create a uniform understanding of sanctions. In this book I seek to correct the ambiguities of the present approaches in understanding sanctions. Because of the political nature of sanctions and the universality of these measures there are simple terms such as "threats to peace" and "security" that are given as understood widely. Chapter three of this book opens with a discussion of these terms in order to either dissect a relevant meaning based on the UN Charter or to leave alternate meanings exposed enough that readers can form their own understanding.

In dealing with a topic as relevant and politically charged as economic sanctions, it becomes important to address definitional problems. In chapter three terms such as "peace," "politicization," "efficiency," and "humanitarian consequences" in third parties, and the relevant normative judgments are identified and discussed.

In discussing humanitarian concerns, special attention is given to avoid conflating humanitarian objectives; I try to steer away from posing any value judgments and urge the reader to view such notes in economic terms. In other words, in writing about bed nets, the reader shall value the bed nets in economic terms and take into account the costs associated with the bed nets and economic benefit in minimizing diseases rather than as tools protecting groups of children from malaria-carrying mosquitoes. The reason for such analysis is to extend beyond the superficial possible judgment about sanctions and to refocus the outlook on factors that can open the logic behind the decision-making process, considering the extent of cost for all parties involved. It should not be overlooked that by incorporating third-party victims of sanctions the extent of the analysis is broadened exponentially, as it can include states, NGOs, corporations, local businesses, etc. Therefore to keep a realistic approach the discussion must be limited to immediate third parties with direct influence, such as the target's immediate trade partners, bordering countries, and multinational corporations. Furthermore building on the issues that states face in monitoring sanctions' implementation and the costs of third parties, I emphasize the current problems with measuring success of economic sanctions.

Although controversial, sanctions are without doubt "legal" in the sense that they are a fixture of international law, and are imposed by written acts of international and domestic bodies with authority and general consent of the governed.[41] Nevertheless, the legality of sanctions has been questioned from several perspectives.[42] In the context of the choice between direct coercive measures and other means, sanctions provide a method that on the surface would cause minimal societal harm. Though sanctions are claimed to be used as a legal, non-coercive measure, the long term harm and side effect of economic sanctions are analogous to those of conventional force. "Weapons of mass destruction aside, the difference is not so clearly wrought when one compares the effects of sanctions with the effects of conventional force. Economic and trade sanctions have the potential to devastate a civilian population and to rock the economic and political stability of a developing state."[43] International law scholars point out that lawful sanctions may become illegal if applied for too long without achieving meaningful results.[44] From an effects-perspective, commentators have reasoned that sanctions that are "unilateral in theory but multilateral in practice" may violate international law when imposed without the agreement of the Security Council, just as would the use of force in most circumstances.[45] Likewise, the Security Council may violate customary international law in dereliction of its own charter when it imposes unduly harsh sanctions, though this argument suffers from obvious circularity.[46] The principles of customary law at issue would be the principles of sovereignty and the corollary principle of nonintervention.

For purposes of this book, the legal analysis focuses on the legality of multilateral sanctions and the intersection of domestic sanctions legislation with international law. I shall be looking at the UN Charter and outlining the dominant arguments of the "legality" discourse in Chapter three.

1.4.3 State Responsibility and the Sanctions Process

It is not enough to simply declare that sanctions do not work or will not work. The key is formulating the correct benchmarks and understanding the variables involved. Any model of sanctions must also strive to understand and account for past behavior and be able to predict state action. Why do sanctioned countries, for instance, continue with the same patterns? Logic would dictate that either the country is not affected by the sanctions or that the internal well-being of populations in such societies is not of central concern to the ruling elite. Of course the country could face actual financial or economic loss with subsequent impact on the population but this loss may not be directed at the target country's political decision-makers. The target country is one side of the coin; on the other side stands the sender. Gary C. Hufbauer has shown that in unilateral US-imposed sanctions the negative impact of sanctions on trade is actually quantifiable. However when we move to UN-imposed sanctions, measuring impact on the sender becomes much more unrealistic as the number of actors involved multiplies and ambiguity exists as to the exact costs on the UN itself. In Chapter five of this book these ambiguities will be discussed by looking at sanctions in a systematic manner. By identifying the different actors involved in sanction implementation, the road can be paved for understanding the multiplicity of costs associated to sanction implementation, which can consequently lead to sanction failure. Chapter five sets the undertone for understanding the intricacies that exist in political and trade relations and consequently the difficulties that arise in expecting UN member states to self-impose trade cutoffs with a specific target state.

In many instances it is power conflicts in target countries (mostly civil war between rival power centers), which cause the imposition of sanctions in the first place. In conflict zones, local elites, bureaucrats, and private agents pursue their own interests and not the preference of principle; they may choose the principle closest to their self-interest. To counterweigh the power of local actors, the UN ostensibly responds with greater power, in the form of collective action of states. But multilateral sanctions—simply by nature of being collective acts—raise a host of problems, from uncertainty costs to resource allocation (determinations of who pays for enforcement and who benefits from whatever spoils may become available) to problems of enforcement. Even if Judge Guido Calabresi is correct that "[l]aw is not only concerned with reduction of cost, [but] is fundamentally concerned with shaping tastes"[47] how significant are economic considerations in sanctions deliberations? And do sanctions ultimately shape political taste and preferences between states?

In academic literature there are no more consensuses in regards to the effectiveness of sanctions, than in regards to theory. Commentators and critics observe that UN sanctions generally fail yet the UN maintains that they are effective. However, neither side can propose a unified measure for success or failure. This confusion weighs in favor of critics who point to the shifting nature of goals and measures of success as the very reason why sanctions cannot be understood as anything other than a projection of power by stronger states. Then, there is the issue of avoidance, sanctions-dodging, and adaptation over time. After all, if target states have a self-interest for which they will strive and the ability to adapt, they may be able to withstand sanctions over a prolonged period of time. Like a criminal who breaks the law but is able to avoid capture, target states suspected of violating international human rights, for instance, are branded criminals before the international community. But what is the cost of the alleged crimes to the "world community"? And do externalities of sanctions enforcement and impact on third parties outweigh the benefit of ridding the world of the offending regime? The debates range far into economics, social theory, international relations, and sociology. For risk of straying too wide, I limit the scope of analysis to international relations, law and development as I discuss these topics in Chapter Five.

1.4.4 Politicization of Sanctions

The wording of UN resolutions authorizing sanctions along with related correspondence between target states and the UN Secretary General provides a direct glimpse into the actual decision-making processes (most importantly, timing) and can help us answer general questions such as the stated objectives for sanctions. Other facts such as dates and events that precede sanctions are the basis for more specific questions such as the timeframe involved in imposing sanctions. It should be noted that for the purpose of this book I will be grouping embargos and travel bans together with economic sanctions, as although they fall into modern categories as targeted sanctions, they all have an effect on the domestic economy of target states.

Considering that states with strongest economic ties to the target state would not welcome imposing trade sanctions, we should take into consideration the decision-making process leads to UN sanction resolutions. So, how is this decision-making done within the UN? Is there concern in regards to current existing sanctions, and the length of time they have been imposed? Is there consideration given to the parallel sanctions in neighboring states? What does broader criticism of the UN and more specifically the Security Council and their success in clearing the path for worldwide peace tell us about the sanctions debate?

In formulating a response to the above questions, success must be differentiated from effectiveness. Since accurate data, particularly with respect to the impact of sanctions on public health, general social infrastructure, etc. is notoriously difficult to gather,[48] a framework with predictive potential must take into consideration what can be referred to as soft factors such as rationality of sanctioned state or unintended consequences. Each of these soft factors are expounded on in Chapter five.

Ultimately, the main question for policy-makers of the sanctioning country is whether the proposed economic sanctions will work in weakening the economy of the sanctioned country. Chapter six provides evidence that economic sanctions that are placed on a country are not successful in achieving the stated objectives, as stated objectives are ill defined. I argue that the ambiguities in the sanctions process and irrationality of actors involved leads to a snowball effect of sanctions with no specific measures for success or failure. The case studies presented in this chapter illustrate that business concerns find a way around economic sanctions, leading to unbalanced economies and the creation of underground, or "black" markets; on the other hand, unintended consequences of the sanctions flow to individuals and firms unable to cope with them, resulting in widespread loss of productivity. For most political scientists political processes are defined in terms of power or influence, that is, situations in which some people change the actions or predispositions of other people in some way.[49] Power and power politics is a central concept in sanctions analysis. Throughout the book, I will be looking at changes within the sanctioning states as transfer of legal and extralegal control, which is one manifestation of power dynamics. This is a central concept and in fact the reason that states do not want to give up control over past colonies or markets. Power projection and protection leads to the creation of target countries, which in turn leads to sanctions. These themes—a country's thirst for control of a target state's resources and fight for continuous control despite sanctions, the concept of near-war, threats of sanctions—will be explored throughout the book. Chapter six will set the background to evaluate the missing connections between the power of sanctions states and the probably continuation of neocolonial policies.[50]

Finally, in Chapter seven policy proposal for a more efficient sanctions regime is discussed. These proposals and their political nature are to demonstrate the deeper institutional changes necessary before any state can be sanctioned by a process which is not designed to successfully achieve outcomes.

From the outset, the goal of this book is to explore, in theoretical terms, the efficacy of economic sanctions as a foreign policy tool. Although a brief historical analysis of sanctions will be given, the main goal remains in the modern use of sanctions. I try to stay away from explaining the myriad proffered reasons for the existence of economic sanctions and it is not my intention to agree or disagree with any sanction schemes currently in force against any country but rather to approach sanctions on their functionality. I urge the readers of this work to keep in mind the pragmatic points I raise in this book and not read for normative or prescriptive *ethical* conclusions. In this book, an attempt is made to try to refocus academic attention on certain underlying factors, which militate against the use of economic sanctions as an efficient and effective foreign policy tool. An anticipated result of such an inquiry is a more scrupulous evaluation of the intended outcome of economic sanctions, both as a result of taking into account the international organization or sanctioning country's motives and expected results, and also as a result of a more carefully measured and more accurate response from the sanctioned state in response to the sanctions. In short, in this book I urge the readers, whether students of international relations or policy-makers to move away from a simplistic analysis to a more complex, multipronged approach to sanctions deliberations.

2 UN / Unilateral Sanctions Regimes

> Until researchers agree on which questions to ask and on how to seek answers, the sanctions debate is unlikely to produce useful policy-relevant knowledge.
>
> —David A. Baldwin[1]

In 1944, representatives of the Allies after World War II (WWII) gathered for over a one-month period at Dumbarton Oaks in Washington D.C., planning the first stages of what would become the United Nations (UN), an institution with the goals of preventing future war and maintaining peace and security in the world. The UN's predecessor, the League of Nations, was seen as a failed organization as WWII came to an end and atrocities of this war were settled throughout the world. The League of Nations was founded after World War I (WWI) to preserve peace and security; however, WWII provided the proof to see the League as a failed organization.

The UN was formed with a more extensive reach than the League of Nations and became stronger as the number of member states increased over time. Although the UN is structured as an imposing organization armed with the task of managing intracountry conflict, under the UN Charter a country's sovereign rights are to remain protected. In fact the UN would engage in only preventive measures of war, giving each state its mutual independence.[2] This independence and the difficult task of managing conflict are administered through the establishment of diverse institutional organs. More specifically the UN has grown to include five primary organs, of which the Security Council is responsible for selecting measures aimed at dealing with any threat to peace and security.

What exactly are sanctions, and more broadly, how do sanctions work as a practical matter? This question must be distinguished from the related question of whether sanctions actually work. This topic is covered in Chapter six. The current chapter, as well as Chapter three, outlines the existing institutional structure and framework of sanctions. This chapter seeks to answer this question by outlining the current sanctions regime, providing a history of sanctions, introducing the taxonomy and classification of sanctions, and presenting a review of the most influential scholarship on this issue.

2.1 A DEFINITION OF SANCTIONS

A commonly accepted definition of the term "sanctions" refers to an unarmed means of economic coercion for persuading a nation to change its behavior or to penalize that nation for violating international law.[3] These violations could also be identified as deviation from self-imposed treaties signed by the state. The sanctions are subsequently imposed to enforce the state's decision to comply with the restrictions of the treaty, even if the cost of compliance to the state supersedes the cost of noncompliance.[4] Sanctions as a nonmilitary measure increase the cost of noncompliance therefore ensuring that the country meets its international obligations.[5] The nonmilitary nature of contemporary sanctions is the main feature distinguishing modern sanctions schemes from their historical counterparts. However, the literal translation of the term "sanctions" denotes anything from punitive measures to military action against a given country or agent.

The etymology of the word gives guidance to the evolution of the concept and its interpretation in modern times. For instance, it could be stated that the semantic meaning of the word may play into the creation of the concept as a morally ambivalent shell.[6] Further analysis of the meaning would bring other contradictory definitions. Sanctions could mean both "to allow, encourage" and "to punish so as to deter." Sanctions, of course, can also refer to penal sanctions, such as the deprivation of liberty, lack of community service, and other substitutes.[7] Sanctions, as Georges Abi-Saab explains, can be understood as a coercive measure regardless of whether the party applying sanctions is armed or not (military or economic means); sanctions can also be in the form of moral condemnation or censure.[8]

The root of the word "sanctions" drives from the Latin word *sanctio*, meaning "a law or decree that is sacred or inviolable."[9] The Black's Law dictionary provides a curiously circular definition: sanctions are to penalize by imposing a sanction. In English, the word is first recorded in the mid-1500s with the meaning "law, decree," but not long after, in about 1635, it is used to refer to "the penalty enacted to cause one to obey a law or decree."[10] Thus, beginning with its earliest usages, two fundamental notions of law were wrapped up in the term. On one hand, the word represented law as something that permits or approves. On the other hand, the term also meant law that forbids by punishing. The verb form of *sanction* was created in the 18th century meaning "to allow by law," but it wasn't until the second half of the 20th century that it began to mean "to punish (for breaking a law)."[11] The term "economic sanctions" refers to economic sanctions as imposed by the United Nations or an individual state to enforce compliance with specific demands of the enforcer; this is a more modern form of sanctions.

However, as discussed here and its use in common language the term "economic sanctions" refers broadly to boycotts, or embargoes imposed by the United Nations on any target, including travel bans and financial sanctions.

2.1.1 A Brief History of Sanctions

Economic sanctions have a very long history, dating to the earliest wars of civilization. In fact, every military blockade of a given city or port dating back to the ancient Greek city-states' attempts to use their fledgling fleets to cut off trade to rival cities, was in essence an act of economic sanction. As explained by numerous authors, sanctions really are nothing but a variant of the age-old battle strategy of laying siege to a given castle, territory, or population and thereby depriving the citizens of the targeted land of vital trade and other resources critical for the survival of that population.[12] A more recent example is the Nazi siege of Leningrad during World War II. The purported aim of the siege of this city was to prevent Allied troops from staging an effective defensive position on the Baltic Sea. Most historians agree that the true purpose was to starve the Russians into submission and defeat them through the demoralization of the population. In this case and other such examples, the intended consequence of such a blockade was always the capitulation of the sanctioned city, state, nation, or people to the party imposing the sanctions.[13] Failure to surrender or acquiesce to the dominant power resulted in economic strangulation, and eventually in the widespread loss of human life, as the majority of the population was unable to feed itself. Historical examples abound illustrating that most military sieges were, at least in part, absolute trade sanctions (i.e., a total ban on imports and exports) against a given country.

As countries have developed over the past centuries and have sought to become more civilized, the framework for laying sanctions has been revised and reworked to limit sanctions to solely economic proportions.[14] Although this is open for criticism, as sanctions can take other forms including diplomatic sanctions, most sanctions are placed conscious of the economic consequences on the target state. In short, the idea is to restrict trade and isolate the targeted country, thereby achieving certain foreign policy objectives or other goals.[15] This revised framework contains a number of contradictions that are immediately apparent. After all, all economic sanctions carry human costs and have inherent humanitarian consequences, as the decrease in trade and the inflow of vital goods or services is directly correlated to a population's standard of living or access to necessities. The circularity and contradictions of the sanctions regime is discussed further in chapter three.

The first case of the UN imposing economic sanctions involved the matter of Rhodesia in 1966.[16] Though there are several sources that put this early form of sanctions in 1965, Resolution 217 (1965) did not specifically introduce sanctions on Rhodesia but rather took a nonmandatory position on the arms-embargo.[17] Resolution 232 (1966) placed a more specific but mandatory sanction regime in place in regards to Rhodesia. This case was brought to the United Nations Security Council (UNSC) by Great Britain in response to Ian Smith's rise of a self-governing white minority ruling of South Rhodesia, where few blacks were eligible to vote, lasting until 1979. Under this case for the first time in its twenty-year history, the UN invoked articles 39 and 41 of the UN Charter and imposed mandatory economic sanctions on Rhodesia.[18] These sanctions remained in force until December 1979. Though the Rhodesia sanctions were the first set of UN sanctions, before the formation of the UN, the League of Nations had imposed multilateral sanctions against Italy. Incidentally, the Rhodesia sanctions are a widely cited example of failure of the economic sanctions. These sanctions did cause an economic weakness which may have diminished the country's strength in coping with the Rhodesian Bush war.

During the Cold War, the UN was loath to impose sanctions as any attempt to bring sanctions to the attention of the UNSC was vetoed either by the Union of Soviet Socialist Republics (USSR) or US sanctions of a different nature—wholesale embargoes, with the exception of token trade—existed between the capitalist and socialist camps. There were three cases of sanctions, which broke through the Cold War stalemate, including sanctions against Rhodesia, mentioned above, South Africa in 1977 (in response to the apartheid regime), and Iraq in 1990 in response to its invasion of Kuwait. The sanctions against Iraq triggered a new wave of sanctions, in what today is known as the 'sanctions decade': the 1990s. The Iraqi sanctions were the archetype for all subsequent UN sanctions, with increasing severity over a period of thirteen years.

During the 1990s, the UNSC stalemate between the USSR and the US was over. Russia's greatly diminished role in the world that allowed the UNSC to increase its oversight and peacekeeping missions around the world, including in many parts of the world (particularly Africa) formerly aligned with the Soviet Union. In all, over thirteen sanctions regimes were imposed during the 1990s. Of these sanctions, four are complete comprehensive sanctions, seven are target, and all include an arms embargo. The UNSC also increasingly imposed sanctions in response to alleged humanitarian crises in target countries, giving rise to the term "humanitarian sanctions," one of the most controversial forms of international sanctions.

2.2 A TAXONOMY OF SANCTIONS

Having established an understanding of the etymology and brief history of sanctions, we now turn to a summary of several prominent sanctions schemes, or what I refer to in the book as sanctions "regimes." This term follows the nomenclature of the United Nations. A brief overview of these multiple sanctions regimes is important as the structure of the argument in the section rests on a concrete understanding of the specific sanctions regime in place, and precise definitions of the terms used.

First and foremost, contemporary sanctions regimes are almost exclusively international in character, involving the modern nation state as either the sanctioning party or sanctioned party. Although domestic and local parallels certainly exist, it is the international sanctions that pose extensive challenges for the population. Though sanctions may exist in the private sphere, such as when several private concerns collude and refuse to conduct business with a third party, or when an individual company decides to restrict the sale of its products to the subsidiaries of its main competitor, the ambiguous and multidimensional nature of international sanctions gives them a much more political face. Thus, in modern international law, the first breaking point in describing sanctions is whether a given sanctions regime is *unilateral* or *multilateral*. *Multilateral* sanctions are also commonly referred to in the academic literature as well as in popular press as *universal* sanctions. Both these categories of sanctions are in reference to the relationship between political states.

Furthermore, sanctions schemes may be subdivided into the following categories: collective sanctions; indirect sanctions; punitive sanctions; mutual sanctions (for instance, Cold War sanctions); total sanctions; and targeted sanctions (restricting export of a specific goods or type of goods).[19] Targeted sanctions as referred to here are in the same terms as Rose Gottemoeller described in her article "The Evolution of Sanctions," where targeted sanction remains targeted throughout the life of the sanction. The use of this technique is complicated because as the strength of sanctions increase, any subsequent sanction on the target increases the sanction's scope, directing it towards comprehensive sanctions. Because of the often political nature of sanctions and the extended length of time they are imposed, each sanction scheme may also be a combination of, or a hybrid of any of

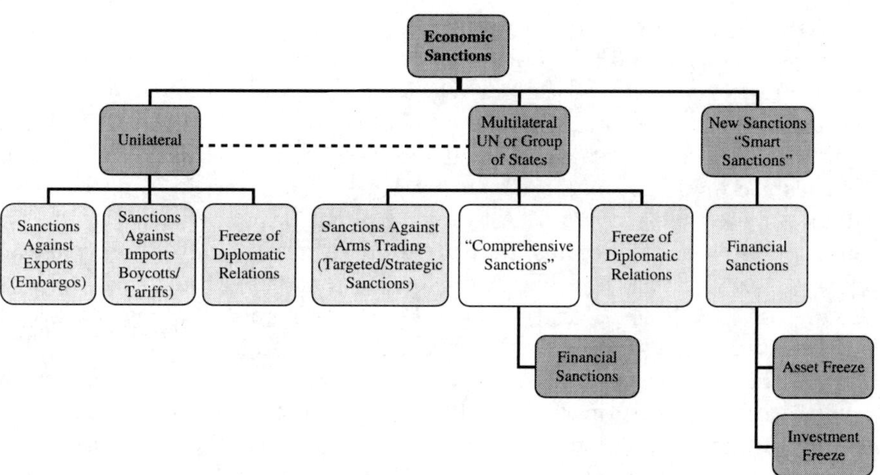

Figure 2.1 Sanctions Classification

the types mentioned above, where over time most sanctions are similar in nature and scope. Collective sanctions are those enacted by a significant number of states (usually numbering more than ten) and apply to a range of goods or services. Punitive sanctions are intended to inflict a directed and specific blow to the sanctioned country's economy. Figure 2.1 lays out the structure and identifies the varied sanctions regimes currently used by politicians and academics alike.

2.2.1 Unilateral Sanctions

As the name suggests, unilateral sanctions are those imposed by one sanctioning state-party against a single sanctioned target. The target can include a state member of the UN or else a group or organization within a state, such as a political or military faction. Unilateral sanctions also often target individuals through the use of travel bans, financial asset seizures, and other methods. These sanctions are governed by the domestic law of the sanctioning country, and usually involve legislation narrowly tailored towards restricting trade in certain products. An example of such products include arms, sensitive high-tech components, cryptography software, or other goods which may allow the sanctioned party to advance its military or other capabilities.[20] Usually, the sanctioning country seeks to enforce sanctions by enlisting the international community through either voluntary cooperation or by means of the more formal conventional international norms (treaties, conventions, and other international agreements).[21]

2.2.2 Multilateral Sanctions

Multilateral sanctions are imposed by several states or by the broader "international community" and are represented by either the United Nations or the collective agreements of regional inter-governmental organizations (i.e., the EU) against a given state. When referring to multilateral sanctions, most times it is the unification of two or more states against another. Multilateral sanctions of this form are very similar to unilateral sanctions. Their potential effect and measurement of success is finite and the same basics apply. This means that multilateral sanctions are self-driven, since all the parties are involved voluntarily and with equal interest in imposing sanctions on the target country. Although United Nations sanctions also fall under multilateral sanctions, they are quite different from other sanctions. With UN sanctions, the UN is a third party that requires all member states to impose sanctions on a target state. Each UN member state is not directly involved in sanctions deliberation but is directly affected by sanctions. This is because the sanction measures to be imposed are chosen by a select few who also make decisions for all other member states. The Secretary General along with the nine votes from UN members establishes resolutions that are passed as binding decisions. The Security Council has a total of fifteen member state representatives, five of whom are permanent members with veto power. Affirmative decisions of the council are made by nine votes, thus including the vote of nonpermanent members and giving voice to the broader international community in council decisions. The nonpermanent members, who are appointed every two years, are elected alphabetically with attention to representation from different continents. Though the decisions are ultimately made by these nine members through UNSC resolutions, these resolutions do not only affect the fifteen members but rather they have an effect on all other UN members as well as the broader international community. Therefore, UN-imposed sanctions are much more intensive and complex than other forms of multilateral sanctions.

The multilateral sanctions in practice are not effective in a multipolar world because extensive intercontinental trade counteracts them in a globalized environment. Since more countries are less dependent on a small group of powerful countries (due to a breakdown in hegemonic power centers and development of regional trade centers) and are more diversified in their choice of trade partners, this growing world of bilateral and multilateral agreements diffuses the effects of multilateral sanctions. Therefore, the sanctioning countries need to analyze their own domestic economic loss before imposing such sanctions. The same multipolar phenomenon affects UN-based sanctions. In the case of UN sanctions, it is the UN that needs to act as watchdog to oversee every step of the implementation of sanction resolutions or just trust all member states to comply on their own domestic front. UN sanctions during the Cold War were much different than those of the post-Cold War era, as they were based on a bipolar political environment. This was the reason for the limited number of UN sanctions during this period.

2.2.3 The Actual Form of Sanctions

The actual measures referred to in the definition of "sanctions" may take many forms. Collective economic measures are frequently used to attempt to influence a nation's leaders. Economic sanctions can be characterized as: a) restrictions on the flow of goods; b) restrictions on the flow of services; c) restrictions on the flow of money, capital, securities, credit, etc.; and d) control of markets in order to reduce or nullify the sanctioned state's chances of gaining access to them.[22] This form of sanctions can also include *monetary* sanctions "aimed at destabilizing currency values (inducing inflation or deflation) in order to upset economic planning and cause psychological distress."[23] As an example, the International Monetary Fund (IMF) can prescribe sanctions against a state, which changes the par value of its currency without respecting the rules of Article IV(6) of the Bretton Woods Agreement.[24]

The most expansive form of sanctions is known as comprehensive sanctions. Comprehensive sanctions are a cumulative program of embargos, boycotts, and financial sanctions aimed at completely subduing a target state. As a result of growing concern over the humanitarian impact of comprehensive sanctions, the Security Council thus far has arguably stopped fully imposing these comprehensive sanctions after their negative consequences on Iraq, the former Yugoslavia, and Haiti; instead, the United Nations turned exclusively to the use of financial, diplomatic, arms, aviation, travel, and commodity sanctions with the purpose of targeting the belligerents and policymakers most directly responsible for reprehensible policies.[25] The form of sanctions can determine their influence, cost, and implementation process. All UN sanctions are governed by an international law framework, but are enforced by individual member-states.[26] As a practical matter, the implementation of sanctions is a domestic matter, despite the form and type of sanctions imposed.

2.3 SANCTIONS AS FOREIGN POLICY TOOLS

Economic sanctions are used as a major foreign policy instrument because of their perceived significant impact or seemingly less coercive character. Sanctions, and in some cases, the mere threat of sanctions, have been shown to force a ruling body of a country to modify their political behavior or comply with a certain set of international norms—such as in certain human rights cases or when the international community is ostensibly concerned with the humanitarian rights of the sanctioned country's own citizens. The UN Security Council working group on sanctions formulated the official position thus:

> Sanctions are a powerful expression of the collective voice and the collective will of the international community. As such, their symbolic impact is undeniable. Their practical impact has been demonstrated in several cases where sanctions have helped to prod conflicting parties towards compromise. [. . .]
>
> Sanctions have demonstrated that they have a sobering effect on targets. Even the threat of sanctions can have a preventive effect. But only if the threat is perceived as *credible*, and carries the clear message of a willingness to act as necessary. Sanctions, imposed in a manner that signals the unity of purpose and determination of the international community, can achieve results without the use of force.[27]

One theory posits that economic sanctions are sometimes placed on countries with the knowledge that they will not be effective, either to force coercion or for alternate strategic ends. For instance, a study has found that the *threat of sanctions* is often more powerful than the sanctions themselves.[28] At other times, sanctions are imposed for purely ideological reasons. For instance, the United States' sanctions against North Korea, stemming from the Korean War (which itself was prolonged and ultimately stalemated), were largely construed as an act of political grandstanding. It was an act of a large and politically powerful state against a much weaker and politically more vulnerable state. Likewise, during the height of the Cold War, the US and the USSR's mutual spheres of influences in advancing their political presence, created indirect sanctions regimes. Thus, due to the USSR's *de facto* control over the Soviet Bloc nations, the US and its allies limited trade with the Communist states, creating indirect economic sanctions. Of course, the same sanctions applied reciprocally from the Soviet Bloc states to capitalist states and were broken only by mutually agreed to but small-scale trade negotiations through official channels (AMTORG, USAID, etc.).

Importantly, several international conventions forbid the use of economic sanctions as a foreign policy tool. For instance, Article 16 of the Organization of American States (OAS) Charter clearly states:

> No State may use or encourage the use of coercive measures of an economic or political character in order to force the sovereign will of another State and obtain from it advantages of any kind.[29]

This injunction comports with the spirit of the UN Charter and customary international law. For instance, Article 55, entitled "International Economic and Social Co-Operation" mandates that in striving for peaceful and friendly relations among nations, the UN shall promote:

> a. higher standards of living, full employment, and conditions of economic and social progress and development;
> b. solutions of international economic, social, health, and related problems; and international cultural and educational cooperation; and,
> c. universal respect for, and observance of, human rights and fundamental freedoms for all without distinction as to race, sex, language, or religion.[30]

These international treaties reflect the principle that the most effective method of resolving actual or potential conflicts rests with mutual cooperation and that economic partnerships form real bonds between states. As a corollary, economic coercion both conflicts with the international principle of sovereignty, as well as acts as an unconscionable tool by which stronger regional actors may subvert the will of weaker states.

Yet despite these injunctions, sanctions appear to have lasting power on the world stage as a tool of foreign policy, both on a global and a regional level. Sanctions were in fact accepted practices in the international community, both in the West as well as former Socialist states.[31] Regionally, unilateral or multilateral non-UN sanctions are even imposed without approval by the Security Council. Furthermore, since states are not precluded from imposing sanctions that were not approved, it is evident that states are under no legal obligation to impose sanctions.[32]

In choosing to impose sanctions, the UN Security Council is limited by its own charter, first, and then by customary international law. Article 39 of the UN Charter requires that the Security Council determine "the existence of any threat to the peace, breach of the peace, or act of aggression" before deciding what measures are necessary to "maintain or restore peace." Article 39 reads "The Security Council shall determine the existence of any threat to the peace, breach of the peace, or act of aggression and shall make recommendations, or decide what measures shall be taken in accordance with Articles 41 and 42, to maintain or restore international peace and security."[33] There is wide consensus that the UN Security Council is not allowed to impose sanctions for any other reason, save to restore peace, though there are wide interpretations regarding the meaning of a "threat to peace."[34]

Article 41, which is established as the source for determining power of Article 38, extends to the Security Council the power to authorize individual states to take action against rogue nations. Imbedded in Article 41 are two separate frameworks of power distribution. In its first segment, "(T)he Security Council may decide what measures not involving the use of armed force are to be employed to give effect to its decisions. . . ." The Security Council is taking on itself the power to decide what a threat to peace is and which coercive measures are appropriate in dealing with such threats. The second segment of this Article, "and it may call upon the Members of the United Nations to apply such measures" delegates the task of carrying out coercive (nonmilitary) measures to member states. The countries have interpreted this provision to mean that they are individually entitled to impose unilateral sanctions against targets that may have been censured by the UN, and they are free to influence other members into compliance with such unilateral measures. Article 62 further broadens the scope and power of the UN to propose policies and recommendations, which may ultimately result in sanctions, either multilaterally through the UN, or unilaterally through the member states. Article 62 provides as follows:

1. The Economic and Social Council may make or initiate studies and reports with respect to international economic, social, cultural, educational, health, and related matters and may make recommendations with respect to any such matters to the General Assembly, to the members of the United Nations, and to the specialized agencies concerned.
2. It may make recommendations for the purpose of promoting respect for, and observance of, human rights and fundamental freedoms for all.
3. It may prepare draft conventions for submission to the General Assembly, with respect to matters falling within its competence.
4. It may call, in accordance with the rules prescribed by the United Nations, international conferences on matters falling within its competence.

The problem with the interpretation of Articles 62 and 39 is that they raise issues concerning overlapping powers: on one side it is the Security Council that is responsible for determining any measures of "threat to peace," and on the other side Article 62 gives the evaluation power to the Economic and Social Council, while Article 41 entrusts enforcement power to member states. To understand the dynamic of this power conflict, we can chart out the differences (similarities) between US-imposed and UN-imposed sanctions.

2.4 CURRENT ECONOMIC SANCTIONS PARADIGM

There are different views on the effectiveness of sanctions from a unilateral view and there are also questions on their effectiveness from a multilateral perspective. What is still lacking is a rigorous legal analysis under the international economic law of sanctions, not only as direct contributors to the degradation of the economic system of the targeted state and of third states, but also of their long-term impact.[35]

Generally speaking, despite the origin of a given sanctions scheme, or the number of international organizations or member states participating in the economic sanctions at play, the current sanctions paradigm is based on a dual-agent model in which the main players are the sanctioning body "sender" and the sanctioned country "target."[36] Further defined the sanction*ing* body is the proponent of the sanctions whether it is the UNSC or a specific state, whereas, the sanction*ed* country is the intended beneficiary of the given sanctions regime. Thus in the context of multilateral sanctions, the UNSC is considered the sender and participating states become third party beneficiaries.

The current sanctions paradigm rests on a series of ambiguous policy goals. Instead of putting these goals forth affirmatively, it may be easier to imagine them as general guidelines, whereby the policy-makers wishing to impose the sanctions ask the following questions: 1) Is the goal of the economic sanction to weaken the sanctioned economy? 2) Will economic sanctions work in either weakening the economy or changing the sanctioning country's policies? The following ancillary questions also arise: 1) What is the measure of "success" of a given sanctions regime? 2) Under what circumstances will economic sanctions work or be likely to fail? 3) If the economic sanctions are aimed at restricting the sanctioning country's export of natural resources, to what extent will the sanctions impact the rights, and/or interests of third parties? 4) Does the sanctioning country have other means of providing for the sanctioned country's citizens' basic humanitarian needs, i.e., medicine, basic foodstuffs, sanitary water?[37] More generally, will the economic pressure on the sanctioned country's society necessarily create a popular response and a call for change in the sanctioned country's political regime?[38] Or, as has been shown historically, is the society going to be capable of withstanding economic pressure, with the end result of the sanctions being the creation of uncertain and unpredictable political and economic realities in the sanctioned country?

2.4.1 Current US Sanctions

Currently, the US has sanctions in place against a number of countries.[39] Table 2.1 illustrates the current US sanctions regime including the type and duration of the sanctions, the reason for their imposition, and the year imposed.

Table 2.1 Select US Sanctions

Target Country	Year Original Sanction Imposed	Reason	Type of Sanctions/Duration
Sudan	1989	Imposed in response to Sudan's failure to end support for *jan-jaweed* militias in Darfur. Human rights, civil war and democracy.	Barring of 30 new companies or entities from doing business with the US, including Sudan's largest oil exporter and central bank. Sanctions are current. This includes Sudan's telecommunications companies Sudatel and Al-Sunut, Advance Mining Works Company Limited, Advanced Petroleum Company, Arab Sudanese Blue Nile Agriculture Company, Arab Sudanese Vegetable Oil Company, Assalaya Sugar Company Limited.
Myanmar/ Burma	2007	Imposed as an answer to gross international human rights abuses.	Restriction of visa rights to senior members of the government and military; freezing assets held in the US.
Iran	1979	Imposed because of state support of terrorism.	Designation of Bank Melli, Bank Mellat, and Bank Saderat as supporters of terrorism.
North Korea	2001	Placed on the axis of evil list after September 11 attacks.	Embargo of all goods. Sanctions are currently imposed.
Cuba	1960	Castros relationship with USSR and acknowledgement of Marxist-Leninist affiliation.	Comprehensive sanctions on all imports and exports. Sanctions are current.

(*Continued*)

Table 2.1 (*Continued*)

Target Country	Year Original Sanction Imposed	Reason	Type of Sanctions/Duration
Syria	1986	To protect against future terrorist acts, sanctions were imposed on Syria after sanctions on Libya.	Ban on chemicals that may be used for production of weapons, also ban on military equipment, and helicopters. Sanctions are current.
Democratic Republic of Congo	2006	Extraordinary threat to US foreign policy.	Ban on trade of any military equipment. This ban is specific to persons on OFAC list of individuals/ organizations involved in terrorist activities in Congo. Sanctions are current.
Zimbabwe	2002	Promotion of democracy and human rights. Violations from Mugabe government.	Travel ban which was then extended to arms embargo. Freeze of assets, by 2009, extended economic sanctions on individuals and entities. Sanctions are current.
Liberia	2000	Unstable political situation. Charles Taylors support of Revolutionary Unified Forces that increase domestic hostility.	Sanctions are not against the country or the central bank of Liberia but against Charles Taylor and his government. Sanctions are current.
Cote dIvore	2006	Violation of human rights and humanitarian law.	Ban on any transactions with any person, entity, or organization involved in arms trade, and causing threat to peace. Sanctions are current.
Belarus	2006	Non-democratic. Extended term of presidency by Alexander Lukashenko.	Targeted financial asset control.

It should be noted that above are the list of sanctions currently posted on the Office of Foreign Asset Control website. The US has been the most active user of economic sanctions as a foreign policy tool. Since 1945, the US has imposed over one hundred sanctions versus seven sanctions imposed by the United Kingdom, seven by France (of which two were in conjunction with the EU), three by China, and twelve by the USSR/Russia.

Although some of the sanctions that are imposed by the US are in order of compliance with the UN resolutions, most are placed before any UN action and specifically in response to domestic policy. As the wording of the US sanctions resolutions is clear, the sanctions are imposed because the target country poses a threat to US foreign policy.

2.4.2 Current Multilateral (UN) Sanctions

To open the analysis of UN sanctions and generate a comparative view of sanctions, Table 2.2 lays out the type of current UN sanctions regime and established the reason and duration of these sanctions.

There are several noticeable differences between the sanctions imposed by the US on a unilateral basis and the UN-imposed economic sanctions: 1) US sanctions are specific, directed, and extremely detailed, 2) the reasons for imposing the sanctions are identified, and 3) the national interests of the state are identified and protected.

On the other hand, UN sanctions, which are to protect the interests of several states, do not carry such a directed tone and standing. This lack of specificity of UN sanctions is typical of the resolutions and the difficulties that arise from imposing sanctions through an international institution serving the national interests of multiple states. With the advent of targeted sanctions and terrorist lists, the UN has tried to increase the ambiguity of economic sanctions; however, even with such tactics, the UN is left with the problem of interstate political interest.

Table 2.2 UN-Imposed Sanctions

Target Country	Year Original Sanction Imposed	Reason	Resolutions	Duration	Type of Sanction
Rhodesia	1965	Minority ruling	Resolution 270 (1965), Resolution 232 (1966), Resolution 333 (1973), Resolution 460 (1979)	14 years November 20, 1965 to December 21, 1979	Comprehensive sanctions, complete ban of all goods from Rhodesia.
Iraq	1990	Occupation of Kuwait; weapons of mass destruction destabilization, military impairment, release of hostages	Resolution 661 (1990) and Resolution 778 (1992); terminated pursuant to Resolution 1483 (2003) of May 22, 2003, Resolution 1518 (2003) active Arms Embargo.	13 years August 6, 1990 to May 22, 2003	Oil and arms embargo, further extended to include all imports and exports, removed after the United States invasion of Iraq
Yugoslavia	1991	Internal ethnic conflict between Serbs, Croats, and Albanians	Resolution 713 (1991) Resolution 724 (1991); terminated pursuant to Resolution 1074 of October 1, 1996	5 years and 1 month September 25, 1991 to October 1, 1996	Arms embargo, followed by general trade embargo
Former Yugoslavia	1998	Violence between Serbian police in Kosovo and Kosovo Liberation Army	Resolution 1160 (1998); terminated pursuant to Resolution 1367 (2001) of September 10, 2001[1]	3 years March 31, 1998 to September 10, 2001	Arms embargo and UN administration of territory (Res. 1244)

(Continued)

Table 2.2 (*Continued*)

Target Country	Year Original Sanction Imposed	Reason	Resolutions	Duration	Type of Sanction
Serbia/ Montenegro	1992	Internal ethnic conflict, part of former Socialist Federal Republic of Yugoslavia	Resolution 757 (1992), Resolution 787 (1992), Resolution 820 (1993);suspended indefinitely pursuant to Resolution 1022 (1995)	3 years and 6 months May 30, 1992 to November 1, 1995	Full ban on import and export, flight ban, reduction of diplomatic presentation
Bosnia (Serb Party)	1994	Continuous hostility in Bosnia Herzegovina by Serb party, refusal of peace plan	Resolution 942 (1994); suspended indefinitely pursuant to Resolution 1022 (1995)	1 year and 3 months September 30, 1994 to November 1, 1995	Non-recognition of state, trade sanctions, travel bans, freeze of assets.
Haiti	1991	Military coup, incompliance with resolution 861	Resolution 841 (1993), Resolution 873 (1993); terminated pursuant to Resolution 944 of September 29, 1994	1 year and 3 months June 16, 1993 to September 29, 1994	Oil and arms embargo which was further extended to all commodities.
		Democracy	—		

Somalia	1992 First time was in 1988 against civil war and human rights violations.	Factional fighting, military coup, divided government. From one side the rebel group Somalia National Movement and on the opposition the United Somali Congress)	Resolution 733 (1992), Resolution 751 (1992)- Resolution 1519 (2003)-Current	10 years 11 months January 23, 1992 to December 16, 2003 and continuing	Arms embargo, Resolution 1772 (2007); excludes transitional federal government from embargo
Liberia	1992,2 1995 - 2001		Resolution 788 (1992), Resolution 985 (1995);3 terminated and replaced by resolution 1343 (2001) further extension 1478(2003)- Current	8 years 3 months November 10 1992 to March 7 2001Continuing	Arms embargo, Resolution 1343 increased the arms embargo and added tougher travel restrictions and ban on import of diamonds from Liberia
Libya	1992	Lockerbie bombing (terrorist bombing investigation)	Resolution 748 (1992), Resolution 883 (1993) terminated pursuant to Resolution 1506 (2003) of September 12, 2003	10 years and 6 months March 31, 1992 to September 12, 2003	Air and arms embargo extended in 1993 to include freezing of funds and band of oil refining equipment
Angola (UNITA)	19934	Civil war between UNITA & MPLA Democracy	Resolution 864 (1993); 5 terminated pursuant to Resolution 1448 (2002) of December 9, 2002	9 years September 15, 1993 to December 9, 2002	Travel ban, arms embargo, and ban on diamond trade.

(Continued)

Table 2.2 (*Continued*)

Target Country	Year Original Sanction Imposed	Reason	Resolutions	Duration	Type of Sanction
Sudan	1996	Sponsor of terrorism, situation in Darfur.	Resolution 1054(1996); Resolution 1556 (2004)	April 26, 1996 to current	Diplomatic freeze, arms embargo (2004).
Congo	2003	Internal hostilities, East Congo conflict; human rights violations and humanitarian law violations	Resolution 1493 (2003)	Current	Arms embargo; financial freeze; travel ban; ban on military technical assistance
Eritrea/ Ethiopia	2000	Arms embargo; continuation of hostilities between Eritrea and Ethiopia.	Resolution 1298 (2000); terminated pursuant to Presidential Statement S/PRST/2001/14 of May 15, 2001.6	1 year May 17, 2000 to May 15, 2001	Arms embargo against the two countries
Rwanda	1994	Ethnic cleansing, killing of civilians.	Resolution 918 (1994) concerning Rwanda; 6 terminated pursuant to 1011 (1995) and further resolution 1823 (2008) of July 10, 2008	1 year May 17, 1994- 1995 The Security Council Committee on Rwanda was terminated on July 10, 2008	Arms embargo, in 1996 extended only to non-governmental forces

Sierra Leone	1997	Civil war	Resolution 1132 (1997); terminated pursuant to Resolution 1156 (1998);renewed pursuant to Resolution 1171(1998) and Resolution 1446 (2002)	6 years October 8, 1997 to 29 September 2010-All former embargos were lifted pursuant to Resolution 1940 after demobilization of armed groups.	Oil and arms embargo, ban on import of diamonds without Certificate of Origin (expired on June 4, 2003)
Cote divoire	1999	Internal conflict, avoidance of cease-fire; conflict with Liberia	Resolution 1572 (2004) Resolution 1584 (2005)	5 years 1999–2004	Arms and equipment trade embargo, funds freeze, diamond import ban
Afghanistan	1999	Terrorism	Resolution 1267 (1999), Resolution 1333 (2000), to be followed in more general terms with Resolution 1368 (2001) on act of terrorism, Resolution 1455 (2003)	Over 4 years October 15, 1999–2002 Ongoing only on select individuals listed as engaging in activities classified as terrorism or those supporting terrorism.	Flight ban, freeze of Taliban funds, arms embargo, in 2003 an extension on

(Continued)

Table 2.2 (*Continued*)

Target Country	Year Original Sanction Imposed	Reason	Resolutions	Duration	Type of Sanction
Iran	2006	Nuclear Proliferation	Resolution 1737 (2006) Resolution 1747 (2007) Resolution 1803 (2008) Resolution 1929 (2010)	Current	Financial freeze of assets; ban on nuclear technology and uranium enrichment technology; travel ban. Extended to arms embargo. 2010 sanctions extended previous arms embargo and asset freezes. The sanctions are also extended to control of shipping lines, freeze of the assets of the Revolutionary Guard, prohibit the servicing of Iranian vessels, prevent financial institutions from operating in Iran,
North Korea	2006	Nuclear proliferation	Resolution 1718(2006) extended by Resolution 1874 (2009),	Current	Arms embargo and ban on sell of material use in development of nuclear weapons

Syria	2005	Widespread human rights violations and massacre of civilians	Resolution 1636 (2005)	Current	Freezing of funds and economic resources of persons suspect of planning, sponsoring or perpetrating murder of Rafig Hariri (Prime Minister of Lebanon)

[1] UNSC Sanctions Committee Established Pursuant to Resolution 1160, available at http://www.un.org/Docs/sc/committees/res1160/1160ResEng.htm.

[2] Resolution 788 (1992) imposed the arms embargo on Liberia; Resolution 985 (1995) subsequently established the Security Council Sanctions Committee.

[3] Security Council Committee Concerning the Situation in Liberia Pursuant to Resolution 985 (1995), available at http://www.un.org/Docs/sc/committees/LiberiaTemplate.htm

[4] Security Council Committee established pursuant to resolution 864 (1993) concerning the situation in Angola, available at, http://www.un.org/Docs/sc/committees/AngolaTemplate.htm

[5] UNSC Committee Concerning the Situation Between Eritrea and Ethiopia Pursuant to Resolution 1298 (2000), available at, http://www.un.org/Docs/sc/committees/EritreaEthiopia/EthiopiaResEng.htm6 Security Council Committee established pursuant to Resolution 918 (1994) concerning Rwanda,

2.5 CONVENTIONAL SANCTIONS "THEORY"

There are many uses for sanctions, but most scholars recognize that the main purpose is to "impose costs on the objectionable policies of another state, without attempting to unseat its regime, occupy its territory, or destroy its infrastructure–in short, without going to war."[40] The logic of conventional sanctions maintains that economic pressure on civilians will translate into pressure on the government for change. The multiplicity of purposes and methods of sanctions makes such a theory useless except as a general analytical, descriptive tool. For instance, there are multiple instances when, despite an inordinate amount of pressure on civilians, the targeted leaders, sometimes expressly intended to be ousted by the outraged citizens of their countries, have managed to continue pursuing policies that violate international law and pursue whatever means necessary to stay in power.[41] Likewise, sanctions may be imposed against a given country for no reason at all, other than for domestic, political, or economic reasons of the sanctioning country.[42] For instance, the US may wish to enact a particular sanction, or a limited trade embargo against Chinese toys based on the professed grounds that Chinese toys are unsafe. In actuality, the true purpose of these sanctions may be solely to boost the domestic toy industry. Early sanction studies concluded precisely thus—many times, sanctions served to solve internal political dilemmas on the sanctioning side, no matter how adverse their effects may have been on the recipient.[43]

Nonetheless, insofar as mainstream sanctions theory persists in the policymaking discourse and within the academic literature, it is important to summarize the expected results of sanctions on the target, no matter the ostensible reason for their enactment. There are two specific results that can be reached through economic sanctions; however, the severity, number of sanctions states, and the length of sanctions work hand in hand to help us determine the result of sanctions. Sanctions are imposed on average for terms of five years, but can last in duration from 0 to 21 years. Thus, there are three external forces of the type and duration of sanctions, along with the target state's internal economic strength, which would yield specific results.

As Table 2.3 shows, traditional sanctions theory neglects numerous unintended but significant consequences of the sanctions. For instance, scholars have documented several cases where economic sanctions helped to actually empower the government of the sanctioned country. Iran nicely illustrates the defects in our current analytical scheme concerning sanctions.[44] For instance, despite numerous rounds of international sanctions, spearheaded by the United States, Iranian newspaper reports continuously announce economic sanctions as a means for the Western world to repress the success of the Iranian economy.[45] The Iranian government validly argues that through the restriction of the flow of necessary construction and infrastructure components, the sanctioning countries are attempting to slow construction in Iran and hence hamper production of heavy industrial products (particularly in the aviation, automotive, steel, and energy industries).[46] Furthermore the

Table 2.3 Sanction Classified by Type, Duration, and Possible Outcome

Type of Sanction	Duration (Years)[1]	Sanctioned Country (GDP)	Result (POV of Sanctioned State)
Collective Sanctions	<5	Weak	Possible Failure/ Success
	>5	Weak	State Failure
	<5	Strong	State Success
	>5	Strong	Possible Failure
Unilateral Sanctions	<5	Weak	Possible Success
	>5	Weak	Possible Failure
	<5	Strong	Possible Success
	>5	Strong	State Failure
Indirect Sanctions	<5	Weak	State Success
	>5	Weak	Possible Failure
	<5	Strong	State Success
	>5	Strong	Possible Success

1 See Iona Petrescu, Rethinking Economic Sanction Success: Sanctions as Deterrents (April 18, 2008), available at www.people.fas.harvard.edu/~petrescu/ (last accessed September 12, 2008).

state's control of all media outlets gives them an added advantage in driving the society's opinion.[47] The discrepancies and control of media is even more evident in recent times. For example, on September 18, 2009, Muslim countries around the world celebrated the last day of Ramadan by holding protests in unity with Palestine. During this period, the Islamic Republic of Iran had several popular uprisings. On September 18, numerous videos and pictures were released through unofficial means, which showed protests against the internal regime with antiregime slogans stating that internal problems need to be addressed before any foreign influence. On the same day, Iranian news agencies reported that protests in the streets of Iran were for solidarity with the people of Palestine, neglecting to mention any of the antigovernment protests. In fact, the solidarity position was used as a mean of discrediting sanctions and the West's force towards the country. To the point that despite the international community having taken these steps, the Iranian popular opinion remains that Iranian growth will not stop under these pressures but will rise to overcome the effects of sanctions and that self-sufficiency will be restored and maintained.[48] The newspaper headline read, "despite the West's reports on instability within Iran and to overthrow free governments, our people filled the streets in support of freedom for Palestine."[49]

Thus, beyond significant humanitarian concerns in Iran, it is easily apparent that the full-scale strangulation of a national economy did not necessarily produce equivalent economic torment for the government leaders who were responsible for the reprehensible policies that the world had condemned via sanctions. Further, sanctions have unintentionally contributed to the emergence of black markets, creating huge profit-making opportunities for the ruling elite and their collaborators.[50]

2.5.1 The Economic Inefficacy of Sanctions: Extrema 1—State Failure

Are sanctions schemes truly effective in pressuring governments to make modifications that bring policy in the sanctioned country in line with that of the sanctioning body or country? Or, is the economy of the sanctioned state able to withstand the sanctions? What are the proper measuring parameters for making this determination? How do sanctions affect the economy, and do they force the sanctioned country's economy to be more self-sufficient? How can researchers measure the efficacy of sanction schemes, and the negative costs of their unintended consequences? As always, it is easier to answer these questions by starting with an analysis of the respective extrema—such as cases where sanctions have caused absolute state failure.

It is axiomatic that a lack of vital resources can destroy a nation's economy.[51] Sanctions have the potential of inhibiting a nation's economy from sustaining the basic food and related humanitarian needs of the given population, leading to both economic and social collapse. Such collapse extends to all sectors of society. It crosses all classes because of the state's inability to sustain its basic infrastructure, such as the provision of energy, foodstuffs, and the protection of core channels of transportation. Thus, no member of the population is exempted when a nation's economy is paralyzed.

Furthermore, an even more puzzling feature of the modern sanctions regime is the fact that sanctions are often threatened against, or imposed on, presently failing states. To cite a recent example, the international community's response to the genocide in the Darfur region of Sudan was to threaten Sudan with sanctions, though there is recent indication of a likely policy shift.[52] In fact, six of the targeted states under UN sanctions since 1990 have remained in the top ten of the Failed State Index list prepared by the US based think-tank, Fund for Peace, and published by Foreign Policy magazine.[53] This index determines the state's well-being and ranks states based on lawlessness, delegitimization of the government, economic decline, terrorism, insurgency, crime, and violations of human rights. The contradictory nature of threatening sanctions against a country already in civil war has not been adequately studied. Nevertheless, suffice it to say, the conditions precedent to failure of a state or government can arise as a result of external factors such as natural disasters, dramatic changes in the world economy, or the withdrawal of a patron nation's support.[54] Moreover, conditions of state failure frequently also result from internal war caused by the intersection of factional, ethnic, or regional leaders or groups.[55] To combat the brutality of the groups or leaders who instigate internal conflicts, the

UN imposes sanctions on failing states. This may be seen both as a direct retaliation, ostensibly on behalf of the victims of the war or conflict, and as a deterrent against future brutality.[56] And this division intricacy within the society deals directly with economic instability and the level of control.

2.6 UNILATERAL SANCTIONS

The classic examples of unilateral sanctions in the twentieth century are US sanctions against Cuba, North Korea, Iran, etc.[57] In each of these instances, the United States imposed harsh trade embargos against the particular countries due to the given country's opposition to, or political incompatibility with, the United States' foreign policy agenda. Similarly, in recent times, the Bush Administration openly discussed and threatened the option of sanctioning Venezuela for President Hugo Chavez's rampant anti-American rhetoric, and for President Chavez's energy policies, which threaten US strategic interests in the region.[58] Similar sanctions have been discussed against President Evo Morales' regime in Bolivia, again due to the country's actions of taking steps inconsistent with American business interests in the region. These policies have been carried over into the Obama administration.

For present purposes, it is also crucial to distinguish between *de jure* multilateral sanctions, which are in actuality unilateral sanctions. These sanctions, through diplomatic means, are able to garner other states' support, but are essentially unilateral actions. Scholars have long documented cases where sanctions are controlled by one or two powerful countries. Where so-called universal (or multilateral) sanctions have been imposed, with mandatory obligations stipulated by the League of Nations or the United Nations, the impression of consensual policy is always illusory: one or more powerful states, particularly in the UN Security Council, have been able to suborn the organization into support for their own foreign policy objective.[59]

It is also important to understand that even countries that do impose unilateral sanctions may prefer to obtain the cooperation of the international community, ideally resulting in the imposition of UNSC sanctions. Thus, for instance, Stuart Eizenstat, the Deputy Secretary of the US Treasury Department, states the official US policy thus,

> If and when economic sanctions are deemed necessary, multilateral sanctions supported by the United Nations are likely to be the most effective in producing desired outcomes. Multilateral sanctions send a stronger message to the target government, are more difficult to circumvent by shifting trade and procurement to third countries and impose fewer costs on US agricultural and business interests, which are at least able to compete on a still-level playing field.[60]

2.7 HUMANITARIAN SANCTIONS

Humanitarian sanctions are UN-imposed sanctions on a country whose leader deprives its citizens of fundamental human rights or other humanitarian rights. Of the various different types of sanctions, humanitarian sanctions are some of the most controversial, due to the circular logic underpinning their justification.[61] The now infamous Iraq sanctions (pre-1992) and the effect of these sanctions over the ten-year period from the first Gulf War in 1991 to the 2003 Iraq War provide stark evidence of the human cost which these sanctions extolled, and their absolute countereffectiveness in re-entrenching Saddam Hussein in power.[62] In essence as Iranian foreign minister Ali Akbar Salehi stated in an interview with *Al-monitor* and *Times* magazine with respect to a new round of sanctions on Iranian "you cannot claim your eagerness for democracy, human rights and all of these things and through unilateral sanctions, try to put all sorts of suffering and hardship to other people. This is a contradiction." This statement carries much weight with respect to unilateral and multilateral sanctions. To protect human rights and to coerce leaders to protect the human rights of their own citizens by causing depravation of basic necessities to the same citizens is unsettling. This problem is substantiated further with the results of sanctions that were imposed on Iraq. High child mortality rates and an increased level of malnutrition cause long-term impact on the population of a county.

2.7.1 Hidden Ancillary Costs

The scholarship concerning the sanctions against Iraq made significant inroads into the traditional sanctions theory by highlighting dozens of hidden but direct costs of the sanctions on the people and economy of Iraq.[63] Nevertheless, literature which sought to monetize the real costs of the sanctions remained by and large marginalized, as though the costs were too tenuous or did not directly flow from the sanctions. The case of Iraq, where the only source of basic societal need, medicine, *etc.* were provided to the population through continuous requests by the Iraqi government from the Security Council, is also illustrative of institutional problems within the UN, as will be shown in section 4.1.[64]

2.7.2 Infant Mortality Rate

Several other well-known studies concerning the sanctions against Iraq sought to analyze the impact of the sanctions by looking at demographic indices, such as mortality rates, literacy rates, and related demographic indicators. For instance, several UN studies examining the human costs of the sanctions against Iraq concluded that 500,000 infants died as a direct consequence of sanctions from 1991 to 1998.[65] These types of studies, while certainly scientifically valid and rigorously conducted, nonetheless lack the punch of more traditional economic cost-benefit analyses. After all, as cynical as it appears, it is clear to most scholars that the main function of sanctions in the minds of policymakers is the likely cost and the anticipated benefit of a given scheme. It is within this framework that the following analysis proceeds.

3 UN Security Council and Protection of Peace

> [T]o establish conditions under which justice and respect for the obligations arising from treaties and other sources of international law can be maintained, and to promote social progress and better standards of life in larger freedom, [. . .] have resolved to combine our efforts to accomplish these aims. Accordingly, our respective Governments, through representatives assembled in the city of San Francisco, who have exhibited their full powers found to be in good and due form, have agreed to the present Charter of the United Nations and do hereby establish an international organization to be known as the United Nations.
>
> —UN Charter, *Preamble*

> Law set between nations is set by general opinion. The duties which it imposes are enforced by moral sanctions: by fear on the part of nations or by fear on the part of sovereign of provoking general hostility, and incurring its probable evils, in case they shall violate maxims generally received and respected.
>
> —Kenneth W. Abbott[1]

The UN via the UN Security Council (UNSC) imposes multilateral sanctions for an increasingly diverse range of stated purposes, including reversal of aggression, restoration of democratic systems of government, protection of human rights, the ending of wars, efforts to combat terrorism, and support of peace agreements.[2] But how does the UNSC actually go about the process of deliberating and imposing sanctions? This chapter outlines the organizational aspects of UN sanctions, including an analysis of the functional aspects of the UN Security Council (UNSC) sanctions committees. This chapter's analysis is divided into four parts. Part one examines the role of the UNSC. Part two outlines the major challenges confronted by the UNSC in determining what constitutes a "threat to peace" sufficient to warrant sanctions. Part three looks at the inner workings and struggles of the UNSC sanctions committees, drawing on primary research from the personal papers of Paul Conlon, the former deputy secretary of the Iraq Sanctions Committee. Finally, Part four examines the decision-making process required to sanction a country.

3.1 THE UN SECURITY COUNCIL

The fundamental purpose of the UN system is to maintain peace between nations; in its preamble, the UN defines peace as a condition in which countries employ a state of tolerance.

> We the people of the United Nations determined to save succeeding generations from the scourge of war, which twice in our lifetime has brought untold sorrow to mankind. [. . .] And for these ends to practice tolerance and live together in peace with one another as good neighbors.

The United Nations Charter, which reads with the same sense of urgency and hope as the US Constitution certainly tends to employ an equivalent unity and long-term trajectory and the shifting of responsibility of peace from the institution to the sovereign members. This shift is later on in the charter reversed back to the institution and in particular the Security Council as one of the primary organs of the United Nations through Article VII, which reads,

> There are established as the principal organs of the United Nations: a General Assembly, a Security Council, an Economic and Social Council, a Trusteeship Council, an International Court of Justice, and a Secretariat. Such subsidiary organs as may be found necessary may be established in accordance with the present Charter. UN Security Council works directly with general assembly and secretariat in decision-making process.

Thus the UNSC is established as the executive organ of the UN and commands decision-making authority. In the words of the official British commentary to the Dumbarton Oaks proposals, "the powers to be conferred on the Security Council are greater than have ever before been given to an international body."[3] Or, as the chairman of the US delegation later summed up at the United Nations Conference on International Organization (UNCIO) in San Francisco during 1945 meetings, "The Security Council's powers are thus equivalent, in substance, to those of a supreme 'war-making' organization."[4] A brief historical note about the creation of the UNSC may be in order. The UNSC was intended to be a reasonable check on the will of the General Assembly, despite what critics later came to see and understand as an antidemocratic power center. The UNSC was to guarantee the equal rights of all the members despite its power; the structure of the UNSC also meant that the exercise of power would be separated from other nations or powers, further legitimizing the UN. The presence of veto power during the Cold War era was a form of balance creation within the council, as the Soviet Union fully used their veto power to restrict the Security Council from making one-sided decisions. America's exercise of the veto power similarly gridlocked but also guarded the UN from taking one-sided measures.

It can be deduced from reading the preamble and Article VII that the UNSC, both in practice and in doctrine, is the organ responsible for peacekeeping and control, but key questions still remain unanswered. Is there a price that societies have to pay for peace? And, at what point in their political life must they pay this price and by whose determination? Are states by their act of becoming members of the UN signing away the right to economic sovereignty?

Based on Article 52 (2) of the UN Charter, all members are to inform the Security Council/UNSC agencies of any problems that cause a "threat to peace and to the security of nations." Further, based on Article 54, the UN members and regional agencies act as indirect organs of the UN that have the responsibility to inform the Council of activities they have undertaken for the maintenance of peace and security.[5] This article also implies that all members are to report the measures they have undertaken to implement any UN resolutions that require action on their part in order to achieve a state of international peace. However, no rights are given to regional agencies in regards to decision-making or taking steps without UNSC involvement. Further, in UN General Assembly Resolution 290, accepted in 1949,[6] guidelines are given in order to maintain international peace, but there is a gaping lack of definition in the charter on the notion of threat to international peace.[7] Indeed, the difficulty in defining what constitutes a "threat to peace" or an armed conflict is one of the greatest challenges in contemporary international law.[8] The difficulty of defining threats to peace leaves states open to taking an increasingly political position and of course the states with more influential power at the UNSC are able to drive sanctions. In the past ten years, multiple instances of the threat of a military attack have been directed towards several countries; however, such threats have not been established or even questioned as a threat to peace and security. A more recent example is Israel's threat to take military action against Iran. Though the Iranian regime's nuclear ambitions have been classified as threats to peace, the degree of which threats to peace and security are classified is completely ambiguous and at times arbitrary. So which is actually considered a threat, Iran's ambitions or Israel's position? As Russia's deputy foreign minister, Sergey Rebakov, warned in an interview "[a]n attack on Iran would set off deep shocks in the security and economic spheres that would reverberate far beyond the boundaries of the Mid-east."[9] This position though, which may not represent the political position of the West, does open up the perspective on the true politicized meaning of threats to peace and security. In such cases where there are parallel intimidation tactics, where the involvement of UN peacekeeping forces or UN monitoring could begin to influence the potential of a military conflict, the UNSC seems to remain silent. It is in such instances, which represent a juncture of coercive actions, that the UN monitoring of a conflict is absolutely necessary. The discussion of monitoring conflicts will begin in Chapter 4 of this book; however, it is important that we keep in mind that the problems with sanction implementation begin with more basic definitional problems and the foundation of the UN Charter.

3.2 WHEN IS A "THREAT TO PEACE" SUFFICIENT TO WARRANT SANCTIONS?

In giving an explanation for the meaning of threat to international peace and security, Prof. Henkin states, "the threat to international peace and security is not capable of legal definition but only of political determination by a political body."[10] To this end, Article 39, Chapter VII of the UN Charter leaves the Security Council responsible for making the decisions on measures to restore international peace. Logically, in order to understand what constitutes a "threat to peace or security," we must unpack what is meant by the word "peace" and further "security" and the conditions that define this at once simple as well as ambiguous concept.

3.2.1 What is Peace?

What is the definition of "peace"? To understand the meaning of the concept under international law, we need to first explore its everyday, common meaning. Then, to define the concept in positivist terms, we must study its form and base our definition in theory. I choose to begin this stream of analysis from an unorthodox position intentionally, moving towards more positivist interpretations later. In 1989, the Dalai Lama analyzed the concept of peace thus,

> Peace, in the sense of the absence of war, is of little value to someone who is dying of hunger or cold. It will not remove the pain of torture inflicted on a prisoner of conscience. It does not comfort those who have lost their loved ones in floods caused by senseless deforestation in a neighboring country. *Peace can only last where human rights are respected, where the people are fed, and where individuals and nations are free.*[11]

In his speech accepting the Nobel Peace Prize, the Dalai Lama continues, "Peace starts with each one of us. When we have inner peace, we can be at peace with those around us. When our community is in a state of peace, it can share that peace with neighboring communities, and so on."[12]

In everyday parlance, peace is understood as a state of mutual harmony between people or groups, a state of tranquility or serenity. Peace, by another definition, is "the freedom of the mind from annoyance, distraction, anxiety and obsession."[13] Webster's defines peace as follows: "A state of security or order within a community provided for by law, custom or public opinion."[14]

Therefore, based on this definition, it is the respect for and compliance with legal norms that consequently leads to a state of security, order, and ultimately to peace.

Surprisingly, there is no clear definition of peace in international law.[15] Since no clear definition of peace exists in international law, as a consequence, some have suggested that a negative definition of peace—such as "the absence of armed conflict"—should prevail.[16] As outlined in section 2.3 *supra*, peace appears in the UN Charter in Article 39, but is left undefined in the Charter, the *travaux préparatoires*, customary international law, and treaties.[17] The concept of peace in international law is defined by the lack of the presence of its antonym, in other words, the absence of war. This negative definition presents several theoretical problems. First, since war is traditionally defined as conflict between states, then peace, which is the absence of war, should exist when there is no *state* conflict. This is patently false, however, since threats to peace, of course, exist in the form of civil wars, domestic genocides, and the like.[18] The situation in the Democratic Republic of Congo after the 2006 elections, for example, is a case of extreme conflict that does not involve formal conflict between states.[19] Second, the failure to define peace makes definitions built upon the concept unstable. If we do not know what peace is, how can we define the concept of a "threat to peace"? Chapter VII of the UN Charter with an underlying presumption that peace is already understood concerns members with "Actions with Respect to Threats to the Peace, Breaches of the Peace and Acts of Aggression".[20]

From a positivist perspective, there is no clear understanding or guidelines regarding peace. The same can be said regarding what constitutes a threat to international peace or how to evaluate such a threat. However, international lawyers are increasingly working to formulate a more concrete definition of peace. According to Kristen E. Boon, professor of law at Seton Hall,

> A fuller understanding of the contours of peace has emerged only recently, in no doubt influenced by the simultaneous fragmentation of the concept of war. It is now acknowledged that peace is not simply created by a *de jure* agreement like a peace treaty, *but requires consolidation, such as compliance with peace agreements, monitoring cease-fires, demilitarization of former combatants, repatriation of refugees, mine clearance, and the reform of police forces*. Like the "positive obligations" that inure with economic and social rights, the establishment of

a durable peace is based in part on conditions that make it practicable, including aid, economic reconstruction, the provision of food and medical care, and mechanisms to address accountability for past atrocities.

A useful analogue is Article 55 of the UN Charter, which indicates that maintaining international peace and security requires not only banning force, but also actively promoting international social and economic cooperation "with a view to the creation of *conditions of stability and well-being which are necessary for peaceful and friendly relations among nations* based on respect for the principle of equal rights and self-determination of peoples."[21]

Assuming that peace is the practice of acceptance and that neighboring countries are lenient towards one another, the Security Council is left with a skewed appraisal of future conflict circumstances. Lacking an objective, under the positivist conception of peace, the Security Council is left to substitute its own subjective interpretation in lieu of formal conceptions of peace. This has led to the fair critique that the decisions of the Security Council under Chapter VII are outcomes of political consideration, not legal reasoning, nor are its proceedings subject to judicial procedures.[22]

Other commentators have suggested that politicized, fact-based conceptions of peace may actually be the more accurate determinants of threats than concrete legal-based definitions.[23] However, this determination will still stay open to a subjective interpretation of peace until there is a concrete definition of the term.

If the Security Council is subject to criticism for failure to understand peace, does it at least have a procedure for foreseeing potential threats to peace? What is the *process* of evaluating a "threat to peace"? Whether or not the assessment of a "threat to peace" is a political act is not necessarily of importance, but it seems more vital to realize that some assessment does proceed before decisions are made regarding sanctions. Some light may be shed on the assessment process through continuous evaluation and comparison of the past causes of threats to peace. Such evaluation might even lead to the Security Council instituting procedural and systematic changes in imposing measures. Furthermore if *states*, like the UNSC, use their own subjective interpretations of threats to peace, what should be the proper role of the UN in reconciling competing interpretations?

3.2.2 The Concepts of Security/Force/Order

If peace is defined by the absence of war, then security can be defined as the promulgation or protection of peace. From the vague description given by the UN Charter regarding peace and the importance of the Security Council's decision concerning which legal measures are to be taken—measures that directly impact domestic law, it may be wise to refrain from perusing the causes of threats to peace but look, rather, to threats to the international legal order, which in turn include treaties and declarations on human rights.[24] These are not necessarily identical. The dichotomy between law and peace was first analyzed by Kelsen soon after the formation of the UN in 1950. The question essentially is whether the UN should work to maintain peace or law.[25] In its most extreme form, the question asks what we should do when confronted with a genocide situation: should we force nations to comply with their international obligations or intervene to stop the killing? Other commentators believe law and peace are synonymous; the implication of observing law is that a nation is at peace. This debate continues into the present time. Since the international legal order is a concept with more defined terms, and as treaties are parts of such order, measurement against such definitions can be objective and precise.

Some countries define the concept of security as stability. Similarly in UN practice, security is defined in a much similar way, as seeing the two as equals and synonymous rather than two ideas that exist in a causal relationship to the other.[26] If law is considered a coercive order, then within international law it is the implementation of law that in fact gives validity/legitimacy to any legal order, norm, or rule. Whether or not those confined under any rule are in accordance with their decree or not, it is in fact the collective action of others through a legal entity that gives root to the accepted legal norms and conduct. If there is a collective agreement against torture, then unless those who have broken the agreement have been punished for their behavior then such agreement does not exist. Additionally, all parties involved in the collective agreement should be subject to the same punishment for the agreement to have a uniform effect. Sanctions are a common form of coercive measure used in order to enforce against undesirable actions of states, groups, or individuals.[27] Sanctions are a forcible interference in the sphere of interests that are normally protected by law.[28] Based on the above explanation, sanctions are the punishment for causing a "threat to peace and security." However, the definition of this threat has not been established and, furthermore, it is questionable whether sanctions are imposed equally across all conflict states.

3.2.3 Re-evaluation of the Concept: Threats to Peace and Security

All nations are to refrain from making threats or using force against other states.[29] Does it follow that the threat to the use of force is equivalent to a "threat to peace"? Or can the two concepts be weighed on separate scales?

Some scholars interpret the Charter as not prohibiting states from threatening international peace and security;[30] therefore, as they are not forbidden from threatening the peace and security of other sovereign states, this leads to an ambiguity in assessing potential threats that would lead to acts of aggression.[31] Leaving the question, what defines a permissible threat from an illegal act of aggression?

There is wide debate in the literature regarding whether economic sanctions themselves constitute a "threat to peace and security." In other words, are economic sanctions consistent with the letter and spirit of the UN Charter? Critics like Vera Gowlland-Debbas contend that sanctions are not proscribed in the UN Charter and are contradictory to the economic cooperation mandate of the UN.[32] Critics also argue that the UN determination of the nature of threat and peace is also highly politically driven. For instance, during the early stages of the Balkan conflict in the 1990s, the UN's response to the conflict illustrates its inability to coordinate an effective measure of a "threat to peace" and to implement a protection policy.[33] In this conflict situation in several circumstances, the Bosnian foreign minister asked for protection for his states based on Article 42 of the UN Charter.[34] However, because of an intensified situation, the UN actually closed the UNPROFOR (the protection unit) headquarters and left behind a staff of 120.[35] This highly volatile conflict situation was heightened with continuous disagreements from Yugoslav and Bosnian leaders in response to the increased aggression and with respect to who was the responsible party.

Scholars defending sanctions as an appropriate extension of UN power respond by pointing out the need to have an effective coercive tool. In the words of David A. Baldwin of Columbia University,

> The dominant concern of the drafters of the UN Charter was 'to save subsequent generations from the scourge of war,' it was not to save them from economic pressure; it was not to depoliticize the world; and it was not to eliminate all forms of coercion. The fact that subsequent charter provisions refer to the 'threat or use of force,' 'threat to peace' 'Breach of the peace' and 'acts of aggression' did not mean that the drafters wanted to proscribe all forms of intense coercion. It means that they wanted to prohibit war whether it was legally so defined or not. To get bogged down in the technicalities and intricacies of the Charter while losing sight of this preeminent and overriding concern with war is to obfuscate rather than clarify the meaning of the Charter. And a fourth reason to doubt the assertion that the peaceful settlement provisions of the Charter were intended to prohibit the use of embargoes, boycotts, and other means of economic pressure is that the regulation of trade had long been regarded as among the sovereign rights of an independent state. If the drafters of the Charter had intended to proscribe such an important right, it seems reasonable to assume that they would have done so in a more explicit and forthright way.[36]

The more immediate problem, however, is that there is also a disproportionate interpretation of what constitutes a "threat to peace." Similar conduct by two or more unique states will be interpreted differently by the UNSC and involved states. Here the reference is to the magnitude of an act of aggression and interpretation if a violation of a legal order is subjective. Some states may not see acts as warranting sanctions as severe as might be proposed by other states that are directly affected by the offender. Accordingly, while a state might see their action to be a sovereign right, they will be chastised for the same deed. For instance Iraqi sanctions in response to a threat of nuclear proliferation were much more severe than those imposed on North Korea today for the same offense. In other cases, the severity of sanctions is disproportionate to the threat the sanctions have caused to peace as political situations change; therefore, each case requires a unique approach and implementation, which requires extremely flexible organizational and constitutional capacities to correlate each international conflict with the appropriate course of action. Such difficulties may only be overcome if there is a specific guideline as to the exact course of action that will be taken in accordance to each specified "threat to peace" which would only be possible if we define "threat to peace" as a threat to legal order.

3.3 THE UN CHARTER AND PEACE PROTECTION

The past decade has seen a radical expansion of the definition of what constitutes a threat to international peace and security. The debate over the expanding range of threats led to the formulation of a UN High-Level Panel on Threats, Challenges and Change.[37] Anne-Marie Slaughter summarizes the consensus reached by the UN High-Level panel as encompassing the following threats,

> 'new security consensus' that will underlie a 'new comprehensive collective security system.' The new consensus rests on the common recognition of the actual security threats 'we face' in the twenty-first century. These threats 'go far beyond States waging aggressive war.' As indicated, 'They extend to poverty, infectious disease and environmental degradation; war and violence within States; the spread and possible use of nuclear, radiological, chemical and biological weapons; terrorism; and transnational organized crime.' They arise from 'non-State actors as well as States,' and threaten 'human security as well as State security.'[38]

The following sections analyze the substantive provisions regarding peace protection as well as challenges posed to formulating a strategic approach to peace monitoring, enforcement, and the application of economic sanctions to peace enforcement situations.

3.3.1 Substantive Provisions on Peace Protection

The concept of security may have changed but how does the UN react to what constitutes a "threat to peace"? Based on the preamble and Article 41, it is clear that any procedures decided upon in order to restore peace should not include armed force by the Security Council. The preamble to the UN Charter states,

> [. . .] and to unite our strength to maintain international peace and security, and to ensure, by the acceptance of principles and the institution of methods, that armed force shall not be used, save in the common interest, and to employ international machinery for the promotion of the economic and social advancement of all peoples [. . .][39]

The positive tone of Article 42 is, however, contradictory to Article 41. Article 41 gives the Security Council the right to take actions by sea, air, or land forces, also opening it for members to take action independently.[40] The 2003 military attack on Iraq and the 2009 raid off Somalia by French forces, are examples of states practicing their rights under Article 41. This leads to the question, is the Charter mechanism for peace maintenance through the UNSC and the concept of legal sanctions substantial?

3.3.2 The Evolving Role of the UNSC

It may not be clear how to measure threats to peace and security, but the Security Council, through deployment of missions to potential unstable areas, continues efforts to restore peace in areas of conflict within limits allowed by the Charter. The UNSC relies mostly on its subsidiary organs such as the UNSC committee, a few larger international organizations, and member state representatives as it carries out its force. However, the UN and its subsidiary organs are the most conservative and archaic parts of the UN system in regards to the relationship with any NGO entities inside states or public opinion.[41] There are other means through which the UNSC may become aware of the needs or preventive measures to be taken against conflict situations. Judge Mohammad Amin Vaghad first introduced the need for a protection army, which sought the help of the UN against the Taliban in 1994.[42] However, appropriate measures were not introduced against the Taliban until 1999.[43] This unfortunately is the lack of responsive actions that are necessary for any form of success in diminishing international conflict.

The UN possesses a juridical personality pursuant to international law, as well as the national laws of the member states. Juridical personality means that the UNSC is subject to legal duties and legal rights, is capable of performing legal transactions, and of suing and being sued at law.[44] However, the United Nations has immunity against any legal actions, unless it waives this immunity explicitly.[45] In the United States, the immunity of the UN is "absolute unless waived."[46] This at once gives the UN more power and control, thus, prevents it from being subject to true and enforceable criticism.

Although the UN is an international organization, which could feasibly have complete transparency, it is quite a closed environment. This lack of transparency is extended so much that the archives of the United Nations, and in general all documents belonging to it or held by it, shall be inviolable wherever located.[47] As the deputy secretary of the Iraq Sanctions Committee (ISC) states, the ISC "was operated with so little transparency that no person or entity outside of its immediate environment could perform any internal assessment; if the ISC did not assess its own work, no one else could."[48]

The UN's lack of transparency and its immunity extends to all UN organs (including the Security Council). This makes the institution inaccessible to the public and devoid of public scrutiny. Hence, it takes on a more political character and consequently becomes vulnerable to outside political influence. The lack of oversight or a participatory organ gives the institution a political character instead of preserving its neutral role as an international peace-making (or peace "enforcement") body. The problem with a political United Nations is that it may, as any political entity, from time to time act in a manner beneficial to its internal health, which would challenge its underlying reason for existence. As Paul Conlon remarks, speaking on the ISC's relationship with the different UN organs,

> the Security Council, the most conservative of all UN organs, the Committee (ISC) kept to the traditional practices of the Security Council, in regarding it almost as below its dignity to address itself to any entity beneath the evolutionary status of the sovereign state. Since all its communication was limited to states, it also kept to archaic methods and styles of communication, including a heavy dosage of *langue de bois*.[49]

Oscar Schachter identifies the Security Council as a political body and further stresses that neither precision nor logic are values for political bodies.[50] As seen above, the UN, and more specifically the UNSC, are politically driven actors. This is commonly understood. What is less understood is how this politicization affects the UNSC decision-making process. It is troubling that the task of imposing economic sanctions, which require such precise measures as they impact every aspect of a country's health, is executed by an organ that may lack specifically such elements as precision and logic in their nature.

Furthermore, a body such as the UNSC that is of a political character opens itself up to being used as a tool for economic statecraft by other political entities, while remaining subject to decisions that may be categorized as economic statecraft.[51] As it is political states that are involved in the decision-making process, a central issue is the use of UN decisions towards a state's own interest. As members use their veto power primarily in their own national interest,[52] it is to say that all decisions may fall along the same line of reasoning. This is problematic because the sanction decision is one that is meant to resolve and not to gloss over a solution. Furthermore, this makes the link between Charter mechanisms for peace maintenance and the concept of legal sanction tenuous.[53]

3.4 UNSC EVALUATION OF "THREAT TO PEACE/SECURITY"

3.4.1 Legal Framework of the UN Security Council

The Charter gives the UNSC the power to investigate any dispute or situation that might lead to international conflict (threat to peace). Upon the realization that a situation may violate international law and cause a "threat to peace," the UNSC is required to use any nonmilitary means necessary to prevent or stop aggression. The common nonmilitary measure used to fight against conflict is sanctions, which are binding on all states.[54] All of these steps raise concerns of legality, and having resolved legality, effectiveness. They also raise the following issues: 1) the sovereign rights of a target country that are affected; 2) the legal implications of sanctions regimes (after the decision to sanction has been made); 3) implementation (covered in Chapters four and five); and 4) measurement of success (Chapter six). Legality and the review of UNSC resolutions and implementation has emerged as a highly complex field within international law, and deserves significantly more attention than is given in this book.[55] Aspects of legality and judicial review of UNSC resolutions, however, are addressed in Chapter 6 of this book. Another approach involves a call for increased General Assembly supervision. Nevertheless, several preliminary remarks must be made regarding this important issue.

Are sanctions against a target country "legal" when imposed by the UNSC? What procedures and remedies does the target country have to challenge the legality of these sanctions? There are several problems in determining legality. From the perspective of the target states, sanctions come as a total violation of that state's right of sovereignty and the customary legal principle of nonintervention. From the perspective of third parties, implementation and enforcement of sanctions is also constrained by both target states' and the third parties' sovereignty.

The UN system's law-making abilities are bound to that of the multilateral "norm-creating" treaty as an instrument of law-making.[56] However, even a unanimously adopted declaration has diminished authority if it is not accepted by the states particularly affected.[57] When a question of imposing sanctions arises, choices have to be made in regards to issues of sovereignty, independence, and "threat to peace."[58] Hufbauer also alludes to issues of sovereignty and interpretation of sovereign rights, especially after the Cold War era. Prior to the Cold War, issues concerning the internal affairs of states were of less concern to the international community as evident through only three cases of UN sanctions from 1945 to 1990 compared to thirteen cases after the 1990s. However, from the 1990s, it is observed that instances of civil war and other forms of internal strife are also seen as a threat to the international peace.[59] Issues of sovereignty are vulnerable to critique from all sides, as limits to a state's control over internal affairs is not clearly defined in international law. Furthermore, if sovereign rights are observed, humanitarian jurisdiction can still be questioned. As in the case of Rwanda, human rights' issues overtake the sovereign right of Rwanda. To be sure, this issue is not unique to the concept of economic sanctions. The same issues of sovereignty were involved in the implementation of the special tribunal for Rwanda, the International Criminal Tribunal for Rwanda (ICTR). There, it was decided at the UN and among the international community that the crime of genocide trumped any issues or claims of sovereignty. In fact Article 2(7) of the Preamble must be read along with Article 13. However, Article 2(7) states that "nothing contained in the present Charter shall authorize the United Nations to intervene in matters which are essentially within the domestic jurisdiction of any state or shall require the Members to submit such matters to settlement under the present Charter."[60] Though this language secures final sovereignty of states, Article 13 (b) raises the question of the responsibility of the General Assembly in "promoting international co-operation in the economic, social, cultural, educational, and health fields, and assisting in the realization of human rights and fundamental freedoms for all without distinction as to race, sex, language, or religion."[61] Thus from one side, the sovereignty of a state must be protected but on the other side, conflict that is posed against citizens' natural rights falls outside of the roam of state sovereignty, broadening the scope of UNSC sanctions to cases of extreme violence against native citizens of a state.

The rationales for imposing sanctions have broadened during the time period from 2000 to 2008. This is especially true in the wake of September 11, when "security" considerations took on new form. The Bush Doctrine–which dramatically expanded the threshold for military threats–coupled with the new conception of "security" as having socioeconomic, environmental, and humanitarian roots, meant that issues which would previously be within a state's sovereign rights were suddenly fair game for UN or unilateral sanctions schemes.[62] This in fact is the expansion of the concept of "countermeasure" which is now introduced as an international conflict.

Despite an increase in UN-imposed sanctions, the success rate has stayed quite limited. Only two cases with limited successful intervention can be pinpointed. One is the case against Libya and the other is the sanction imposed against Yugoslavia over the civil war in Bosnia.[63] This lack of success can be artificially linked to different factors including globalization, an increased ease of communication between states, *etc*. However, because there is virtually no basis of comparison from before the 1990s, correlation cannot be shown.

3.4.2 Policy Considerations Regarding the Decision to Sanction

As analyzed above, virtually any activity including planning, preparation, initiation, or the waging of wars of aggression can be classified as a violation against peace and humanity and can be interpreted and argued to constitute war crimes. The expanded definitions of genocide, human rights, crimes against humanity, and threats to peace have resulted in a parallel expansion of conditions, which are likely to trigger sanctions deliberations. Therefore, the situations or cases under which nations would refer cases to the UNSC under Article 51 of the UN Charter is substantially increased, as any cases related to peace will be sent to the UNSC.

Paradoxically, expanding the definition of threats to peace does not serve the cause of peace. This is because UN actions or interventions in target states will lack precision of purpose, leading to ambiguity in implementation (as will be seen in Chapter five). Therefore, concrete definitions of peace and security, along with what type of conduct rises to the level of danger sufficient enough to constitute a "threat to peace" are necessary. Few proponents of sanctions, even humanitarians genuinely seeking sanctions to prevent the escalation of violence, seem to realize that the definitional problem may only aggravate the underlying situation. An illustrative case is the sanctions against Darfur. Conflict in Darfur started in 2003, after rebel groups, the Sudan Liberation Army (SLA), and the Justice and Equality Movement (JEM) accused the government of favoring black Africans over Arabs. The conflict between the rebel groups and the Sudanese government has resulted in 400,000 deaths as reported by the Coalition for International Justice.[64] The UN Human Rights Council called on the Security Council to make an urgent decision to protect Darfur civilians. Thus, taking the tragic situation in Darfur, humanitarians calling for sanctions against the Sudan are mistaken in assuming that sanctions will stop militias by depriving them of necessary arms. The legal pretense for sanctions was the genocide in Darfur. Yet, as will be explored in Chapter five, absent a clear definition, what has started as genocide or ethnic cleansing may evolve into a full-fledged civil war or humanitarian disaster of a *much greater* scope than the original horrible situation if necessary supplies are prevented from reaching the country. This is because rival groups will necessarily begin to compete for finite resources, like foodstuffs, and other necessary supplies. In countries that are under sanctions, despite the assumption that the populace will be influenced by hardships imposed by the sanctions, there is an outreaching expectation that they *will* attempt to influence the ruling elites towards change, a countervailing internal force. However, as the government will adjust to the sanctions, the population will also begin to adjust to the new environment, restrictions, and practical effects of the sanctions, not only making the period during which sanctions are imposed longer and less effective but also breaking up the society further into two economic groups–those who are able to resist the sanctions (or maybe even benefit from the sanctions) and those who are harmed. Through deductive reasoning, it can be derived that the longer the period of time sanctions are imposed, the less effective they will be in achieving an end result related to the populace. Likewise, the longer sanctions are in place in the target country, the higher the likelihood of stratification along economic lines based on the ability to withstand sanctions. The length of sanctions would in particular hinder chances of successful future ruling regimes. As the economic strain on the country continues, the new generations faced with difficulties of progressing through a natural life become weary and distrustful of the sanctioning body and internalize the country's potential for success. Remarkably, in his speeches to the Iranian population after the 1979 revolution, Ayatollah Ruhollah Khomeini would emphasize that the new regime was not afraid of sanctions but afraid of cultural and economic dependence on the West.

Reform of the UN Charter to reflect the definitional problems stated above is not impossible, but would prove to be very difficult. There were several reforms proposed by the UN after the Oil-for-Food scandal unfolded. These reforms, which included reallocation of political responsibility, were suggested by a team that was delegated by Kofi Annan were not approved by seventy-seven developing countries who are signatories of the "Joint Declaration of the Seventy-Seven Countries" otherwise referred to as the G-77.[65]

The UN's conservative and path-dependent Secretariat, as well as its sprawling bureaucracy, embodies Newton's law of physics: the organization and its constituent parts continue in a state of rest or of uniform motion towards applying ambiguous policy directives unless they are compelled to change that state by force impressed upon it. The stronger the force applied, the greater the magnitude of the expected change.[66] Nevertheless, as noted above, the soft and inconsistent nature of the UN and international law conditions triggering sanctions mean that they continue to be invoked based on politicized premises, without *a priori* specific start conditions, end conditions, and more importantly, lacking a definite goal. The fact that the "United Nations," in the sense of the Secretariat, General Assembly, and Security Council exists, has tended to obscure the fact that the "United Nations," in the sense of a community of states committed to a common program of purposes and principles, does not exist.[67] Lacking common goals and definitions, the UN is left to urge member states to comply with its sanction resolutions and only hope for positive results. From the perspective of the UN or the imposing party, when economic measures are used as sanctions, the objective should be to deter or dissuade states from pursuing policies, which do not conform to accepted norms of international conduct.[68] However, since sanctions are often poorly defined or not defined by specific terms or with specific objective, the length of time that they are imposed can become extended to the point that the objective of the sanctions may disappear. Yet without a clearly determined end point (that is, a condition for determining when sanctions have, for instance, "accomplished their intended objectives"), UN policymakers continue to enforce sanctions for indeterminate terms, resulting in humanitarian crises. Unfortunately, the humanitarian crisis or the true impact of extended sanctions is not apparent until the target state resumes its neutral presence in the international order. These sanctioned states, weakened by sanctions remain vulnerable to postsanctions external influences on their policies vindicated by the arrival of development funds from more powerful states. Thus leaving the unanswered the question of "how can UN ensure sovereign rights of states are protected in implementation of sanctions?" In the following chapter I seek to analyze the trajectory of the implementation of economic sanctions.

4 Implementation
Strength of Sanctions and Domestic Policy

> Members were not clear what they were doing and why, nor what the real interpretive functions of the Committee should legitimately be, nor what the real issues were.
>
> —Paul Conlon[1]

The development of the UN and the increase in its membership has created a potential for an effective and forceful organization. Despite this potential, the implementation of UN-imposed economic sanctions remains an *ad hoc* process and the effectiveness of these sanctions has remained unclear. However, the UN has not ceased using economic sanctions and thus far the steps that have been taken by states or the UN to resolve the effectiveness question has not led to a clear response, as conflict situations and threats to peace continue in the same notorious conflict zones.

Do the trade sanctions imposed actually affect the target country or are they a gateway to black market development? Considering that economic sanctions are historically imposed on undeveloped countries, the economic effects on trade are of less immediate importance than their role as a cause of infrastructural failure. Though, before the question of effect is answered, there is the matter of the strength of the sanctions. How strong do sanctions have to be to cause a noticeable change in the target's economy? How is this strength measured and by whose standards? We can refer to this strength as the "strength of threat," referring to the threat that is created by imposed sanctions. The underlying assumption of sanctions is that the consequences are equal regardless of the target's position; however, if a country is more isolated from the world economy and does not have many natural resources or bilateral contracts then its economy is less influenced by economic sanctions. Although Mongolia does not represent an autarchy, its overall trade volume relative to other countries makes it a good base for comparison. Economic sanctions on a country like Mongolia (with an economy not dependent on imports or exports) is hardly the same as imposing sanctions on Iraq, which is directly dependent on oil exports. Therefore, the implementation process is highly dependent on the target's economic and political position, which can be the basis of evaluation for strength of sanctions.

Can the effectiveness of sanctions be quantified based on sanction strength in particular if the target is expected to change its policies? Although Hufbauer *et al.* answered this question with respect to US the measure of this strength is questionable, particularly for UN sanctions, since an economic impact cannot be directly measured due to the series of external factors, such as third party relations. Therefore the measure of the strength of sanctions is highly indeterminate and biased. Scholars have started connecting the problems of measurement in the sanctions domain with the lessons from peacekeeping operations. For example, in the overwhelming number of sanctions cases there are other factors which militate against an easily quantifiable analysis, such as: 1) the complexity of conflict situations; 2) the extensive involvement of nongovernmental parties (such as the dispute over the Gaza Strip and continuous violence in Sudan); 3) the frequent political support and military assistance of one or more of the permanent members to one or another of the parties in conflict; and 4) the growing multiplicity of military, civilian, and governmental functions undertaken by peacekeeping operations.[2]

Besides the question of the strength of the sanctions, in order for sanctions to motivate any change in the target's policy, there needs to be a general acceptance of the authority of the sanctioning group, which would minimize the resistance or retaliation of target states. In practice, since it is not always states that are the cause of conflict, the authority of the UN in dealing with the nonstate actors is questioned, resulting in an ineffective sanctions regime. Additionally the UN's authority is jeopardized, since implementation is theoretically an international measure and in practice it depends on domestic legislation. To complicate this matter ultimately individual member states are given the right, by the UN Charter, to use force preemptively, which means that they may act unilaterally if they see a "threat to peace and security" without waiting for the Security Council's approval.[3] Beyond consideration for the heightened power that is given to member states on such delicate matters of intervention in what may sometimes be a matter of sovereignty (a classic debate in international law), the freedom of action of individual states diminishes the UNSC's authority, especially in cases where sanctions are imposed for a prolonged period of time. As sovereign states, each UN member and nonmember state strives for more control and higher profitability for the state and its citizens; consequently, it becomes questionable whether is it in the best interest of member states to give up this power in-exchange for exercising their internationally given right.[4] Therefore, it is the member state's implementation of sanctions that would be the determinant of the strength of sanctions.

Returning to the Iraqi sanctions regime, Conlon notes that the freezing or impounding of assets—as the act was conceived in the resolution authorizing sanctions—did not have the intended effect of stopping trade. Though it was meant to be a "distinctly preventive" measure rather than carrying a punitive function, directed more at Kuwaiti assets than Iraqi ones,[5] neither financial sanctions nor traditional trade sanctions had much effect as states were able to circumvent the resolutions by either trading illicitly, or applying for broad licenses from the Sanctions Committee. Almost immediately after Iraq accepted Resolution 687, which welcomed restoration of Kuwait,[6] Iraq sought to resume oil exports under paragraph 23 of that resolution. Included in the decisions of this resolution was that upon approval by the Council of Iraqi compliance with the resolution, the prohibition against the import of commodities and products originating in Iraq and the prohibitions against financial transactions related thereto contained in Resolution 661 (1990) had no further force. Iraq requested that the UN "unfreeze" assets totaling $1billion in order to begin trading under paragraph 23. Conlon continues,

> After debates at several meetings over related non-issues, the Committee decided to inform a number of states (identified by Iraq as holding frozen assets) that assets frozen on the basis of the resolution [*sic*] 661 could be unfrozen, provided that the unfrozen amounts were used to pay for humanitarian imports under the provisions of paragraph 20 of resolution 687.[7]

Over the next year, $1 billion was authorized by the committee under the humanitarian waiver provisions of the resolution authorizing sanctions. This was directly related to the Iraq Sanctions Committee's infamous Oil-for-Food scandal. Paul Conlon admits that "to some extent the Committee's own behavior was responsible, for outgoing clearance letters continued until June 1993 (eight months after the adoption of Resolution 778) to contain a now obsolete passage suggesting that assets could be unfrozen for humanitarian goods." The importance of the above example is that if a case as highly managed and deeply politicized as the sanctions against Iraq in the early 1990s can fall prey to workarounds and circumvention by states and firms eager to benefit from lucrative sanctions-dodging schemes, then what is to be said of smaller states, or less visible UN sanctions? If a $1 billion scam can be orchestrated in front of the eyes of the world, indeed, through the very halls of the United Nations headquarters, than the ability of neighboring states (which account for great majorities of trade volume for any given country) to continue trade should be self-evident. Therefore it is the interplay of state relations and state's communication with the UN that would provide support for the correlation of sanction strength and implementation. The hypothesis identified here is that a multilayered process leads to an unequal implementation and increases the ineffectiveness of these sanctions. This hypothesis is dependent on what shapes domestic implementation and how states can position themselves to overlook international sanctions based on their power structure within the international community. An understanding of implementation of economic sanctions is not possible without understanding how states inform the UN of their cooperation, and what implementation techniques are used domestically.

4.1 COOPERATION

As previously alluded to, individual cooperation of all member and non-UN member states is required for sanctions to have any effect. This cooperation is different amongst member states based on their formation, structure, constitution, and economic interests. For instance the European Union (EU) block states in general do not have the power to terminate binding enforcement measures of the UN based on the principle of "parallelism of competence." This principle determines that when a constitution invests in the decision-making power of a given organ, the power of revoking such decision lies with the same organ.[8] Therefore, the EU members are bound to UN Security Council sanctions. The situation differs when dealing with states other than EU states. For instance, in response to continued efforts for sanctions against North Korea, China–due to its strong trade ties with North Korea–did not succumb to sanctions until North Korea's second nuclear test.[9]

There are other issues that arise in the realm of cooperation. In many instances, trade relations are challenged by sanctions due to their pre-existing nature. A demonstration of this situation comes from a letter to the UN commission by five African states. The letter, dated October 15, 1990, questions the validity of sanctions on pre-existing contracts. These African countries had trade relationships with Kuwait before UN sanctions were imposed on the country. The five African countries asked for permission to continue trading oil with Aden (an oil producing city in Kuwait), in spite of existing sanctions placed on the occupying Iraq regime. Resolution 661 of 1990 issued sanctions against Iraq, *after* Iraq's occupation of Kuwait. The sanctions were imposed on the trade of any goods that were at the time controlled by the occupying regime. The African countries based their argument on the date of their signed agreement with Kuwait.[10] Although the UN and UNSC found this date argument legally irrelevant, a series of overlooked issues came to the surface during UNSC committee discussions.

These subsequent issues were discussed in terms of sanctioning states with extensive trade of natural resources:

1. In regards to natural resources such as oil, who should receive control of the resource post sanctions?
2. What are the specific measurement criteria for determining when and how much of the resources had left their original destination?

3. Who receives the revenues from shipments that occurred before sanctions were in place?
4. Are any of the contracts signed before sanctions are imposed executable?[11]

The above arguments have continually been addressed since the 1990s as they have not been defined and clearly understood due to the nature of sanctions. The date of the contracts between the nations does not actually matter but, rather, it is the date of export that needs to be regarded as the basis of analysis for the implementation of economic sanctions. Therefore, it is the member states that would have to provide documentation and information in regards to their previous trade with a particular target country. Since these states could have an absolute need for the imported production (oil, gas, or other resources), they may be hesitant in timely cooperation. This issue surfaced numerous times during sanctions against Iraq.[12] The question arises on what specific system does the UN have in place for overseeing or controlling this implementation process?

4.2 DOMESTIC IMPLEMENTATION OF UN SANCTIONS

A key requirement for a successful sanctions regime is domestic or national implementation of UN resolutions authorizing the sanctions. Implementation is governed by Article 25 of the UN Charter, which identifies that incorporation of UNSC resolutions is left to the domestic states.[13] States, as a matter of theory and practice, have different approaches to international law generally, and sanctions enforcement in particular.

In the US, for instance, national legislation pertaining to UN sanctions is further complicated by the various unilateral sanctions schemes.[14] Different countries not only understand their duty to comply with UNSC resolutions in different ways but they have also developed a distinct vocabulary for describing their implementation process (or lack thereof). In mandatory reports to the UN, member states use varying phraseology to describe their level of implementation. Here is a list of selected terminology:

- Uruguay declares that it is in "general agreement" with UN sanctions;
- Jamaica "advises its ministries" of UN sanctions
- Thailand, Laos and Bahamas state simply that they "will comply" with UN sanctions resolutions.[15]

The permutations of synonyms for compliance are endless:

- Poland issues a "statement of cooperation";
- Uruguay, Venezuela, and the United Arab Emirates issue a "general agreement";

- Burkina Faso issues a statement of "Full Support" for a given sanctions resolution;
- Israel "will act accordingly";
- Cuba is "taking steps" to implement sanctions resolutions;
- India has "advised authorities"

Such vague compliance requirements show the minimal importance given to actual implementation, leaving the oversight to the UN. The costs and the number of large states that would need monitoring diminish the possibility of oversight.

Other states take a much more serious stance on implementation. On a country-by-country basis, Sweden is one of the leaders in domestic implementation, with specific enforcement of UNGA and UNSC resolutions even when such enforcement entails harming the interests of its own citizens.[16] Reporting of the *actual progress of implementation*, is different from reporting on *how* a given country will implement a particular sanctions scheme (see above), is also subject to vastly differing approaches, resulting in asynchronous levels of enforcement and domestic implementation. For instance, in reporting on their compliance with UN sanctions against Iraq, states used various forms of "compliance." Slovenia, for instance, published a text of Resolution 757 (1992) in its official gazette with additional instructions. In its letter to the Secretary General, Slovenia mentions that these measures have a negative effect on its economy but that they would proceed with the sanctions nonetheless.[17] England reports their level of compliance in great detail (12 points of change), Liechtenstein enacted legislation on June 5, 1992, Finland produced a nine-paragraph report detailing their enforcement and implementation of UN obligations, Germany'seight-paragraph report declared full compliance, Italy's report proclaimed "EU compliance," Czechoslovakia issued a"full compliance" report, and the Russian Federation vowed "full cooperation."[18] A review of UN documents reveals that the same language and forms of reporting were in use as of 2009. Though there is no direct enforcement of a sanctions implementation, some states, such as the US, have a much more stringent process. Though the US leaves room for waiving implementation for national interest, it takes a unilateral enforcement mechanism even on UN sanctions.

4.3 IMPLEMENTATION IN PRACTICE

4.3.1 The US and Problems with Sanctions Implementation

The US implementation of UN sanctions is a complex theme. For instance, there is well-known strong opposition in the US to the United Nations, which some conservative commentators see as an infringement on US sovereignty and independence.[19] Klein states that "[t]he globalists, of course, are not content with just trying to suborn our foreign policy decision to the UN's, or to subject our duly elected leaders to the compulsory jurisdiction of the play-actors peopling their manufactured 'international court."[20] Though Klein's discontent with the UN's role in US foreign policy, and US responsibility as a member of the UN may seem extreme, some US politicians and decision-makers actually follow a similar line of reasoning. Klein continues, "even stripping the US Treasury by way of 'global taxes'—or 'assessments' or 'duties' or 'moral obligations' or 'ransom' or other phrases globalists use to cloak their intentions—would not satisfy these do-gooder parasites."[21] Discussions of the role of the UN, US compliance with UN resolutions, veto power of Russia and China, and US funding of UN activities had actually set a policy platform for the Republican presidential candidate during the 2012 elections. Despite these political positions, the US does have a strong implementation process for both unilateral and multilateral UN sanctions. The US as the most active sender of unilateral sanctions needs to be evaluated to give us a better picture of how sanctions implementation takes place from the point of view of a sanctions advocate.

Though the complexity of domestic implementation of UN sanctions is not in question, a multipronged process further complicates the US implementation. Complication in the US stems from the large number of agencies that have oversight over sanctions implementation and the shifting nature of US foreign policy and the specific sanctions regimes.[22] Sanctions implementation in the US is carried out by the Department of State, Department of Treasury, and the Department of Commerce with sometimes overlapping and competing monitoring, enforcement, and oversight functions. Maneuvering through the agencies, the US implements UNSC sanctions but also imposes what it deems are reasonable restrictions on these sanctions in order to conduct foreign policy. In the wake of terrorist attacks, for instance, America's stated need to conduct a vigorous and multifaceted foreign policy has meant changes to the law to give the executive branch greater flexibility in administering aid or directing foreign trade. This was not merely a policy of the Bush administration in the wake of September 11, 2001, but actually extended earlier into the Clinton administration. To gain a better understanding of US implementation of unilateral and multilateral sanctions and the intertwined involvement of administrative agencies, we must study the congressional statutes that relate to economic sanctions. The US domestic legislation covering *sanctions* is multidimensional and can affect US businesses that operate in neighboring states to the target country whether or not the sanctions are unilateral.

A review of the pertinent sections of one legislative package is useful to illustrate how sanctions are implemented on the domestic level and the interplay between multilateral and unilateral sanctions schemes.[23] The *Foreign Operations, Export Financing and Related Programs Appropriations Act,1997*, enacted by the 104th Congress, prohibits US foreign aid to any country not complying with UN sanctions against Iraq and Serbia-Montenegro. Section 536 of the Act provides that any state that does not comply with the UNSC sanctions against Iraq, Serbia- Montenegro will not be eligible for foreign aid assistance under the Foreign Assistance Act of 1961. Additionally the Sanctions Act of 1997 sets out restrictions on funding and the conduct of US representatives and firms with respect to sanctioned countries. Section 570 prohibits new investment in Burma pending progress on human rights, and requires US representatives to international financial institutions to vote against spending for Burma. Section 533 prohibits US foreign aid to any country not complying with UN sanctions against Iraq and Serbia-Montenegro. It also authorizes the president to ban US imports of goods from countries that have not enacted trade restrictions against Iraq and Serbia-Montenegro. Section 553 puts conditions on the release of foreign aid to the Palestine Liberation Organization.

This act in essence transforms any unilateral measures taken by the US into multilateral sanctions, which is of particular importance when targeting neighboring countries that are vulnerable to major changes within the region. Such countries are faced with the choice of minimizing their economic relationship with the neighboring state or foregoing assistance from the US. Therefore their dependency, on both sides, places the target's neighboring state with the challenge of selecting a side, meaning, the country must determine how they can gain the most economic benefit. This type of decision-making would in effect increase the country's dependency upon selecting one side or another, since their choice would inevitably mean a partial economic loss.

Along with the Foreign Assistance Act of 1997, the *Antiterrorism and Effective Death Penalty Act of 1996,* prohibits foreign aid to any country that provides assistance to terrorist list countries. Interestingly section 234 of this act diminishes the power of UNSC resolutions and solidifies the US as the responsible state in dealing with international terrorism. This section reads "...the United Nations has been an inadequate forum for the discussion of cooperative, multilateral responses to the threat of international terrorism; the President should undertake immediate efforts to develop effective multilateral responses to international terrorism as a complement to national counter terrorist efforts."[24] Such complementary activities include covert operations and military force. The power shift evident in this act not only provides a strong background on the US position towards the UN but also provides evidence of the passive look the US has towards UN resolutions. Furthering that even in cases where the binding mandatory UN resolution removes sanctions from a state, the US will continue with economic force to ensure compliance.

A US law that provides us with specifics of how the implementation process is executed is the *Iran and Libya Sanctions Act of 1996 (ILSA).* Three years following UN-mandated sanctions restricting sale of aircraft and oil-refining equipment to Libya, the US imposed this law. This act, which expired in 2006, did not result in the sanctioning of any specific firms. Although this act was primarily on Iran and Libya after its expiration in 2006, the introduction of the Iran Freedom Support Act (P.L. 109.29) limited the act to only Iran. Several presidential waivers were added through this act; however, sanction on Iran continued on petroleum and weapons of mass destruction development. Additionally funds and political assistance for individuals or organizations active in promoting democracy and nonproliferation were made available. This act, similar to other sanctions regimes (unilateral or multilateral), was formulated to impose sanctions on the most vulnerable sectors of the target country. In the Iranian case, the petroleum sector, which was the source of 20% of the GDP, was targeted. Even after the Clinton presidency when in 2006 the *Iran Sanctions Act* (ISA) targeting only Iran was introduced, the US faced hesitation from their allies in stopping all investment in Iran. Although, since the 1979 Revolution, the Islamic Republic of Iran has had a continuous interest in maintaining independent control of their resources. The government introduced a buy-back investment program, which allowed investment in the country without giving any equity stakes in the Iranian industry to foreign firms. Using this process, the French oil and gas multinational, Total S.A., and other competitors, the Gazprum of Russia and the Petronas of Malaysia, agreed to a $2 billion contract with Iran. Realizing the continuation of these investments and their political position, US President Clinton decided to waive the ILSA sanctions on these countries.[25] In effect, the *Iran Freedom and Support Act* was the result of congressional member's recognition of foreign companies' deviation under ILSA.[26]

The ISA, which was introduced in 2006, was to strengthen the secondary impact on any foreign investment in Iran and limit flexibility. Future provisions have been proposed to further remove any possibility of these sanctions on third party investment in the target country. To further diminish the desire of investment in the Iranian sectors, a bill was passed in 2007 which would protect fund managers from shareholder lawsuits, in cases where the fund manager divested from firms that have made ISA-sanctionable investments.[27] As demonstrated here, the ILSA and ISA demonstrate the multitiered difficulty of imposing sanctions not only on a target state, but investment firms in the sender country, allies, and subsidiaries of US firms. The ISA thus far has faced several extensive revisions because of the inability to control profitable long-term contracts made by third parties in a sanction regime. Since the US is the driver of the sanctions in this case, they are in fact not only sanctioning the target state but they have a secondary target, which would not only weaken the economy of the primary target, in this case Iran, but would also hinder economic development through investment in the second tier target. Such multitier targeting is also present in the sanctions against Cuba. In addition the complexity of enforcing sanctions with the side effect of hindering relations, the implementation of sanctions is extremely challenging as the targets will search for alternative supply sources from third parties. Several other US-initiated acts that impact implementation of the UN sanctions are:

- *United Nations Participation Act of 1945* (This act defines US representation at the UN and identifies the selection criteria for a representative. It does limit the actions of the representative to those permitted and communicated by the US president. Interestingly, Section 287(c) gives the president broad powers to impose economic sanctions, but only those mandated by the UN Security Council);
- *Iraq Sanctions Act of 1990* (comprehensive trade embargo on Iraq following Iraq's invasion of Kuwait);
- *Iran-Iraq Arms Non-Proliferation Act of 1992* (law applies to Iran the same export license prohibitions applied to Iraq in the Iraq Sanctions Act of 1990);
- *International Security and Development Cooperation Act of 1985* (prohibits export of goods and technology to Libya)[28]

The Office of Foreign Asset Control (OFAC) carries out the implementation of sanctions in the US. The *International Emergency Economic Powers Act of 1977 ("IEEPA")*, gives the US president broad authority to deal with unusual and extraordinary international threats; this is also the act that establishes the US Department of Treasury Office of Foreign Assets Control. The OFAC is responsible for issuing regulations to US federal agencies concerning US implementation of UN and unilateral sanctions. For instance, concerning the sanctions against Iraq, the 1990 sanctions implementing a United Nations resolution block financial assets in the United States of the Iraqi government. They prohibit most US exports and re-exports of US goods and technology to Iraq, US imports of goods from Iraq, and financial transactions with the Iraqi government. Unilateral US sanctions also prohibit exports of US services to Iraq and block all property assets in the United States of the Iraqi government. The OFAC regulations of December 1996, implementing a later UN resolution, authorize US companies to seek licenses to buy oil from Iraq; the revenue is intended for the purchase of humanitarian supplies for Iraqis.[29] Additionally under the IEEPA, OFAC administers sanctions against nations and individuals pursuant to federal law. As of 2008, the OFAC administers sanctions against the following states:

- Iran (since 1979 for the Iran hostage crisis and subsequent sponsorship of terrorism);
- Myanmar also known as Burma (since 1997 for repressing democratic opposition);
- Sudan (since 1997 for human rights violations and sponsoring terrorism);

- Russia (since 2000 to prevent export of weapons-grade uranium. These sanctions are listed under non-proliferation sanctions);
- Zimbabwe (since 2003 for undermining democratic institutions);
- Syria (since 2004 for sponsorship of terrorism and pursuit of weapons of mass destruction);
- Belarus (since 2006 for undermining democratic institutions);
- North Korea (since 2008 for risk of the proliferation of weapon-usable fissile material);
- Haiti (President Bush in 1991 used his authority to freeze all the assets of de facto regime in Haiti and prohibit any trade with Haiti. These sanctions are no longer active).[30]

Since implementation is a state matter, and because of US extensive sanctions process, we would be able to draw more specific correlation between the language in the UN sanctions and unilateral sanctions. One of the longest-term US unilateral sanctions is the Cuba sanctions regime. These sanctions began by the initiation of the *Export Import Bank Act (1945)*, which prohibits Export Import Bank credits to Marxist-Leninist countries, such as China, Cuba, and former Soviet Bloc countries. Further sanctions were imposed on Cuba by the *Cuban Democracy Act of 1992* and the *Cuba Liberty and Democratic Solidarity Act of 1996*.

The *Cuba Liberty and Democratic Solidarity Act of 1996* (Helms-Burton Act) is a comprehensive trade embargo against Cuba and subtracts from US aid to Russia an amount of money equal to Russia's support for the intelligence facility at Lourdes in Cuba. This act also calls on the US representative to the United Nations to seek multilateral UN sanctions on Cuba. However, the purpose of this act is 1) to assist the Cuban people in regaining their freedom and joining the community of democratic countries in the Western Hemisphere, 2) to strengthen international sanctions against the Castro government.[31] As it stands, the first two purposes of this act contradict one another. Although the goal seems to be the ultimate freedom of the Cuban citizens, the second purpose seems to suppose that the best means of reaching this goal is through further depriving the people of economic prosperity through sanctioning the government for an extended period of time. Though international sanctions against Cuba have not been imposed to date, trade with Cuba remains limited. The importance of this act and Cuba in general to our broader discussion with respect to UN sanctions is the continuous circularity in argument with respect to the use of sanctions for the ultimate goal of freedom. Looking further at this act, we can demonstrate the secondary impact of sanctions on third parties (countries). Under the Helms-Burton Act, there are certain safeguard measures that are put in place to ensure that Cuban made products or products made with Cuban material are not imported through Mexico or Canada. Further impact on countries that trade with Cuba could be sanctions as described in section 1704(b)(1) of that act. Such barriers to trade make this act beyond a limited foreign policy tool against Cuba and a much broader multilateral sanction regime to alienate not only Cuba but what the US would call unfriendly nations towards US policies.[32]

Although the US has had long-term sanctions imposed on communist countries, there have been instances where such policies were waived because of national interest. Notably, China received a national interests waiver in 1980 (see waiver section below) following Richard Nixon's successful China-US summit.

An area of study that has boomed since the September 11, 2001 terrorist attack on the US is concerned with terrorist activities. Prior to these attacks there were different regulations that established the country's position on terrorist activities. One notable regulation, which was enacted prior to the events of September 11, 2001, is the National Defense Authorization Act for Fiscal Year 1996 prohibits the Defense Department from giving aid to countries on the State Department Terrorist list. Additionally, the Department of Defense (DOD) Appropriation Act of 1987 prohibits the DOD from entering into contracts of $100,000 or more with any company owned or controlled by the government of a State Department terrorist list country, and the Arms Export Controls Act of 1968 restricts arms exports to countries on the State Department terrorist list. These acts in essence strengthen the sanctions and broaden their power whether multilateral or unilateral.

Prior to the UN, "international" sanctions were governed by the Smoot-Hawley Tariff Act of 1930, which prohibits US imports of goods mined, produced, or manufactured by convict labor, forced labor, or indentured labor and the Trading With the Enemy Act of 1917 that gave the president authority to control foreign transactions and property interests during war. The IEEPA amended this legislation to give the president power and more control over foreign trade during peacetime and emergency situations.

The IEEPA also contains a sweeping policy regarding multilateral economic embargoes against governments in armed conflict with the United States. According to Section 1707,

> It is the policy of the United States, that upon the use of the Armed Forces of the United States to engage in hostilities against any foreign country, the President shall, as appropriate—(1) seek the establishment of a multinational economic embargo against such country; and (2) seek the seizure of its foreign financial assets.[33]

There are several provisions which complicate consistent US implementation of UNSC sanctions, one of which is the presidential waiver. There are three circumstances under which the US president can waive the enforcement of unilateral sanctions. The president can waive the imposition of sanctions if a waiver "is important to the national interest of the United States."[34] Additionally *Human rights and security assistance* code, (22 U.S.C.

§ 2304) allows for the presidential waiver to be applied in extraordinary circumstances or cases where an improvement in the democratic process has led to an improvement in the human rights record.

According to Raj Bhala of the University of Kansas, School of Law,

> This waiver authority appears to be quite broad; it is not limited to a national security interest, but rather can be invoked for any sort of national interest. The legislative history indicates that the President might consider use of this waiver authority if the imposition of sanctions would threaten US intelligence sources and methods, hinder the international cooperation and the international obligations of the United States, or lead to unacceptable costs to US economic interests. For example, the *President* could find that imposing sanctions is contrary to national interest because it would result in an unacceptably high loss of sales or profits to US businesses or cost too many Americans their jobs.[35]

The Antiterrorism and Effective Death Penalty Act of 1996 prohibited US nationals from supporting terrorist organizations and engaging in financial transactions with governments named on the State Department's terrorism list including Cuba, Iran, Iraq, Libya, North Korea, Sudan, and Syria.[36] Importantly, however, US sanctions legislation allows the president to waive sanctions under the law for national security reasons.[37] Raj Bhala writing about the president's waiver authority explains "the President can waive sanctions if the imposition would harm the US government's ability to obtain critical goods and services."[38] The definition of goods and services remains subjective, which in effect broadens the president's authority further.

Glenn H. Kaminsky and Charles G. Wall of the US Department of Commerce, Office of Chief Counsel for Industry and Security, state it bluntly:

> In practice, the interaction between these powers [US President, Congress and the United Nations] in restricting trade often leads to confusion, as harmonizing everyone's wishes with regard to these very sensitive destinations isn't always possible.[39]

As demonstrated in this section the US is quite stern on the sanction implementation process. Furthermore, the comparison between unilateral sanctions and UN-imposed sanctions shows that they both carry secondary power, by threatening nontarget states for noncompliance. However, the presidential waiver authority, gives the US a way out of implementing UN sanctions forcefully. As Kaminsky continues,

> "[in] some instances, sector-specific or comprehensive sanctions mandated by the United Nations Security Council (UNSC) have resulted in the imposition of new US controls or tightening of the licensing policy

for existing controls, for example with UNSC Resolution 1718 on North Korea. In most cases "because of US foreign policy reasons or because of statutory requirements, US sanctions have differed in scope or duration from those mandated by the UNSC."[40]

By maintaining the rights to act unilaterally in enforcing implementation, the US preserves its position as a political power. The inconsistency even on a domestic level of implementation is evident as the US, one of the proponents of sanctions, can use presidential waivers to divert from their general legal obligations under international law. Furthermore the exceptions made under national interest and for maintaining their political position with their allies, demonstrates the inconsistency of implementation of both unilateral and UN sanctions.

4.3.2 Unilateral Sanctions Legislation in Implementing UN Security Council Resolutions

A comparative analysis of other nations' implementation procedures provides a better picture of what is the best implementation method. In Australia, UN resolutions are rapidly implemented, with few restrictions or limitations.[41] Australia implements UN sanctions[42] thoroughly grounded on the Charter of the United Nations Act 1945, which details the manner in which Australia will apply sanctions based on the decisions of the Security Council.[43] This act binds all Australian citizens including those residing abroad in complying with Security Council resolutions, which consequently bind Australia. The act provides that the Governor-General may make regulations, which are binding until the Security Council ceases to enforce the resolution on Australia. Furthermore, the Customs Act of 1901 enforces the sanctions dealing with the import/export of goods. Australia defines that the breach of UNSC resolutions would result in financial liability. The penalty upon conviction for offenses dealing with noncompliance of sanctions implementation in Australia would result in ten years imprisonment or a fine. The fine would be either an amount three times the value of the transaction in the breach of sanctions (if this can be calculated) or a fine of $275,000 for individual offenders. The fine for corporate offenders is either a maximum fine, which is three times the value of the transaction in breach of sanctions (if this can be calculated) or a fine of $1.1 million, whichever value is greater. False or misleading information in relation to Australia's UN sanctions enforcement law would also have severe consequences.[44] Australia's sanctions implementation measures are much more detailed and in-depth than those of many other nation states or of even the Security Council. The existence of the consequences of noncompliance in implementing sanctions makes Australia's implementation much more structured. The UNSC can use the same structured format in regards to compliance in order to have specific compliance rules, which would lead to much more effective implementation of member and nonmember states. For example because of Australia's position on sanctions, they have implemented multiple unilateral sanctions against North Korea in implementing UN sanctions, making compliance measures much more severe.[45]

In the European Union, UNSC resolutions that are adopted as EU directives by the EU's Common Foreign and Security Policy have a direct effect on constituent domestic jurisdictions to the extent that they are implemented as European Commission (EC) regulations.[46] The EC is not a direct member of the UN. Binding resolutions of the Security Council are addressed to the UN member states, not to the EC. However, the concurrent membership of all members in both the EC and the UN makes the EC responsible for taking note of UNSC sanctions resolutions.[47] The process is two-fold: first, the European Council adopts a so-called "common position"; second, the position is implemented through an EC regulation.[48] An example of such EC regulation is the Council Regulation (EC) No 337/2000 of 14 February 2000 concerning a flight ban and a freeze of funds and other financial resources in respect to the Taliban of Afghanistan.[49] The specific measures that the EC regulation calls states to enact are described in the EC regulations, which resemble templates. These regulations read,

1. The approval of the said Committee should be obtained through the competent national authorities of the Member States, whose names and addresses should, therefore, be made available and annexed to this Regulation.
2. For reasons of expediency, the Commission should be empowered to supplement and/or amend the Annexes to this Regulation on the basis of pertinent notifications from the said Committee.
3. The competent authorities of the Member States should, where necessary, be empowered to ensure compliance with this Regulation.
4. Violations of the provisions of this Regulation should be penalized and Member States should impose appropriate penalties to that effect.
5. The Security Council calls for the measures to be applied notwithstanding any rights conferred or obligations imposed by any international agreement signed or any contract entered into or any license or permit granted before the entry into force of the relevant paragraphs of Resolution 1267 (1999) enter into force.
6. The Commission and Member States should inform each other of the measures taken under this regulation and of other *relevant information* at their disposal in connection with this regulation, and cooperate with the said Committee, including by supplying information to it.[50]

At first glance, the vague EC regulations appear identical to the wording of UNSC resolutions, which could lead to the perpetuation of bureaucracy; in other words, the UN passes the responsibility to the EC, which in turn passes the requirement of implementation onto member states. However,

EU members have the most rigorous reporting responsibilities to the UN in regards to actions they have taken to implement UNSC resolutions. The situation is even more complicated if the member states are federal bodies, such as Germany. In such cases, this theoretically creates a multilayered legislation scheme in which enforcement, monitoring, and reporting are required, but due to the complex structure of the bureaucracy, very little actual enforcement can take place. The EC has been able to minimize this bureaucratic structure through the introduction of specific guidelines for all states within the framework of Common Foreign Security Policies.[51] The US, EC, and Australia are examples of a strong domestic implementation process. However, not all states go through a thorough domestic implementation of measures equally. Therefore, realistic implementation of sanctions is dependent on the smallest common denominators under the assumption that the world is an organization with the parts related to the whole functionally.[52]

4.4 DIPLOMACY

Considering the difficulties and inconsistencies that arise from implementation of sanctions, it may be a best practice for the UN to attempt to prevent or minimize conflict. To prevent conflict, the main strategy, and one enshrined in the spirit of and letter of the UN Charter, is to use diplomacy and take diplomatic measures to prevent disputes from escalating into conflict. The use of preventive diplomacy in the form of mediation, conciliation, and negotiations or preventive disarmament is, in theory, what the UN promotes when faced with any conflict situation.[53] However, such measures have in numerous instances led without much deliberation to economic sanctions and even military measures. Though some scholars have stated that in the case of Yugoslavia diplomacy was effective in conflict prevention;[54] throughout the 1990s, there were sanctions placed against former Yugoslavia and there was also military deployment to the area, which led to escalated conflict that is still impacting the region. In particular, Kosovo has not yet gained recognition as an independent state and conflict continues in northern Kosovo, especially in the Mitrovitsa region.

According to the UN publications, "the United Nations carefully monitors political and other developments around the world to detect threats to international peace and security, thereby enabling the Security Council and the Secretary-General to carry out preventive action."[55] Still the effective monitoring of threats to peace are questionable, due to the compound task of monitoring and the danger that monitoring units may face. Granted that in cases such as in the Congo, North Korea, Iran, and others, the UNSC has been aware of the potential for future conflict; the monitoring has been taking place over a long period of time (seven to ten years), meaning that the countries have had the time to adjust to difficulties that occurred or any future difficulties that may arise. The weakness of sanctions increases with the added fact that time elapses between when conflict is recognized and sanctions are implemented. New forces, trade partners, and other potentials for conflict have become part of the target country's status.

Accordingly, the UNSC, after delayed decision-making while *staying seized in the matter,* allows too much time to elapse before they resort to mandatory sanctions. This is considered a tool to enforce decisions, overlooking the idea that the target states (those responsible for the recognized conflict) have stayed alert about the future decisions of the UNSC and that sanctions may be placed on their state. Therefore, the target country will prepare for sanctions before they are even imposed; consequently the UNSC does not benefit from the element of surprise in imposing the sanctions. The delay in decision-making and reaction can be minimized by better planning and stronger implementation. The next chapter will identify the methodical problems that impact sanction implementation.

5 Implementation
From Theory to Practice

In 1919, President Woodrow Wilson declared that "a nation that is boycotted is a nation that is in sight of surrender. Apply this economic, peaceful, silent, deadly remedy and there will be no need for force."[1] As seen in the multiple empirical studies of the 20th century sanctions schemes, the application and enforcement of sanctions is not a simple or straightforward matter. Wilson continued,

> It is a terrible remedy. It does not cost a life *outside* the nation boycotted, but it brings a pressure upon the nation which, in my judgment, no modern nation could resist.[2]

This short quote carries imbedded within it the expectation of harm on the population of a target state. It also crudely identifies the force of sanctions as a pressure that no nation can resist, thus identifying sanctions as a coercive tool. Though Woodrow Wilson classified sanctions as a controlled source of harm, which would only impact the target state, Iraqi sanctions have shown that sanctions do cost lives but do not necessarily bring a state to compliance. Sanctions in fact have been a precursor, rather than substitution to force, in the case of Haiti, Bosnia, and Iraq.[3]

In more recent years, as we previously discussed, sanctions have again become the preferred foreign policy tool of the UN, and threats of sanctions in response to nuclear proliferation and state support for terrorism have become almost commonplace. In addition there is little consensus in scholarly or policy circles in regards to the decision to sanction or even what constitutes a threat to peace. In this chapter, I explore a similar phenomenon at the UN. What institutional ambiguities exist in the implementation process and what steps can be taken to resolve these problems? What legal changes do countries have to make to implement sanctions domestically and to actually stop trade with a sanctioned country (target)? How will these sanctions be administered? These questions will entice us to think and maybe respond to what Kenneth Abbott calls the "two main features of international life: the *actors* whose decisions and conduct shape outcomes, and the *factors and processes* that cause, influence, or constitute decision, actions and outcomes of compliance and noncompliance with legal rules".[4] This chapter presents the problem in the lack of institutional guidelines, concluding that the lack of institutional guidelines and the deliberately ad hoc process leaves sanctions without a time-frame, and diminishes their authority and influence.

The following chapter seeks to answer these questions from several perspectives. Part one (section 5.1 *et seq.*) takes a pragmatic, policy-oriented approach to sanctions implementation and represents the main factors affecting implementation from three sides of the sanctions transaction, the target state, and the sanctioning body (sender), and third parties. Part two (section 5.3 *et seq.*) analyzes the main concerns in implementing sanctions without any final effectiveness benchmarks or standards and finally gives alternative ways of approaching the sanctions deliberation process. The conclusion outlines the different approaches to sanctions implementation and compares responses to sanctions decisions by the UNSC.

5.1 FACTORS AFFECTING IMPLEMENTATION

Many important, but oft-neglected, factors influence policymakers' proclivity towards sanctions as a foreign policy tool. To understand the process of sanction implementation, it is necessary to see the role, function, and effects of sanctions on parties involved in the sanctioning system. Who are the parties (actors) involved? There are three primary actors involved in the sanctions process, the UNSC, the 193 members implementing sanctions domestically, and the target country, where the former two work unanimously as senders. Other than these three main actors, there are numerous other actors that are involved in the process of sanction implementation and their complete cooperation is needed in order to drive a sanctions scheme forward.

The institutional branch most directly involved in sanction implementation is the UNSC Sanctions Committee. The Sanctions Committees are established pursuant to the particular UNSC resolutions authorizing sanctions on a target states. Sanctions Committees are involved in the specific process and the implementation of the sanctions. They are involved in day-to-day monitoring of operations, reporting to the UNSC, as well as operationalizing subsequent UNSC resolutions (amendments) pertaining to the target country. The committee, though directly involved in the implementation process, is not solely responsible for effective implementation; states and corporations that have a relationship with the target country are also vital factors. In addition, there are third party contractors, who may hold strong economic ties with the target country and would have a direct influence on the implementation process. The list continues to third party states charged with implementing sanctions on a domestic level, including individual NGOs and multinational corporations.

Due to the number of different actors involved, the process of sanctions deliberation needs to be a planned and a well-coordinated action. Historical evidence demonstrates that implementation is anything but a coordinated, well-planned, or capably executed endeavor. Quite the contrary, a review of primary materials, including the notes of Paul Conlon, reveals striking confusion, disorganization, and remarkable lack of centralized oversight in the implementation of the sanctions. We can review UN sanctions-in-practice by examining specific, commonly accepted *factors* affecting implementation and their practical aspects.

5.1.1 Clearly Defined Goals

Similar to any other planned action, the UN's decision to sanction must start with a specific outline of goals, followed by procedures for implementation. The process of sanctions employment is complex and involves the application of international law, where the general claims to the application of general international law are historically challenged by the notion of special regional variations or exceptions.[5] Although as Edward McWhinney, discussing the legal effect of United Nations General Assembly resolutions identifies, resolutions "are not, of course listed among the formal sources of law established under article 38 of the World Court status, whose adoption had long preceded the formation of the United Nations."[6] These UN resolutions are accepted by customary international law but they are challenged by regional application and the lack of concrete procedural goals, making them destined to fail. As Oscar Schachter states: "the enforcement powers of the Security Council under Chapter VII of the UN Charter contemplate action in particular cases rather than by adopting general rules."[7] One of the major downsides of this case-by-case method is the increased ambiguity in individual state implementation.

The importance of concrete procedural goals and structure is specified in Roger Fisher's formulation of the goal of peace. He states the necessary steps as:

a. *Concentrating on Crisis Prevention*: attention of the policy-makers should be given to the big picture rather than the crisis of the day.
b. *Developing a System*: meaning the law must consist of substantive and procedural rules. International system is deficient in process.
c. *Avoiding the Criminal-Law Model*: a UN system that is strong enough to punish a state is bound to create more crisis and confrontation.
d. *Applying Successful Domestic Experience:* drawing on local experience of NGOs[8]

Since in theory sanctions could be imposed to deter a crisis from escalating, a clear and concise system would need a goal centric decision, which could alleviate the crisis. On the contrary an undefined process fuels the situation as states scramble to establish means of complying with the UN resolutions, leaving room for formation of alliances between the target and neighboring states. Clearly defined goals would allow the policy makers a chance to re-evaluate the sanctions over time enabling policy-makers to develop a timeframe for sanctions implementation and removal. In 2000 France and other nations, as a part of an initiative for improving the sanctions process led by the Bangladeshi diplomat Anwaru Chawdhurry, argued for a timeframe for removing sanctions. Such a timeframe would help in reinforcing goals and streamline the implementation process. According to Roger Fisher, crisis prevention is a systematic evaluation of internal and foreign affairs. Fisher states that there are ways that law can help in the midst of a crisis just as medicine can with a disease. In medical situations the physician approaches the patient with an exact course of action to cure the disease; however, the right medicine prescribed at the wrong time can be deadly. Similarly if law is represented by sanctions without being applied with precision and consideration for the situation, it cannot be effective. Fisher continues that, "The client-statesman needs to revise his perceived goal from that of an *ad hoc* solution for an international crisis to that of a functioning system for coping with disputes before they become crises."[9] Such revisions will help the statesmen make decisions that diminish the circular sanctions process, where no clear guidelines for implementation or duration of sanctions are identified. Thus the steps taken in sanction deliberation must define structural goals for effective sanction implementation.

5.2 TIMELINE (FROM SANCTION TO IMPLEMENTATION)

The speed with which UN sanctions are implemented is an influencing factor in the likelihood of success. The swiftness in implementation would signal the strong will of the UN and constituent states to enforce or punish international violators of peace.[10] Bergeijik, professor of international economics at Erasmus University, analyzed success rates over an extended period of time, and was able to show that sanctions take an extended period of time to show signs of success. Thus, he argues that the idea that theory should take into account the stochastic outcome of situations in which sanctions are threatened or applied. An example of time involved in the sanctions process are the two decades that the US Congress and several US presidents circled around each other on how to manage sanctions the US had imposed on Vietnam. Ultimately, these sanctions lasted for nineteen years from 1976 to 1995.[11]

As demonstrated in Figure 5.1 the sanctions process begins by a qualifying event. The qualifying event is any act that the UN or member states would consider as a "threat to peace and security." The process then continues on consequence-based decision-making where decisions are made, upon sender's presumption that threats to peace have increased, whether or not the actual conflict is fully recognized. Illustratively, furthering sanctions

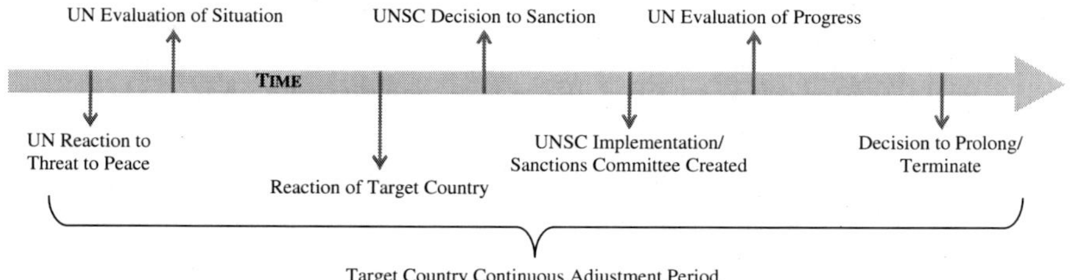

Figure 5.1 Linear Sanctions Timeframe Representation

against Iran has continued to be on the US foreign policy agenda on the basis of ten years of potential conflict, which has not fully surfaced.

Returning to Roger Fisher's procedural goals outlined in section 5.1.1, by concentrating on the conflict, the UNSC's attention is diverted from a broader perspective of reaching a stated objective. Within this linear process, there are discrepancies and ambiguities, which limit the UNSC evaluation of the source of the problem. One scholar refers to this vagueness as "studied ambiguities"[12] of the Security Council, alluding both to the existence of ambiguities and their political nature. However, if the UN sanctions are intended to be effective, the constantly changing conflict situations require a more flexible and fast-acting Security Council and these ambiguities limit the UNSC's response in addressing the conflict in an efficient manner.

Arguably, the most important factor in conflict prevention is the continuous evaluation of the situation, which requires an incessant monitoring and remains the most inefficient part of the conflict prevention process as it depends on individual member reporting.

The time component of the sanctions process as discussed above can be listed as:

a. *Evaluation* (the most prolonged and yet important for discovery of best methods to address escalating conflicts);
b. *Source finding*: To evaluate where resources used for conflict are coming from (as a recent analysis has shown, weapons used in Darfur are US, Chinese, and Russian made);
c. *Forecasting*: Further regulating gun control may be in order;[13]
d. *Decision* (time between problem recognition and UNSC decision), time sensitive and time critical;
e. *Adjustment* (unintended allotted time for target to adjustment to sanctions. This is a consequence of implementation inefficiencies);
f. *Implementation* (member implementation which an unclear process and difficult to measure).[14]

An example that illustrates the time components discussion above that arises from lack of a clear time-line is the current sanctions against North

Korea. The first time the question of sanctions in regards to North Korea's nuclear proliferation was introduced was in 1993, and further back in 1992 the International Atomic Energy Agency (IAEA) had reported evidence of the diversion of North Korea from a civilian nuclear program. Sanctions were not introduced in North Korea until 2006, (Res. 1718), allowing North Korea over ten years of adjustment from the time the problem was recognized.

One of the least time-consuming components of the sanctions process would need to be the decision-making, which is then executed by all the parties involved. However, because of the political nature of sanctions and the lack of uniform procedural standards by the UN, the sanction decisions are left in the hands of the five veto members. Therefore, their political agendas and differences causes endless political maneuvering to ensure that the UN agenda is in line with the state's agenda which allows the target country a clear adjustment period.

An alternate method of envisioning an improved structure for the sanctions process can be presented in a targeted systematic diagram:

The Figure 5.2 presentation gives the target country less of an adjustment period as decisions are made quickly. However, it is the evaluation (the ongoing evaluation process), composed of each constituent period, that must evolve throughout the term of conflict. The two elements of the decision-making process are: 1) the determination of facts or events; and 2) and the actual decision to react, which may not be operated by

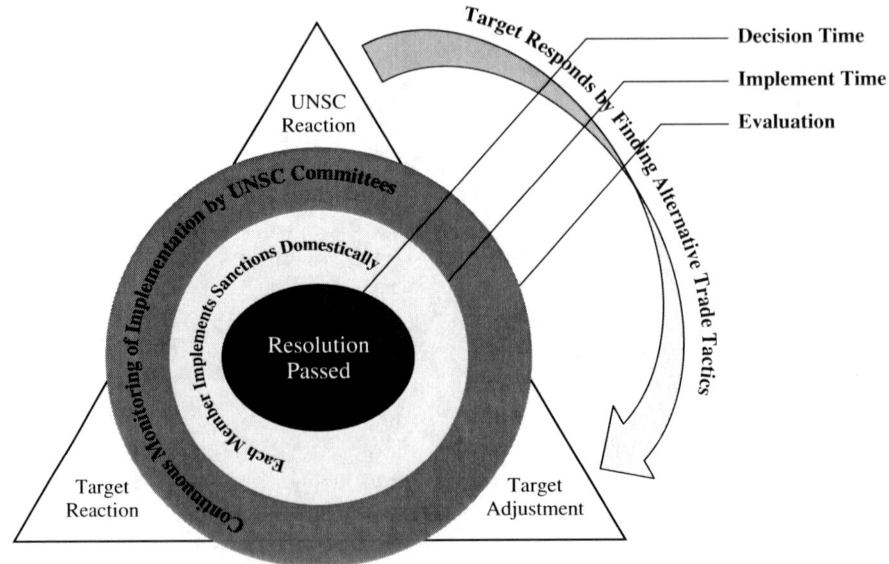

Figure 5.2 Visual Representation of Revised Sanctions Implementation Process

the same organ.[15] Consequently, this increases the time needed in the decision-making process. In Figure 5.2, the task of determination of fact falls under the evaluation process, making the actual decision less time-consuming.

5.2.1 Reaction Time

As a threshold matter, it is widely agreed upon that there is a need for urgency in matters that are brought to the UNSC's attention.[16] The start of a conflict could result in major casualties; thus, each week spent in the evaluation phase could mean hundreds or thousands of lives. Or else, as Hufbauer concludes, slow or incremental sanctions may simply strengthen the target government at home as it marshals the forces of nationalism.[17] This is illustrative of the need for a speedier UNSC decision-making process.

The time between the recognition of conflict and decision-making is a determinant of the outcome. As Margaret Doxey explains using the South African sanctions case, the international organizations took years in framing and implementing a program of economic sanctions, which as a result created opportunities for South Africa to build immunity to the sanctions.[18] The period of time elapsed between the recognition of a problem and decision-making is due to diverse factors, some of which include: 1) the existence of an overly centralized decision-making body, 2) lack of guidelines for implementers, and 3) lack of understanding of the decisions from the perspective of the implementer. These factors play a major role in increasing the time of reaction to conflict.

To illustrate the importance of time in sanctions deliberation, we can refer to the resolutions that brought sanctions to the former Yugoslavia after the fall of the Soviet Union and the Yugoslav division along ethnic lines. On November 27, 1991, the UN imposed Resolution 721, which did not envision the deployment of UN peace-keeping operations despite the request by the Yugoslav government. Resolution 721 followed Resolution 731 (September 19, 1991) and urged all parties to comply with the agreement they signed in Geneva on November 23, 1991. The agreement was intended to bring a ceasefire to the area. Resolution 721 also approved the possibility of establishing a UN peace-keeping mission in Yugoslavia. However, conflict in the area continued and six months later, based on a letter from the Bosnia and Herzegovina Minister of Foreign Affairs to the UN, there continued to be civilian casualties and ethnic cleansing.[19] In this same letter, the Minister of Foreign Affairs, also pointed out that humanitarian supplies had been looted away from the airport upon arrival and that no aid had reached civilians. He specifically stated "desperate humanitarian tragedy *cannot await the outcome of economic sanctions*, pleading for international control of the Sarajevo airport and international supervision of Yugoslav weaponry."

It was not until the end of May that a second resolution went into effect introducing further sanctions against Yugoslavia. By mid-June, member states started informing the UN of measures they had taken to implement these sanctions. By that point, another letter had already had been received from Bosnia and Herzegovina reporting that 50,000 individuals had died in the atrocities resulting from the Yugoslav conflict. A tenth of the casualties had been children and 1.4 million people were homeless.[20] It should be noted that the time that elapsed between these events is as short as one or two months. However, the situation was changing on a daily basis. Therefore, speedy international action was vital for survival of thousands of human lives.

Again, on June 5 1992, Yugoslavia sent a telegram to the Secretary General stating their compliance with Resolution 767 (1992) and 757 (1992), further stating that Resolution 757 (1992) was based on a misconception and restating that the Federal Republic of Yugoslavia was not involved in Bosnia and Herzegovina. The Yugoslav letter posited that any one-sided approach to the conflict would have led to a tragedy.[21] Only one day later, a letter was received from Bosnia that the aggression had increased.[22]

The above stream of communication signifies the inconsistency in discussions, the questionable outcome of economic sanctions, and the extended period of time required before any results become evident after sanctions have been imposed. Because the outcome of sanctions is directly dependent on decisions of the Secretary General as well as on implementation of members on actions such as arms embargo to deployment of troops, it could be argued that the outcome is neutralized by political and economic changes within a stated target country.

The reaction time of the UN and the member states has been fundamental in this case, where there was a state of emergency. Even when it comes to UN protection forces, response time is of the essence. Reaction from the UN forces has been historically slow due to an extremely hierarchical, centralized decision-making process. Such a hierarchical process occurred in Bosnia in 1993, when, operations had to be cleared not only through military commanders but also through a cumbersome UN political process.[23]

The UN's responsibility in the protection of peace is also highly dependent on the reaction time of all the parties involved. The UN, member states, and the target country can be seen as pillars needed to achieve a final result of protection of peace and security. Since the entire pillar would have to work together on precise timing to avoid civilian casualties, it can be derived that reaction time alone is one of the reasons why sanctions are not effective.

5.2.2 Implementation Time

For sanctions regime to comport with goals that were established before the implementation stage, the combined time spent by the UNSC and all implementing parties to react, evaluate, decide, and implement must be greater than the adjustment period of target state (defensive actions time) to the situation.

Following with the North Korea examples, which were discussed in section 5.2, the Security Council was made aware of the possibility of nuclear proliferation since the early 1990s. This meant that a threat of sanctions against North Korea existed from that time (*evaluation period*), giving North Korea sufficient time to find the material needed for their program *(reaction period)*. The decision to impose UNSC sanctions against North Korea did not come until 2006 (*decision period*), and sanctions have been implemented since 2006 to the current time (*implementation period*). This means that North Korea, knowing in advance that it would potentially be sanctioned in the future, had opportunity to prepare fully for this change. Therefore, the *target adjustment time* in this case was much larger than the sum of UNSC reaction, evaluation, decision, and implementation periods. This meant that North Korea had a much higher chance of developing or having the chance to develop a nuclear weapon program by the time sanctions were in place. It is, of course, questionable how one can measure the *adjustment time* of each target state in each particular sanctions regime. In this respect, perhaps the most direct factors for planning in foreign affairs concerns the predictability, or likelihood, of events.[24]

It should also be considered that the *implementation time,* as explained here, is the most dynamic of all aspects of the sanctions process because it is dependent on the cooperation of all parties involved. Cooperation could be capricious and also dependent on domestic legal changes to implement the UNSC resolutions.

5.2.3 Illustration

Sanctions against the Democratic Republic of Congo provide a clear illustration of the *time sensitive* factors in sanctions implementation. The Democratic Republic of Congo (DRC) has been in civil war since its postcolonial period.[25] Although DRC has had a central government since its independence in 1960, regional tribal leaders had maintained power throughout the 60s and 70s. The central government has remained in turmoil since, as neighboring rebel groups have entered and now occupy the country. The unstable control of the central government means that implementation of economic sanctions in any form must be accompanied with strong procedural and administrative controls. Although since the 1960s and the presidency of Mobuto, the first elected president, numerous cases of the violations of human rights have been reported, UN sanctions were not imposed on DRC. The importance of the Congo region in analyzing sanctions implementation is two-fold. First, the international community has acknowledged conflict in the region, in particular DRC, since decolonization. Second, due to the ambiguities on recognition of "threat to peace and security" and no clear guideline as to when it becomes vital to place sanctions on the state, international sanctions were not placed on DRC until 2003.[26]

The consensus is that sanctions that were imposed on nongovernmental groups in DRC in 2003 were in response to the second civil war in the country, which started in 1998. Prior to enforcement of these sanctions and the onset of civil war, UN peacekeeping forces were sent to protect civilians; however, they were not able to stop the violence that caused 2.5 million deaths. The in-country extensive evaluation of the conflict should have begun in 1995 when the anti-Mobutu rebel groups led by Laurent-Desire Kabila initiated their activities. This period would have set the *evaluation period* for this conflict. However, the first instance of the UN's investigation of the massacres by Kabila's forces was in mid-1997 by a UN human rights team. Therefore, this historically conflict driven region had been preparing for *reaction* to future UNSC sanctions (arms embargo) from the onset of conflict in 1995 allowing it two years of adjustment. The slow reaction from the UN to impose any form of sanctions on DRC until 2003 is evidence of the extended *decision time* employed in the UN decision structure. Additionally although the first arms embargo was imposed in 2003, it was not until 2005 that the UNSC imposed further arms embargos and travel bans on the rebel strongholds in eastern, northern, and south Kivu and Ituri, allowing rebel forces to increase or transfer their arms trade.

To illustrate the importance of time in the decisions by the UN, in a letter dated November 9, 2005 from the neighboring Ugandan president to the UN, the brief amount of time spent by the UNSC mission in the region was questioned.[27] The letter stated that the time the UN mission spent in the region was too short to get a good sense of the situation (referring to short *evaluation time*). In addition to the minimal time dedicated to the evaluation of the conflict, the Ugandan president brought up other significant and often neglected themes within the UN evaluation of conflict situations. He stated that there is a continuous need for better collaboration of the UN and the regional representatives as those in the region have better *knowledge* and a *vested interest*.[28] Though since the 1990s there have been developments in the sanctions process, with the creation of expert panels and special investigative groups, the involvement of the nation states in the conflict zone in determining the direction that the sanctions process should take remains limited.

In recent years the UNSC has attempted a more controlled implementation processes. In 2009 a group of experts were selected to develop specific guidelines for exercise of due diligence by importers and other active traders in DRC who could be subject to the arms embargo.[29] The guidelines are very highly specific but still neglected to address the matter of timeframe for deciding to invoke sanctions and implementing them. The established guidelines requested that all member states take appropriate steps towards compliance.[30] Under Resolution 1807, the implementation was to be enforced by the member states with the Sanctions Committee's administration.[31] Though these guidelines established a strong framework, the reporting requirements did not bound member states to a compliance timeframe or specify negative consequence for noncompliance. These guidelines read ". . .call upon states to take appropriate steps to raise awareness of the due diligence guidelines. . .and to urge importers, processing industries and consumers of Congolese mineral products to exercise due diligence by applying the aforementioned guidelines, or equivalent guidelines."[32] This language leaves states deciding on the severity of their compliance based on immeasurable data.

By giving the Sanctions Committee an administrative character, the guidelines attempted to peel away the layers of complexity and ambiguity in the sanction implementation process providing specific criteria for actions. Taking into account the dominance of the mining industry in DRC and its role in fuelling conflicts, the guidelines established that any stock of material left from prior to the introduction of the mining ban must be sold and the profits be used to finance traceability and environmental and social projects in the affected provinces. Such specific administration of profits is a positive move towards implementation and will be discussed further in chapter seven. Additionally the guidelines warned that the oil companies with interests in blocks in eastern Congo should take note of the complex security environment and ensure that exploration and eventual production operations do not directly or indirectly benefit armed groups or criminal networks within the Military Arms of the DRC (FARDC). Though importantly these guidelines identified that corporations are active actors in the sanction implementation process they still fail to discuss specific outcome, any timeframe for implementation or possible removal of sanctions.

Another area where such guidelines excel but can fail in final implementation is with respect to third party actors. Resolution 1807 obligated member states to notify in advance regarding shipment of arms and related material to DRC, establishing guidelines such as identifying the end-user, the proposed delivery date, and the itinerary of shipments. This is a step towards more successful implementation of the arms embargo; however, the shortcoming is in the lack of central oversight and re-evaluation of the circumstances. The progressions of the sanctions in Congo attest to the complicated nature of conflict that would warrant sanctions. This case also demonstration the ability of armed rebel groups or sanctioned governments to circumvent sanctions and fuel conflicts, which is eased by the slow response from the international community.

5.2.4 Target Country Defensive Move

Most diplomacy is time-sensitive and consists of short but intensive interaction. By the same token, the type of legal or administrative work that the Sanctions Committees perform requires slow but persistent effort, as well as thorough scrutiny and collegial discussion.[33] The time that is required for the implementation of sanctions creates a perfect opportunity for the target country to prepare for the sanctions and adjust accordingly as the sanction strengthens on the state through additional resolutions. The question of how much damage can be inflicted on the target depends to a large degree on the target's (in)flexibility as it reacts to the sanction. This reaction by the target is either to defend its position in the international community, avoid sanctions, or to comply with the requests made by the UNSC.

Since the UN Sanctions Committee and all the parties involved in implementation are not flexible enough to forego quick changes, the target states are given a *leeway time* in preparing and making changes necessary to their economic structure.[34] Thus, as tension and discussions on furthering the sanctions increase, so does the need of the target country to find alternative sources for coping with the measures enforced. Especially since rigidity of economic structures is a short-term phenomenon, it appears probable that the passage of time erodes the economic impact of sanctions.[35] During the timeframe that implementation is taking place or decisions for sanctions are finalized the target country is given leeway time to find alternate trade partners and more creative ways of bringing supply (monetary or otherwise) into the country. Illustrative of this type of target behavior is the case *Mastafa v. Australia Wheat Bd. Ltd.* This case brings to the attention of the court that in 1999 the Hussein regime had demanded that AWB (an Australian wheat exporter to Iraq under the "Oil-for-Food" program) pay "inland transportation" and other service fees to the Hussein regime in order to be allowed to deliver humanitarian goods. In a four-year-period these service fees amounted to over $220 million.

The results from oil smuggling during the time of Iraq sanctions have manifested themselves after the fall of Saddam's regime. The results show that in total, smuggling generated nearly $11 billion in illicit revenues for the Iraqi regime.[36] Of this $11 billion, more than $4.5 billion was paid in cash and the equivalent of approximately $6.5 billion was largely paid in goods although some portion might be still owed to Iraq.[37] Such systematic measures can be employed by target governments to reach their political agenda, whether or not their agenda involves the economic health of their nation. A case that surfaced in 2008 is illustrative of both the black market and the methods that Saddam Hussein used in bringing in illegitimate funds. The background of *Karim v. AWB Ltd.* tells a revealing story.[38] "Starting in 1999, the Hussein regime began demanding that humanitarian goods suppliers, including AWB, pay '"inland transport'" and other service fees to the Hussein regime as a condition for their continued sales to Iraq under the OFP. Plaintiffs allege that the payments by AWB and other suppliers of such fees were in fact kickbacks intended to transfer funds to the Hussein regime in violation of the UN sanctions. In total, plaintiffs allege that humanitarian goods suppliers, including AWB, paid at least $1.5 billion in such kickbacks to the Hussein regime. Plaintiffs allege that AWB USA, Commodity Specialists, and BNP collaborated in and/or facilitated the payment of kickbacks by AWB and other suppliers to the Hussein regime." This telling case is representative of many other similar circumstances that revolved around kickbacks to the regime during the sanctions. It is inevitable that target governments are interested in pursuing ways through which they may achieve their international political agendas. Consequently, even if the sanctions have any considerable economic impact, they produce little political compliance from the leaders but increase hardship on the population.[39] As discussed above the Iraq, Haiti, Yugoslavia, and North Korea sanctions are good examples of cases where the governments do not succumb to political compliance despite rigorous sanctions regime.

The target's "defensive moves" discussed in this section can be presented as such:

a. *Preparatory point*: The period in which the UNSC is made aware of the problem and starts the process of decision-making.[40]
b. *Leeway time*: The period of time that the Sanctions Committee and the member states need to implement sanctions.
c. *Adjustment stage*: The period in which the target country adjusts to the new internal situation. (This is continuous and involves expansion on self-sufficiency).

Iraqi sanctions reinforce the importance of determining the *leeway* time that is embedded within the sanctions process. The first time the UN looked at the case of threat to peace initiated from Iraq was in 1980. Resolution 479 was passed documenting the escalation of conflict between Iraq and Iran. The importance of this resolution and the conflict between Iraq and Iran was that it was set as a precursor to the occupation of Kuwait, which resulted in UN sanctions. Therefore, the evaluation and awareness of the Iraqi situation was first noticed as conflicts rose in the region and the situation has been on the UN agenda since 1980. However, sanctions were not imposed on Iraq for ten years, giving Saddam Hussein the opportunity to form a strong army and internal control.

Table 5.1 Sample Cases Representing the Sanctions Process Timeframe

Country	Problem Recognitions	Decision is Made to Sanction	Term of Implementation
Haiti	1991	1993	1994 Lifted – 1 year
Libya	1988 – 4 years	1992	1999 Suspended – 7 years
Iraq	1980 – 10 years	1990	2003 Partially Lifted – 13 years
North Korea	1992 – 10 years	2006 – 1 year	2006 – 09 – 3 years

Table 5.1 shows the "defensive move" timeframe of four chosen target countries. The four cases above demonstrate the time of recognition of the conflict to the time sanctions were imposed. In each of the cases, the target country had over one year to adjust their actions for possible sanctions.

Thus pre-mandatory Security Council resolutions provide hints that the Security Council is on the brink of implementing sanctions; the target country has incentive to build stockpiles and adjust its economic structure in advance.[41]

5.2.5 Term/Duration (Length of Sanctions)

Though the discussion of a timeframe (term/duration) was brought up by several member states at the UN in 2000, sanctions are still imposed indeterminately. This is mainly because of the opposition from the US and England, arguing that targets will be able to sit out for the sanctions period and return to their harmful activities upon termination of sanctions. Aside from the period of time from recognition of conflict to implementation, an important chronological period affecting success/failure of sanctions is their duration. Sanctions, like nations, are not static; they evolve and change to reflect changes in circumstances. They can be short in duration, lasting mere months, or well into decades. (US sanctions against Cuba and UN sanctions against Iraq provide the most dramatic example of the latter.) Sanctions, likewise, can remain in place long after they have been shown to be ineffective foreign policy tools, or when the negative externalities begin to outweigh any likely benefits.[42] McGillivra and Stam, used regression analysis and hazard models to test forty-seven unilateral sanctions events. They concluded that leadership change strongly affects the duration of sanctions only in the case of nondemocratic states.[43] Leadership change in democratic states was shown to be unrelated to the duration of sanctions; however, leadership change in nondemocratic sender and nondemocratic target states was strongly related to the ending of economic sanctions. Of course, this analysis based on unilateral sanctions applies directly to multilateral UN sanctions as well. According to Christopher Joyner of Georgetown University's Institute for International Law and Politics,

> Another lesson of the Iraqi sanctions is that a UN sanctions operation must have some *end game*. Admittedly, strategic logic demands that it is imprudent to set a time limit for a UN sanctions operation. To do so would allow an offending government merely to bide its time until the sanctions expire. However, it also seems desirable for a UN sanctions operation to be implemented with a deliberate, graduated timetable for achieving its objective. Further, the lack of a set deadline does not legitimize a sanctions operation in perpetuity. Indeed, Article 1, paragraph 1 of the UN Charter requires that measures undertaken to maintain

> international peace and security (inclusive of sanctions) must be "effective" and must be "in conformity with the principles of justice and international law."[44]

Joyner continues, "*protracted sanctions* can produce grave impacts that injure innocent persons and society long after the illicit government ends, and *excessively prolonged* sanctions may come to be viewed as ineffective."[45] But how long is "protracted" and after how many years are sanctions considered to be "excessively prolonged"?

Studies looking into the duration of sanctions have concluded that economic sanctions imposed by the Security Council have a tendency to increase in strength over time.[46] It may be the UNSC's aim to impose sanctions with varying degrees of severity over time in an effort to force the target states to negotiate or to put the target country in a position where they are compelled to comply. However, this hypothesis has important policy implications depending on the following factors: 1) the degree of severity of sanctions is indeterminate, 2) the decision as to the strength of the sanctions is subjective to member state's decision, 3) human suffering is overlooked, and 4) sanctions for the same crime vary based on when they are placed on the target country, ultimately leading to the sanction becoming an essentially undefined and continuous measure on an incline to no particular ending point. Therefore, the target country's offense is not only judged by the seriousness of the international community's view of the target's act of aggression but it is also dependent on pre-existing sanctions, where any direct negotiations by the target become impossible. The target ultimately is faced with the option to either make absolute changes to their behavior or to speculate what the next measure of sanctions will be. The council is compelled to stay moderate in the severity of the primary sanctions they impose, as they may need to increase the strength of the sanction at a later time if the target country still does not comply with UNSC resolution demands.

All these problems would be accounted for if the sanctions were to have a term limit (a sort of expiration date), which would clearly define the length of time that the target would be under sanctions and give the target a chance to change its behavior. In case the target does not make any changes to their behavior, then a second step can be taken.

In cases where sanctions are imposed without a limit the severity of the sanctions increases over time and reaches a plateau or, a stagnation point. At this point, no matter how much harm would be inflicted on the population and the state, the regime or the sanctioned groups will not be impacted. However sanctions that have a term limit would be presented in a step-by-step process. This process would allow for changes within the target country with the knowledge of when these changes must occur. The term limit allows the sanction to increase in strength without a stagnation period.

As the sanctioning body reaches each "step" it may modify its sanctioning strategy to match the new circumstances. This provides more flexibility and an opportunity to re-evaluate the situation in the target country. Additionally this method would allow the Sanctions Committee to evaluate if the government has been modifying their trade policy to allow for other alternative sources of revenue-generating trade. Such a process would allow for the long-term implementation and forecast of the target's actions. This refers not only to sustainability, but to long-term effects with a short-term goal-driven perspective.

5.2.6 Minimizing Negative Effects

There are no specific measures to specify the negative effects of UN sanctions. However, for purposes of analysis, we can divide them into three categories: infrastructural, economic, and humanitarian effects. If the side effect of sanctions is negative, then it is evident there are minimal actions the Security Council or any member state can take to reverse it. According to Laurence Boisson de Chazournes, professor and chair of the department of public international law and international organization at the faculty of law, University of Geneva,

> The 'side effects' issue had been raised early on with the adoption of sanctions against Southern Rhodesia, but it was with the imposition of sanctions against Iraq—over a thirteen-year period—that the issue became particularly controversial. Side effects obviously affect the target State (which is the very reason for the adoption of the measures) but not necessarily in the manner in which they are intended. The most harmful consequences generally fall on the civilian population, far more than on members of the government. Third States can also be affected, as a result of the growing interdependence of domestic economic systems.[47]

The three categories of negative effects of economic sanctions are interchangeable. Once the infrastructure of a society falls apart, the economic and humanitarian effects follow. An example of such negative impact of sanctions is evident throughout the Iraqi sanctions regime and the increase in waterborne and poor hygiene diseases such as stunting, wasting, malnutrition, malaria, cholera, typhoid, leishmaniasis, measles, poliomyelitis, tetanus, diphtheria, pertussis, and meningitis.[48] Many UN representatives have voiced against sanctions and their negative impact. The negative impact of Iraqi sanctions on the population, even after the introduction of the Oil-for-Food program which was enacted by Resolution 1302, is what led to resignation of one UN official, Dennis Halliday, who had worked for the UN for thirty years. He compared the dealings of the program and the sanctions to genocidal tactics. In an interview he stated that the Iraqi situation was close to famine.[49]

Economic sanctions, just like any other war or coercive measure, take a toll on the weakest of the economy. Thus paradoxically, instead of directly impacting the ruling class, sanctions carry significant economic hardship on the lower classes with little decision-making ability in a given targeted country. The common narrative is well summarized by Professor Chazournes as such,

> In Iraq and in Yugoslavia, sanctions led to the impoverishment of the middle class, higher crime and long-term economic damage, which contributed to growing insecurity and instability. Embargoes led to scarcity in available goods and, consequently, to an increase in prices in the domestic market. In Iraq, the price of basic commodities increased by around 1000% between 1990 and 1995. The consequences are well known: the impoverished suffer disproportionately and the economic independence of the middle class (a potential source of resistance to the regime) is shattered. The members of the regime and their allies who control the black market profit the most from the situation. In Haïti, for instance, the army had an interest in the continuing imposition of sanctions, as it had seized control of the black market on goods prohibited by the embargo and generated considerable profits.[50]

However, the manner in which the UN can minimize such causes is questionable, as measuring the level at which a country is in absolute need of a good or service is subjective. It is also unrealistic to depend on the UN to determine what humanitarian aid would benefit the country's civilians most. As Paul Conlon states during the Iraq sanctions period in regards to resource allocation to Iraq for purposes of food preparation and food distribution, there were two unresolved issues: *when* such humanitarian circumstances arose and *who* was to make this determination. In this case, there did not seem to be an agreement specifically in regards to aid to Iraq. One side argued that only severe food shortages, such as in a famine situation, would constitute circumstances for help. On the other hand, Cuba argued that it had to be looked at in the larger context of basic human rights.[51]

Such negative impact on civilians are, in many instances, seen as a side effect that is keeping the sanctions from their main objective, overlooking the fact that these side effects have in fact been replaced with the actual objective of the sanctions. For instance, writing in 1997, Sweden's defense minister Anders Björck,

> In cases where economic sanctions have been imposed, it is often UNICEF (the Child Emergency Fund) and the Humanitarian Dept. of the UN Secretariat that are seen as disruptive—*e.g.*, when they produce studies on the devastating effects which sanctions have on children and civilians in the affected country.[52]

Sanctions are in fact placed on the country to cause hardship on the population; therefore, they are seen as an instrument that has side effects on civilians embedded within its tactic. Thus in an environment where negative effects are not only overlooked but are seen as a barrier to a successful sanctions process, it is not a viable practice to minimize such effects. Therefore, realistically attention must be turned more towards implementation and economic impact rather than the side effects of economic sanctions.

5.2.7 Minimizing Effects on Third Parties

As we have seen in section 2.7 *supra*, third parties and innocent bystanders are often harmed by international sanctions.[53] This is a direct consequence of the failure to specifically define the purpose of sanctions and to enforce sanctions schemes in accordance with that purpose.[54] As Major and McGann posit "[d]espite being quite straightforward, there are several flaws in this sanctions-as-punishment hypothesis. Analytically, one danger of using this model *is that imposing heavy costs on the target, rather than achieving the desired policy change, often becomes seen as a surrogate for success.*" Major and McGann, perhaps, unreflectively, also make the same mistake they accuse Hufbauer and others of making; they too fail to focus specifically on the contours of the given policy change. By failing to analyze *specifically* what policy-makers hope to accomplish ahead of time, and asking—before the imposition of sanctions—whether sanctions will further that *specific* goal, Major and McGann also fail the test of determinacy.[55] In this section, focus will be placed on particular states, firms, and individuals in nonsender and target countries and their role as third parties. This is done for several reasons. One of the most important reasons is that the effects on third parties *within* the target countries (civilian populations, ethnic minorities, children, the elderly, *etc.*) have been thoroughly analyzed and documented by leading scholars.[56] This is one of the most important and thoroughly researched subfields in the discipline.

Sanctions also impact nontarget and nonsender states, firms, and individuals. For instance, because every UN member state is responsible for the domestic implementation of UNSC sanctions resolutions, the states necessarily suffer additional costs. These costs can be trivial, such as the costs of reporting compliance, or they can be significant, such as the loss of trade with a bordering state (especially in a subsistence or key commodity like oil). To illustrate this point, Syria and other Middle Eastern countries were negatively impacted by UNSC sanctions against Iraq in the early 1990s, resulting in higher domestic fuel and petroleum-derivative products. Similarly, the complexity of administrative steps to comply with UNSC resolutions should not be underestimated, especially for poorer countries without a strong UN presence or international law bureaucracy. The length and time that a third party country would need to have in order to comply with new

Security Council resolutions can be drawn from the resolutions passed after the September 11, 2001 attack on the United States. In order to comply with these measures, states found it necessary to pass domestic legislation. In her account of Germany's response to Resolution 1373, Kim Scheppele remarks that after much parliamentary debate, the resulting legislation granted increased power for security agencies to demand information, without notice, from banks, telecommunication companies, airlines, and other institutions.[57] It also authorized greater powers to create a central government database of personal information and allowed many ministries access to the information.[58]

During the Balkan crisis, neighboring countries were directly affected by the implementation of UN sanctions. Slovenia, for example, had contracts for goods for which payment had already been issued prior to the resolution which were yet to be delivered. The measures taken in order to comply with UN sanctions made it impossible for Slovenia to obtain goods from Serbia, including goods that were owned by Slovene companies. In this regard, Slovenia complained to the UN, noting that the break in trade caused disruption in production; most of the disruption was caused in the production of electrical machinery and chemical products, which were core industries in Slovenia.[59] As it is manifested by this example, the complexity of sanctions and the imposition of sanctions are not the only aspects of importance, which should be considered from the UN perspective; rather other issues such as the existence of trade between third parties and a target country need to be included in the sanctions framework.

In fact, in Article 50 of the Charter, as we shall analyze below, it is suggested that third party states confronted with special economic problems in imposing sanctions have the right to consult the Security Council.[60] This article sets forth the significance of third party cooperation, as well as the impact of sanction implementation on third parties. The article, however, does not clarify the measures that will be taken by the Security Council to resolve any potential problems that may exist. There are many examples of the third party effect present within different sanctions regimes. One in particular the case of *Filatures Miel, S.L. v. Republic of Iraq* (a case in which priority of contract is of concern and the contract date is overlooked) illustrates a situation when the UN did not guarantee compensation for any monetary losses[61] incurred by Hilaturas Miel (the trader who requested payment for yarn that had been delivered to Iraq, but because it was found to be a nonpriority item, had not left the port for destination). The request of the five African countries mentioned in section 4.1.1 to buy oil from Aden in fulfillment of a supply agreement with the company is another example of third party effect (as alluded to before the Kuwait petroleum company was located in Aden and sanctions were in place against the occupying Iraq regime).[62] The ICS' chairperson made the decision that release of oil would not contravene sanctions because the contract had been signed before the imposition of sanctions.[63] These cases point to the question of what is the risk that third parties (including non-target member states) are taking in the domestic implementation of economic sanctions and how will they measure such risk?

Scholars point out that Article 50 should be read in conjunction with Article 49 of the Charter to give third parties real remedies for economic harm inflicted by sanctions or other measures on the given state.[64] Article 49 provides: "The Members of the United Nations shall join in affording mutual assistance in carrying out the measures decided upon by the Security Council."[65]

Article 50 provides,

> If preventive or enforcement measures against any state are taken by the Security Council, any other state, whether a Member of the United Nations or not, *which finds itself confronted with special economic problems arising from the carrying out of those measures shall have the right to consult the Security Council with regard to a solution* of those problems.[66]

In practice, neither Article 49 nor Article 50 provides a meaningful legal framework for establishing third party state rights and remedies. Article 49 lacks any measure of compulsory assistance, as aid is carried out on a bilateral or regional level.[67] Article 50 gives an amorphous "right of consultation."[68] It does not establish the right to a remedy. Likewise, "[i]n practice, the management of the consequences of sanctions quickly exceeded the framework and scope of Article 50, a provision incapable of proposing an appropriate framework to resolve these issues."[69]

Boisson de Chazournes' analysis of the side effects of sanctions leads to the understanding that absent a legal framework or remedies for addressing third party state rights, these states are left with a decision between the "lesser of two evils," such as the choice between directly suffering from sanctions imposed on a trade partner or violating the sanctions. According to Boisson de Chazournes, absent a legal framework or remedies for addressing third party state rights, these states are left with a decision between the "lesser of two evils," such as the choice between directly suffering from sanctions imposed on a trade partner or violating the sanctions.[70] State practice evidences both choices. For instance, restrictions on flights to Libya in the 1990s as a result of sanctions against the Libyan government led the Organization of African Union (OAU) Member States to cease observing these restrictions.[71] Similarly, the United States' decision to import chrome from Rhodesia in violation of sanctions imposed between 1971 and 1977 serves as an illustration of third parties' remedies in the wake of sanctions regimes that do not consider their interests in the initial sanctions deliberations.[72]

5.3 BARRIERS TO IMPLEMENTATION (TARGET RESISTANCE AND SANCTIONS EVASION)

5.3.1 Internal UN Institutional Conflict

The overwhelming majority of sanctions studies analyzing institutional aspects of sanctions enforcement or implementation ignore a critically important side of institutional conflict and institutional barriers to success: personality politics. Perhaps scholars assume that the individuals working at the UN Secretariat or on the respective sanctions committees are rational actors, executing objectively weighed, democratically crafted public policy decisions. In reality, the sanctions deliberations process and implementation (including such key issues as the *staffing* of the respective committees, and staffing at the UN more generally) are intensely politicized issues. The rationality assumption must also be questioned with respect to the day-to-day operations of a complex sanctions apparatus. Work by cognitive psychologists, such as James G. Blight, is finally starting to enter the mainstream of sociolegal scholarship, deepening our understanding of the human element in these complex decision-making processes. Indeed, more research should be done on this issue at the UN.

Paul Conlon's papers are rife with hints that beneath the formalism and positive law driving substantive sanctions deliberations, quite trivial and sometimes irrational facts determined the actual likelihood of success. In his *Historical Note on Personalities Participating in the Work of the 661 Committee*, for instance, Conlon writes "one irony in view of the committee's appalling record in legal matters was the significant element of legally trained participants."[73] One gets the sense of a major clash between lawyers, economists, and bureaucrats of all disciplinary orientations within the sanctions committees. When combined with the political agendas of these bureaucrats home states (or perhaps their individual political agendas), the conflicts are magnified exponentially.

Aside from commenting on personality conflicts, Conlon also called for broader structural reform, stressing that too much emphasis was being placed on the UN General Secretariat, as opposed to the multilevel autonomous organizations within the UN system.[74] Yet, even within the UN system, conflicts between agencies can and do occur. For instance, the United Nations Development Program (UNDP) is the largest of the UN's bureaucratic programs, controlling as much as $5 billion of the $20 billion plus budget of the entire UN system. The UNDP administers aid programs to many of the countries who are under UNSC sanctions. Critics have pointed to the lack of transparency in the UNDP process. The UNDP has an administrative procedure that allows for cash transfers directly to governments to implement much of its programs "with some cash transfers going to some of the world's worst human rights abusing and terrorist sponsoring states."[75] An example of such expenditure is the UNDP's planned payment of $177 million in aid to Iran, which was heavily criticized.[76]

The Jan Falk Engineering Case described by Paul Conlon nicely illustrates the types of institutional conflicts which arise at the UN and the damaging effect that these conflicts have on sanctions implementation.[77] In this case, the UNSC Iraq Sanctions Committee attempted to open a second escrow account to deal with funding for humanitarian purposes.[78] This was precipitated by the fact that Sweden wanted to unfreeze funds held by the Bank for International Settlements (BIS). These funds were due to pay for services performed by the Jan Falk Engineering Co. for work in improving the municipal water systems. However, there was a disagreement on how a second escrow account should be established so that the project would go forward. The entire matter collapsed when Iraq failed to clarify its intentions as the Chairman left his post and the bank pulled out of the matter for unrelated reasons. These bank accounts, which were controlled by the UN, are immune from seizure by other creditors. Because of the conflict over *which* bank (Iraq insisted on a non-UN, New York bank) would administer the contract and pay the contractor, the deal fell apart. Consequently, the civilians were left without sanitary water. Arguably, this aggravated the humanitarian crisis in Iraq and contributed to the decrease in infant mortality rates.

5.3.2 Target Resistance

Between 1990 and present, over ten UN sanctions regimes were aimed at total regime change and democratization.[79] Faced with such sanctions, the entrenched political and economic elites have no other choice but to further burrow into powerful positions, resist the sanctions in the near term, and to hold out for the maximum amount of time possible in the hope that these sanctions schemes will be lifted. Such was the case with Saddam Hussein's regime in Iraq and the current regimes in North Korea and Libya.

Self-sufficiency, economic strength, and the capacity to reduce vulnerability are unequally distributed among states.[80] However, even between states that are not economically sound, foregoing some advantage is more beneficial to the governing body than losing internal power. Consequently such states would tolerate a high level of sanctions regime for an extended period of time, in most cases putting the burden on the citizens. Margaret Doxey suggests that provided the government of a country remains in power, and its program receives adequate support from the politically significant elements in the population, it will be able to plan effectively for a greater measure of self-sufficiency, even if this involves a sacrifice of some economic advantages.[81] Going beyond this forced self-sufficiency, which arises as a coping mechanism for the target states, the reliance on domestic industries assures the society of the state's position and lends more significance to the government and their political power. Subsequently the government gains additional control of the borders and the domestic industry.

Another form of resistance stems from sanctions-dodging. Sanctions-dodging can be the result of a single state, multiple states, or corporations overlooking specific international sanctions. For instance, in the 1990s automobile manufacturer Khodro—the Middle East's largest auto manufacturer—had publicly stated that it plans to use Sudan as the base for wide export of its products, working directly with Sudan's defense ministry.[82] The case of Rhodesia provides another example. In the 1970s embargos were imposed by Britain against Rhodesia. Rhodesia, however, continued to be able to obtain essential imports and to find markets for its exports. The economy was diversified and sustained economic growth was achieved throughout most of the first decade of sanctions enforcement.

Sheer violence from nongovernmental sources in countries under sanctions also complicates the enforcement of sanctions or provision of humanitarian aid. For example, the opposition forces in Somalia in the early 1990s showed their resistance through aggressive attacks on any humanitarian help that came into the country. On June 5, 1992, a letter from US to the UN in regards to Somalia stated "[if] Somalis do not stop looting, robbing and killing the people who come to their help, the help will go elsewhere. Twenty-percent of the world-wide effort of the international committee of the Red Cross was in Somalia at that time."[83] In response to this situation, the UN called upon factional leaders to exercise strict control. The problem was that a lack of government control had led Somalia to its conflict position, which was the reason for the conflict. Consequently, UN forces (28,000 troops) were sent to make sure that food reached starving Somalians. It is a shortcoming from the UN perspective to have false expectations from local leaders.[84]

Another problem that keeps a sanctioned country from making any changes to its underlying governing strategy rises from their disagreement with the actual cause for the sanctions. In response to a draft resolution against the former Federal Republic of Yugoslavia, the vice president of the republic addressed the Secretary-General stating that they were being punished for crimes they did not commit. Suggesting that the conflict in the region was not instigated by them but rather was rooted within the domestic constitution of Bosnia-Herzegovina.[85] Such disagreements are present in most of the target countries' leader's opinion in regards to the conflict situations, which leads to an even higher resistance to change.

5.3.3 Monitoring Costs/Problems

A last factor in the successful implementation of UNSC sanctions is the monitoring and reporting of domestic implementation back to the UN and the adoption, by the UN, of specific follow-up enforcement measures. This is particularly acute in the field of targeted sanctions, where the human rights of suspected terrorists or other individuals swept up in the dragnet of sanctions enforcement are implicated.[86] According to José E. Alvarez, "a more human rights sensitive Council could opt for a more extreme remedy, such as leaving the actual listing of particular individuals or organizations to domestic authorities, subject to general Council guidelines, accompanied by reporting obligations of member states."[87] Such a decentralized, antihierarchical system may have advantages over the current system in more ways than simply protecting the human rights of targeted individuals. For instance, by decreasing monitoring costs, Alvarez's decentralized system may incidentally increase the incentives for states to implement the sanctions.

Another area where monitoring costs can pose problems in implementing sanctions is with respect to implementation designated to the investor and corporations. An illustrative example is the sanctions that were imposed on Eritrea in 2009 by the Security Council. These sanctions were caused by Eritrea's support of the Islamist militant group, Al-Shabaab. This Eritrea resolution required foreign companies involved in mining in Eritrea to exercise "vigilance" to ensure funds are not used to destabilize the region.[88] The language of the resolution is extremely vague and it is unrealistic to expect the private, profit-driven enterprise would necessarily monitor how funds are distributed. After the first draft of these sanctions, which banned investment in the mining industry in Eritrea, Russia and China, driven by their extensive investments in the region, played an active role in diluting the language of the draft and shifting responsibility to the mere monitoring of funds. In the past decade, China has increased its interest and investment in Africa and Eritrea has not been excluded from the list of beneficiaries to these investments. In recent years the UNSC has established new methods of attempting to streamline and move forward in sanctions implementation despite the apparent problems arising from monitoring, in particular monitoring of third parties.

5.4 MOVING FORWARD WITH UNSC SANCTIONS

The UNSC needs to set out a specific framework to define the reasons behind each measure of sanctions and the goals that are to be achieved in a specific time frame. A definition of domestic implementation needs to be outlined by the UN, not to overlook domestic laws, but rather to give specific measures that need to be taken in order to comply with international law. According to Conlon, to achieve the stated objectives, national implementation is inadequate and it is the UNSC, with its relevant subsidiary organs and the UN Secretariat, which needs to conceptualize, administer, and coordinate the implementation of the sanctions.[89]

However, despite Paul Conlon's insistence on UNSC enforcement and implementation, it is precisely because of the unwillingness or inability of the Security Council to enforce collective sanctions that individual states are faced with the task of implementing sanctions on the international sphere. This lack of central control leads to individual states choosing between their own internal economic well-being and their responsibility to the international body. Consequently, states choose not to take part in stronger measures. The cost of the implementation of sanctions to trade partners of sanctioned countries is a sunk cost which is associated with the need to create organization that would act as barrier to the inflow and outflow of goods to and from their state, which could mean the destruction of certain industries.

Amongst many alternatives in implementation, some studies suggest that nations, in implementing comprehensive sanctions, have a wide latitude in choosing boycotts (*i.e.* prohibitions of exports *from* the target), which are easier to implement and are more harmful to civilian populations than embargoes (*i.e.* prohibitions of exports *to* the target).[90] Others that have suggested "smart" sanctions that would affect only the ruling elite and not the population of the sanctioned country.[91] In all these cases, however, the proposals are overlooking the associated costs, whether it is humanitarian or economic, to all parties involved. The sanction costs are not only listed as the implementation cost, which is high for the UN and other international entities, but also the opportunity cost which the sanctioning countries face. The limitations that are put on the government in the case of smart sanctions actually drive additional power to the elite ruling bodies of the sanctioned state, since they increase their need for control on the internal industries and their sovereign influence. One of the concerns pointed out during the Iraqi sanctions was the potential for the development of extremist rulers. Dennis Halliday was one of the supporters of this rational, stating that "the inward looking future generations coming out of Iraq would have less respect for the application of international law through the UN."[92]

For a more effective administration of sanctions, a comprehensive implementation team is needed, consisting of those providing expertise, decision-makers who are not politically driven, and actors other than instructed delegates, which operate as a council subsidiary body, all working with full transparency. In practice, however, the implementation of sanctions is much more regime-specific with high individual government involvement in the selection process of the commissioner.[93] Such a structure sets sanctions to fail before they are imposed, thus the conflict regions remain in conflict.

This chapter illustrated that the problems that arise in sanction implementation go beyond effectiveness and analyzed effect; this is also what Conlon referred to as unclear guidelines for implementation. For the Security Council to have any effect on conflict prevention, their current methods need to be re-evaluated. And, as will be discussed in Chapter seven, a new preemptive evaluation technique may be in order. But the first step is to set a consensus on what the goals of the Security Council sanctions are, and what specific guidelines states should follow to impose successful sanctions. The question of what is a proper measure of success and failure is the topic of Chapter six.

6 Measures of Success / Failure

> Unilateral sanctions *never work* . . . Multilateral sanctions may take a long time, as they did in South Africa, but you have a better chance.
>
> —US Trade Representative Carla Hills, January 26, 1998[1]

Economic sanctions as a foreign policy tool are and will continue to remain an active option in part because they provide the necessary flexibility for politicians to passively deal with intricate international relations. Economic sanctions are a method of moving a state's political positions forward without war. Just as Plato and Aristotle were concerned with the state of Athens during their time, today's students of law and international relations must consider the problems revolving around the state and state policy. The intertwined economic relationship of states makes it important to take into account the international ecopolitical relations and the role of institutions in this relationship. To create a balanced economic environment the complexities of this relationship must be controlled and maintained beyond nation states. Accordingly as long as state relationships exist economic sanctions will not disappear from UNSC discussions. Here we will continue to probe UNSC decisions as they influence all member states.

The UNSC's decision to sanction carries with it the assumption that all states attempt to implement the sanctions equally and thoroughly. In the previous chapter, we discussed the issues of implementation and concluded that implementation can be influenced by external factors; thus, this assumption does not hold. There are other ambiguities as we move forward with the sanctions process. The final task of the sanctions sender is measuring the success/failure of the particular sanctions regime. How do we measure the success of sanctions? What method should analysts use? And from whose point of view should success be measured? What are the downsides to the unspoken universal assumption that sanctions can be viewed through a positive lens? In this chapter, we will see that the question of success acts as an umbrella question for sanctions analysts because it is on this question that everything depends-from the degree of implementation, to duration, to strategy, and beyond.

Generally speaking, it is unclear what *measures of success* pertain to economic sanctions.[2] There is also minimal consensus on the existence of any specific criteria for success. Leaving the measure of success to an ad hoc evaluation would add to the politicized nature of sanctions with detrimental financial results for the sender (in this case the UN and all member states). Discussing the measures of success, Baldwin explains that just the mere fact of imposing sanctions or as he calls it "taking action" is a form of success as it is better than not having any alternative. Similar types of reasoning are continually discussed in policy debates. Defining success as purely the process of taking an action ignores the intrinsic costs associated with the action and determines success at the initiation of the action whether or not it yields results. Baldwin takes the success discussion beyond the question of choice or alternatives when discussing the *Observability of Success*. His comparative breakdown of military success versus sanction success points to the fact that success may not necessarily be based on economic terms.[3] Although in both military and economic actions, subjectivity and the difficulty of measuring noneconomic success is clear, where they differ is with respect to the dramatized effect of a military attack versus the slow progression of sanctions. Measuring success in economic sanctions is complicated because of their slow effect. The slow effect of sanctions and the extensive interplay between member states, the UN, and the target states, and even further the multinational corporations or other non-governmental actors adds to the ambiguous nature of measuring sanctions regimes.

This ambiguity in measures of success is one of the principal reasons for the heated debate regarding the effectiveness of sanctions.[4] The debate surrounding sanctions effectiveness has spilled over to the popular press as the threats of sanctions has increased since 2009 and the discussion of sanctions against terrorists has widened.[5] Policy analysts and policymakers continue to search for an effective solution to the sanctions debate, some even deviating from the customary sanctions practices in order to propose alternatives. In 2009 US Representative, Paul Findley, recommended controversial sanctions against Israel in the form of withholding $3 billion in foreign aid, which would have acted as an incentive to resolve the Middle East standoff between Israel and Iran.[6] Most political scientists, naturally, analyze the success/failure question through the prism of foreign policy, defining success as simply when sanctions have "achieved their stated objectives."[7] Taking this assumption, leading scholars have been able to empirically analyze duration, and use statistical analysis to isolate specific cause/effect chains and show when sanctions have been effective. Such research most actively conducted on unilateral sanctions allows for re-evaluating stated objectives as policymakers proceed with the sanctions debate. There is significant doubt regarding the applicability of these conclusions in practice. It seems few policymakers use empirical sanctions analysis to formulate their projected sanctions schemes.[8] As McGillivray and Stam observe, one of the reasons for the lack of consensus between policymakers and academics regarding the efficacy of economic sanctions as a tool of coercive diplomacy revolves around the sanctions measurement question.[9] Therefore, the difficulty of defining a measurement of success in empirical terms leaves analytically rigorous work in academic interest rather than any extension to real practicability. Thus, as success and failure rest on accomplishments of *political* objectives, such as regime change, capitulation, *liberalization,* defense of human rights, and increasingly more subjective standards, an introduction of a systematic approach to sanctions may be the only means of bringing together policy positions and the academic study of sanctions. Thus assuming that policymakers will have an interest in achieving one of the policy objectives mentioned above, success would need to be based on measuring the target country's compliance with one of the stated objectives. Quantifying a target state's level of compliance with these standards or benchmarks becomes highly problematic, if not altogether impossible.

Granted, this problem—the difficulty of measuring foreign policy success/failures—is not unique to sanctions. Policymakers have the same difficulty with respect to armed conflicts or humanitarian intervention. For instance, the US war in Afghanistan presented a striking example of the *measurement dilemma*. The *New York Times* in 2009 reported,

> As the American military comes to full strength in the Afghan buildup, the Obama Administration is struggling to come up with a long-promised plan to *measure whether the war is being won.* [...] *Those metrics of success*, demanded by Congress and eagerly awaited by the military, are seen as crucial if the president is to convince Capitol Hill and the country that his revamped strategy is working.[10]

Similar measurement problems arose during other US military invasions. The Vietnam War was one in which success remained undecided even after the war was over. The measurement problem is compounded by multiple other factors when analysts consider the perspective from which we are supposed to view success. The first question that comes to mind is success for whom? Cultural factors, humanitarian factors, geopolitical factors, and a store of other indicators begin to enter the calculation of success at every point of success analysis. If the goal is the implementation of a certain policy by the sanctioned country, then the factors indicating success are wholly different than, for example, in cases where economic sanctions are imposed for the release of a political prisoner. Analysts are thus left making the choice on whether the measure of success should be in economic terms or merely achieving the stated objective despite the economic position of the target or sender. There is an additional point to consider as we discuss any sanction regime. How to differentiate between the effectiveness of sanctions and success? Though often success and effectiveness are lumped in one category, they in fact represent two separate sides of the spectrum. Bergeijk makes a further distinction between the "effectiveness" of sanctions and "success" of sanctions.[11] According to Bergeijk, sanctions are *successful* when they inflict economic harm on the sanctioned country.[12] Sanctions are "effective" when they succeed in changing the sanctioned country's conduct in the manner desired by the sanctioning country. Thus, sanctions schemes may be successful but not effective, and effective though not successful (in cases where the sanctioned country accedes to the demands of the sanctioning body at the mere threat of sanctions, and avoids the negative economic fallout which would have resulted from the sanctions. To extend this position even further success can also be defined as achieving an objective in the most efficient manner without much economic harm to the sender's economy or target's population. In contrast effectiveness is achieving an objective no matter what the cost is, even if the economic cost entails a unilateral military attack on the weaker state. It should not be neglected that in addition to the economic costs, success and effectiveness must take into account the intrinsic costs of sanctions. For example an operation may be effective in destabilizing the Syrian regime; however, a new dictatorial government could be even more harmful to both the target's population and less friendly to sender nations both politically and economically, which would be determined as a failure of sanctions.[13] It should be noted that if economic harm is to be a question in success, then with respect to UNSC, the economic harm on the sanctioned state and all other member states must also be considered in measuring success.

No matter how success is defined, it is still an achievement of some goal that success would depend on. Thus no matter which definition of success would lead us to understanding the true influence that sanctions have on international relations we must first look at the stated objectives of sanctions. Thus as the current standard measure of success employed in the literature tests whether the sanctions "achieve their stated objectives," I explore the theories of success through a lens of stated objectives.

6.1 MAINSTREAM THEORIES OF SUCCESS

The dominant success/failure theory posits that sanctions are successful when they have "achieved their objective." Not only is this tautological, but this means that every episode of sanctions will have its own particularized moment of success. This moment would be further complicated as the sanctions regimes intensify and the point at which success is achieved becomes a moving target. Measuring the success of sanctions is particularly difficult as it is not clear what the sanctions are to achieve. Both the definition of success and the implicit rules used in applying it suggest that costs are an important part of the success concept.[14] Successful undertakings are those without excessive costs.[15] As a way of illustrating the importance of defining success, David Baldwin gives unorthodox examples: "The operation was a success, but the patient died," amputating one's leg to remove a wart from one's toe, winning a nuclear war by destroying life as we know it, and imposing economic sanctions that secure the compliance of the target state only by bankrupting the sender.[16] Scholarly differences exist on whether sanctions are necessary to bring about political change or to give forceful expression to the moral disapproval of policies.[17] The sanctions against South Africa are an example of sanctions that are brought about due to "moral disapproval" of policies, in this case on the grounds of racial discrimination.[18] It should also be noted that the discussion of sanctions against South Africa and the apartheid government were not seen as a threat to peace a year prior to the UN imposing sanctions. In the words of the late Bull Hedley, Professor of International Relations at Oxford,

> Sanctions may be imposed without any precise idea of the results they might be expected to achieve: 'Frequently, when one country imposes a trade embargo or other form of economic penalty on another, it is not as an alternative to going to war or because economic levers are available that might make it possible to bring an adversary to its knees; it is because something needs to be done to satisfy the expectations of domestic or international public opinion.[19]

Although other scholars try to measure the impact of sanctions, especially in reference to unilateral sanctions, there is still significant imbalance in the actual practice of measuring the success or failure of sanctions. In an effort to strategize a measure for sanctions, Hufbauer *et al*, divide success in two particular parts: 1) the achievement of sender's policy outcome, and 2) the contribution of sanctions rather than other factors.[20] This analysis is done through the sender's perspective, where in international sanctions it would be the collection of the Security Council and the member states. Hufbauer *et al.* use a success score which divides success measures into four categories under policy results and four categories in sanctions contribution ranging from failure to complete success in the latter and zero contribution to significant contribution in the former. Two points of interest are that the presence of external factors is not overlooked and that in the worst case scenario the country will be left off worse than it was before the sanctions. In international sanctions, the same categorical divisions are applicable as the intent of international sanctions is the same as the majority of cases of unilateral sanctions.

6.1.1 Achievement of Stated Objectives

Although unilateral sanctions and UN multilateral sanctions are different in character, ultimately the senders in both sanction methods should be interested in whether the sanctions succeed in reaching a stated objective. Otherwise there is really no reason for the imposition of the sanctions. It is much more logical to analyze the less complex and the more widely used of the two sanctions methods. Unilateral sanctions have been much more popularly used in the past sixty years, especially by the US, compared to multilateral UN sanctions. Therefore, an examination of the measure of success in unilateral cases will need to be made before continuing with the measure of success in UN-imposed sanctions.

The number of sanctions imposed by the UN is much lower than the total number of sanctions imposed by the US. The Institute for International Economics (Hufbauer, *et al.* 2007) analyzed 204 cases of economic sanctions in the time period between 1914 and 1990.[21] The study analyzed the stated objectives of the sanctions, as articulated by the sanctioning body, and then, based on historical facts, evaluated whether the sanctions successfully achieved their stated objectives in each of the cases.[22] The Hufbauer survey of economic sanctions since World War I found that about one in three sanctions succeeded in changing the behavior of the targeted regime or changing the regime itself.[23] Furthermore sanctions failed to achieve their stated objectives in sixty-six percent of those cases and were at best only partially successful in most of the rest.[24] Alternatively in the 1970s and 1980s, US unilateral sanctions were said to have worked in only about one in five cases,[25] a decrease of twenty-four percent, since 1973, in the success ratio for economic sanctions.[26] The illustrative point from these cases is the ambiguity behind defining success not the actual measure of success rate. In these three cases success has been defined based on achievement of a stated objective, changing of the behavior of the target regime or an overall question of whether sanctions worked.

Employing the Hufbauer methodology, one scholar has analyzed UN multilateral sanctions and found that sanctions have been successful at attaining their stated objective in only *three* cases,

> The three successful sanctions are League of Nations against Yugoslavia, League of Nations against Greece and United States against Egypt. In the first case, Yugoslavia withdrew its troops from Albania "in order to avoid the dangerous consequences of nonacceptance" (Toynbee 346). In the second case, Greece accepts League of Nations' recommendation to withdraw the troops from Bulgaria and to pay damages. In the third case, Egypt ends aid to Congolese rebels, stops anti-US attacks in the Egyptian press and withdraws support from Arab Jordan River Project.[27]

Thus, using the conventional model, we see that historically, economic sanctions have shown only partial success, and that the given "success rate" is decreasing. Of course, such a test suffers from bias, as we have unbounded time periods for evaluating whether the sanctions achieve their stated objective. Stated another way, sanctions that may cause catastrophic results on a given population within five years of enactment, may later (e.g., twenty years or more) be categorized as "successful" so long as sufficient time is given for the population to recover or rebound from the consequences of the sanctions. Absent a standard time period for measuring results, such studies as the ones discussed above become unreliable. Logically, the main factor accounting for the wide discrepancy between the above studies is the subjective valuation of both the stated goals of the given sanctions scheme and the question of whether the target country has actually complied with the demands of the sanctioning body.

Another statistical survey of the 20th century cases concluded that sanctions provided their users "no bargaining advantage *that was measurable* in terms of favorable outcomes."[28] Furthermore, there is "little to no correlation between the degree of punishment sanctions inflicted and their success in obtaining concessions to a coercer's demands."[29]

Other studies primarily deal with UN multilateral sanctions while looking at the success or failure of particular sanctions schemes rest not on economic, but rather, on humanitarian factors. For example, some scholars actually see the problem of the implementation of sanctions as involving a lack of central coordination. Stated another way, these scholars relate the failure of UN sanctions against Iraq and Yugoslavia to the failure of sanctioning states to actually take concrete actions to implement UN sanctions instead of limiting themselves simply to statements of support.[30] It should be noted that recent scholars see both cases as successful; one scholar refers to Iraq's inability to develop a nuclear program as a result of economic sanctions.[31] Although such scholars completely overlook that the ending of economic sanctions on Iraq occurred through an armed attack by the United States and that there were catastrophic casualties during the thirteen years of sanctions and after.

It is therefore still questionable what the true objectives of sanctions are and why there are such wide-ranging ideas in regards to the number of successful economic sanctions. In fact, it may be that the reason there are such discrepancies in the success valuation of sanctions is the lack of established objectives, which establishes that if objectives are clarified correctly then sanctions would be much easier to measure. It should be kept in mind that the dominant economic models used to measure success specifically concentrate the effects of sanctions on import- and export-based sanctions to and from the US, Japan, and Europe. Not only do these analytical frameworks ignore the myriad costs of the sanctions on third parties (aside from the effect on the sanctioned country's "economy" or the ruling elite), such analyses bring up the fact that sanctions may be imposed for purely monetary objectives above all others. Moreover, these models only analyze unilateral sanctions from a political or economic standpoint and cannot be related to multilateral UN sanctions.

6.1.2 Success as Capitulation

Another measure of success with respect to a given sanctions scheme is when the sanctioned country capitulates to the desires of the sanctioning body. This result is easily identified, usually as a result of the lifting of the sanctions in question. Success in this scenario is measured in terms of the potential payoff to the sanctioning body. It can be assumed that in unilateral sanctions a regime change, though it cannot be the apparent stated objective, could result in an enhanced economic relationship to the benefit of the sender. It should not be overlooked that the same scenario could be deemed true as a benefit to members of the UNSC, in particular those with veto power. The institutional payoff is theoretically associated with the lack of burden on the international community, lower monitoring costs by the institutions, and less cumbersome attention to the issues arising from the target state. For the purposes of a success analysis, this payoff may be quantifiable, only if the issue is isolated and there are no external factors. As an example, the internal assassination of the governing elite of the target country may be seen as the result of sanctions. However, if before the implementation of sanctions there were assassination attempts, then it is questionable whether the sanctions in fact were the driving force behind the assassin's action.[32] It should be noted that there have not been any known assassination attempts that can be directly related to UN economic sanctions. Though in general cases of assassination have not been common, especially in regards to international sanctions, the assassination of the Dominican Republic leader, Rafael Trujillo, in 1961 is an example in unilateral sanctions. The sanctions on the Dominican Republic came from the Organization of American States (OAS) and were the aftermath of Trujillo's interference with the affairs of neighboring countries and his assassination attempt on President Betancourt of Venezuela.[33]

Capitulation could also be a result of military actions launched by the UN or unilaterally. Thus sanctions could be seen as the precursor to armed attack.[34] The British position is representative of the close link between sanctions and armed conflict; Britain, in arguing for sanctions has always suggested that sanctions could not be carried out unless the member states were prepared to face the possible military consequences. As stated by Lord Baldwin and quoted by E. H. Carr, "[o]ne of the many conclusions to which I have been drawn is that there is no such thing as a sanction which will work, which does not mean war."[35] Although the number of cases and the period of time that sanctions have been imposed does not provide sufficient data for a thorough analysis,[36] the trends of war as a game changer in a target country have been evident in Afghanistan, Iraq, Haiti, Sudan, Somalia, and Serbia. In Afghanistan, the primary set of sanctions (Resolutions 1988 and 1989) was imposed on acts of terrorism, Al-Qaeda, and the Taliban regimes from 1998. These sanctions, which were a general in scope were diminished to sanctions on specific individuals after the US invasion of Afghanistan in 2001. Thus, the change or removal of certain parts of sanctions was as a result of a military attack. Similarly in Somalia, where sanctions have been in place since 1992, military force has followed. Operation Restore Hope by the US was carried out in 1992–1993 and continued with the Battle of Magadishu. The last military engagements in Somalia was the Battle of Ras Kamboni 2007; however sanctions continue to remain active on the country but poorly enforced. Additionally, although a full military engagement has not taken place in Somalia since 2007, in June 2011 a drone attack killed several Somali officials and injured others.[37] Other cases of military attacks along with sanctions are Sudan, where the 1996 sanctions were faced with a US military engagement in Operation Infinite Reach in 1998, and in Yugoslavia and Serbia, NATO bombing in 1999; Operation Allied Forces was to stop the conflict. Additionally Haiti, under sanctions since 1991 was faced with deployment of 20,000 US forces in Operation Uphold Democracy in 1995. The most comprehensive sanctions of the 1990s, the Iraqi sanctions, came to an end in 2003, after the US attacked to overthrow Saddam Hussein in Operation Iraqi Freedom.[38] Historically, sanctions cases in which the economic embargo fails leads to an escalation of hostilities and even war. The oil embargos of the 1970s present a similar illustration of armed conflict in the course of the implementation of sanctions; of course, the escalation of sanction to armed conflict also affects the measurement of success/failure (as the case is no longer conceptualized as a sanctions case and becomes a case of outright war).[39] If it is in fact true that sanctions lead to war, then sanctions would seem to violate the letter and spirit of the UN Charter. After all, the preamble of the UN Charter establishes the whole purpose of the UN's existence as a body dedicated to the prevention of war. Keeping to the assumption that the UN exists to prevent war and conflict, it is necessary to look within the changes in today's world order and suggest better alternatives to sanctions or a stronger, more transparent sanctions implementation process. It is argued that the basic paradox at the heart of the sanctions debate is that policymakers continue to use sanctions with increasing frequency, while scholars continue to deny the utility of such tools of foreign policy. Therefore a more pragmatic approach is the key to sanctions implementation in order not to fall trapped in the same paradox. For instance, the sanctions against Iraq that eventually ended with the 2003 invasion of Iraq can be classified as a success (since it led to the capitulation of Saddam Hussein) even though most scholars would probably exclude the case of Iraq from a success/failure analysis and treat it as an aberration/exception or a statistical outlier.

6.1.3 Success as Open-Ended Sanctions Regime

Yet another measure of success commonly applied to sanctions schemes is the alienation of the sanctioned country from the global economy, resulting in neither a net gain to the sanctioning body, nor a specific net loss to the sanctioned country. The end result instead ends up being general economic isolation (imposed autarchy). This type of success analysis, for instance, is currently applied to the sanctions scheme in place against countries like Iran and North Korea. In theory, because they are unable to export their valuable commodities (or in the case of North Korea, open their vast and inexpensive labor pool) to the world market, the sanctioned country is unable to acquire the economic strength which would give it any measure of leverage in world political circles.

An open-ended sanctions scheme can fail because of several considerations. First, the sanctioning partners may lose their political will to continue sanctions. According to Daniel Drezner, "coalitions are *less* effective than sustained unilateral sanctions, since early backsliding by members encourages targets to await the coalition's dissolution."[40] Second, open-ended sanctions schemes are not responsive to the changes or political processes within the target country, since they rest on the implicit assumption that the target country's policies are fixed and immutable. The multilateral sanctions against Iran offer a good example of this paradox. After the 2009 Iranian elections, there were political protests driven by the Iranian population discontented with the excessive religious restrictions and unfair political process and re-election of Mohammad Ahmadinejad.[41] These protests provided an understanding of a growing tide of popular and political opposition in Iran; nevertheless, the inflexible UN sanctions regime was and remains to be incapable of accounting for possible changes or a means to support the population of a country under sanctions drives for change. An open-ended sanctions regime can be conceptualized as successful from the perspective of the sender as it gradually weakens the target state over a prolonged period of time. In unilateral sanctions, the classic example of this is the US sanctions against Cuba, where success was determined by reference to the degree to which the Castro regime was alienated from US trade. As discussed in Chapter four, the US sanctions on Cuba actually went one step further than directed trade embargo on Cuba in the first years of the sanctions. By openly refusing to trade with any country that was trading with the Castro regime, the US was basically implementing a process of increasing force with the hope of diminishing the time period required to bring the target into compliance. A similar policy was behind the UK and the US "Trading with the Enemy Act of 1914." Mainstream models for measures of success do not account for success as an open-ended sanctions regime because states have never stated unrestricted sanctions as an explicit objective.

6.2 CRITIQUE OF MAINSTREAM SUCCESS MEASURES

Numerous critiques have been leveled against the current sanctions success paradigms. Most are grounded in normative analysis, railing against sanctions due to the immense human toll which they exert on the poorest segments of the population of the sanctioned country. Furthermore, the outcome of sanctions is dependent on the structure and behavior of the receiver. As in governments where they have a strong national hold, the sanctions are more likely to extend over a longer period of time with no real successful results, as the leader has more internal manipulative power, such control of media and publications, propaganda, controlled social media, centralized oversight in university activities, etc. In an attempt to categorize the critiques of mainstream sanction success measures, it will first be important to give a brief background of each. After categorizing the mainstream success evaluation, a critique of the current success model will be introduced.

6.2.1 Theoretical/Definitional Problems

This line of critique is oriented around the definitional problem surrounding the notion of success. Professor Wallensteen, a leading international peace scholar while discussing success states "[t]he definition of success is, of course, crucial and can be part of longer discussion. In military strategy it is often two outcomes that matter: victory or defeat. Thus, success and failure of sanctions could be a parallel: either the sender gets the receiver to change goals as desired by the sender (success) or not (failure)."[42] This stream of thought is typified by the work of David Baldwin, who posits that effectiveness itself can be subdivided into three categories: (1) *scope*, referring to the range of issues effected by sanctions; (2) *weight*, which is the degree to which sanctions affect scopes of target's behavior; (3) *domain*, referring to the number of people, countries, or international organization affected by the sanctions.[43] These three categories including *domain*, which is actually illustrative of the number of involved actors in sanctions deliberation, fall under effectiveness of sanctions. While Baldwin excludes *side effects*, in my analysis, they must be added to the definition of effectiveness when UN sanctions are the subject of analysis. Side effects as a category to be considered in defining sanctions allow us to take into account the extended impact of sanctions even after sanctions are removed from a target.

6.2.2 Institutional Problems

As noted above, there are implementation and execution costs associated with determining sanction success. It should further be noted that such costs increase as the institution becomes more multifaceted. The following diagram explains the activity structure of the UN as an institution and its relationship in information-transfer with the Security Council in regards to imposing sanctions.

As Figure 6.1 illustrates the UN Secretary General acts as a hub of information transfer and communication. The most difficult and highest transaction cost is associated with monitoring success and failure, as it filters through the system before it becomes a decisive source of discussion. Monitoring the success and failure of sanctions eventually turns into a decision of

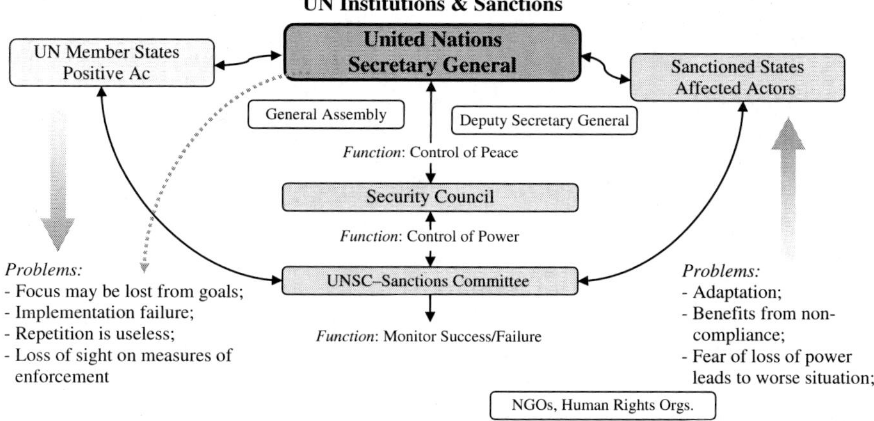

Figure 6.1 Institutional Information Flow Leading to Sanctions

whether or not to terminate sanctions and whether a successful result was reached. In 1997, the Secretary General added an additional layer to the structure by creating the position of Deputy Secretary General of the United Nations. The office was central in administering the Oil-for-Food program during the Iraqi sanctions and was criticized for its actions and a lack of oversight of the program.

The problems that arise from such a multilayer, top-down structure, as demonstrated above, are crucial in the administration of sanctions regimes. A multilayered organization creates a bureaucratic structure and adds complexity to the decision-making. As we discussed in Chapter five, the time frame for decision-making would make a difference in the implementation of sanctions. The more scattered the timeframe for decision-making, the distribution of information, and the implementation is, the less forceful the decision becomes upon execution. The politicized nature of the UN along with the increased bureaucratic structure leads to extensive inefficiencies, including ineffective communication and increased costs. Additionally, in such an organization, the lower level officials' observations are seen as irrelevant. Earlier in this book, I recalled an interview with one of the high ranking UN officials who asked me the relevance of Paul Conlon's papers when he was not the chair of Iraqi sanctions committee. Such line of reasoning is demonstrative of the minimal value given to the work of lower level officials and the bureaucratic nature of UN decision making.

6.2.3 The Critical Colonial Critique

Among the most vociferous groups of opponents to the current sanctions regime are the critical legal and critical colonial studies schools.[44] The increased influence of multinational corporations and the influence of sanctions on trade in particular, of the natural resources of a target, demonstrate that sanctions have been far more facilitating of neocolonial policies than the other way around. There is also validity to the argument that sanctions have been successful in implementing decolonization policies, such as in the case of ending the apartheid regime in South Africa. Critical scholars emphasize that the existing sanctions schemes are, upon closer examination, nothing but a continuation of the West's (particularly Europe and the US') failed 19th and 20th century policies of colonialism.[45] Rohit Chopra, Professor of Media Studies elaborates, "Economic sanctions, or punitive economic measures, also operate as markers of *difference*. They signify the cultural inability of a state—peculiarly anthropomorphized, one might say—to belong to the world of civilized nations."[46] As US state officials noted in 2001, when the administration was considering removing sanctions that had been imposed on India in 1998 after the Indian government announced a series of underground nuclear tests, "the sanctions were symbolic as much as practical."[47] This critique is especially relevant as the UNSC contains four former colonial powers with veto power. UK and France are obvious, undisputed ex-colonial empires. Russia was a colonial power until the Soviet Union, though some even argue that the USSR was a perpetuation of the Russian empire. Whether the US was a colonial power or not is open to heated debate, but most would agree that the four powers exemplified colonial behavior in their recent histories (immediately preceding the formation of the UN). China's recent conduct in Africa can be classified as falling within neocolonial patterns (the same as Soviet actions during the 20th century), though these claims are open to debate. As a more recent example, opponents of the increased Chinese investment in Africa posit that China's veto of sanctions against Sudan is because of China's continued interest in access to Sudanese resources. Such discussions could be substantiated by the extent of Chinese investment in Sudan. In 2005, China invested $351 million in Sudan, which was more than any other country in the region.

Following this line of reasoning one could speculate that strong former colonial powers impose economic measures that are designed to starve developing nations of the manufactured goods and technical know-how, leaving the sanctioned state unable to develop their own domestic industries. As a result, the former colonies are forced to remain in their historic state as suppliers of raw materials and commodities to the developed nations, while spending the bulk of their income on imports of necessary consumer and industrial goods from the colonial power. In cases when sanctions are imposed to bring change within domestic policies of a country, the sender is in effect forcing the target to accept the sender's policies and increase economic cooperation despite any long-term internal economic impact. Antony Anghie does not discuss economic sanctions in the form presented here, but his critique of international law's complicity with the colonial project has grounded the critique of modern multilateral and unilateral sanctions as legacies of imperial traditions. As Anghie appropriately states,

> The practice of cultural subordination and economic exploitation, which are essential aspects of colonialism, are not epiphenomenal aberrations in the international system that were remedied by the project of decolonization and self-determination rather they continue to play a role in contempt international relations and generate important analytic categories.[48]

Although Anghie was referring to the Mandate System and the role of League of Nations, the same logic can be followed with respect to the role of the UN and powerful states in influencing the decisions of the target country. Thus if intended consequence of sanctions is a more democratic state with open and friendlier trade policies towards the former colonial states, and the sanctions are imposed on states that have historically remained under colonial influence, then these actions cannot be differentiated from colonial behavior. It is the conduct of the powerful states that determines this relationship despite the process used, as the consequence is in line with the colonial process. Essentially, the policy is a continuation of the industrialization substitutes imports (ISI) development model of the 1960s and 70s.[49] But whereas the ISI model was discredited in the 1980s by the economists who had advocated it as a development model, ISI as a rationale for sanctions remains firmly entrenched in the academic and policy literature.[50]

If we further look at the dynamic of the relationship between the colonizer and the colony, the colonial power is believed to be the savior rather than the exploiter-colonized state.[51] Such a dynamic continues as the sender state finds itself in the role of a savior not exploiter of the target country. As this role continues to this day, it has transformed and the colonizer (sender) charges forward with the understanding that the colonies are to be saved from their own miserable selves.[52] Though such phrasing of the colonial relation could be crude, it does explain the colonial assumption that the colony's government, social, and legal structure is archaic by Western standards. There is also the further presumption that the colonies are in fact unhappy with their own circumstances, seeking a *better*, more modern, and Western system. From a social aspect, it looks at the society not by native standards, but by imported Western standards. Such standards are then used in reasoning for imposing economic sanctions or carrying out a military attack that would in essence infringe on the sovereignty of the state. As one direct example, the discourse surrounding the military attack on Iraq was bluntly stated to be for saving the Iraqi population of its own misery. Operation "Iraqi Freedom," "Operation Enduring Freedom," or even "Democracy for the Iranian People" set the foundation for belligerent attacks, militarily or economically.

It is improbable to imply that postcolonialism is a clear break from the colonial past. Kohn and McBride clarified this, stating, "post colonialism does not mark the end of colonialism but rather the emergence of the world it created."[53] Thus the formidable power disparities have not disappeared from the interstate relations. Just as today we cannot discuss the struggles of former colonies without looking at their colonial past, the decisions made by former colonial powers cannot be wiped clean of their colonial past. As Machiavelli found in reference to the state of Florence "All foundlings must break away from the past and all foundlings resemble the traces of the past."[54] It is questionable whether a clear break from the colonial history of states is possible, however, if the UN is to carry an authoritative force, there is a need to diminish the power disparity within the UN structure and the mandatory sanctions resolution.

Two events resulted in transition in the colonial power struggles of the 20th century. The first came after the end of WWI and the formation of the League of Nations (the League). The Mandate System, introduced by the League to redistribute territories of defeated powers, brought about institutional colonial involvement and power. The Mandate System, in theory, was established as a means of transferring power back to the former colonized states, by placing them under the control of advanced nations. The advanced nations (England, France, and Belgium) took on these states as their colonies, and there was no process established that would have allowed a transition of full long-term control of the state to the native government. Anghie differentiates between the pre- and post-Mandate System by establishing the progress of colonialism from a positivist approach that led to a mandate based pragmatic approach. He states,

> [t]he classical positivist criteria for statehood—government, population, and territory—are now rendered in the Mandate System, in detailed sociological terms. Thus, for example, in the Mandate System, territory is understood now in terms of resources and economic development; population is understood in terms of health issues, mortality rates, hygiene, and labor concerns; and government is conceptualized in terms of the reform of native political institutions.[55]

Though prior to the Mandate System, the colonizers could directly control the colony, with the new system, they were given more power. The power to influence and change the native, to show them the *right* structure and when the native system is not satisfactory, when the native insists on maintaining control the native is reprimanded by tighter controls. "Put another way, the formal positivist criteria of statehood—government, population, and territory—are transformed from mere criteria, which have to be satisfied, into projects to be undertaken by the Mandate System."[56] The System, empowered by the mandate of the League, required the colonial powers to maintain a system of checks and balances on the colony. This was in essence the first step in the transfer of power from the colonial state to the institution. The punishment was now carried out with institutional force rather than colonial control. Such a system, which was meant to allow states that are perceived to be unable to govern themselves, to develop into full functioning states, was the continuation of the power superiority, economic control, and social influence. The Mandate System represented the shift from autonomous law to jurisprudence based on rules, standards, policies, and administration.[57] This system was not established on a level playing field, and consequently reenforced prior power differences and continued to strengthen the weak-powerful dichotomy.

The second transition was as a result of the failure of the League and the onset of WWII. Even though the interwar period witnessed a slight shift of colonial control, the end of WWII and the formation of the UN brought a new idealist view to international relations. As international law has moved away from the Mandate System to a UN-administered trusteeship system the pragmatic rules based jurisprudence has become an institutionalist law as an interaction of equals. The formation of the UN in 1949 set the basis of what followed, in which, the institution and unanimous consent was to redistribute power. This process in theory allowed for assigning the task of resources distribution, economic development, or in other ways economic independence back to the state through international institutional control. The pragmatic understanding of the population has been transformed to democratic development, financial interdependence, and self-determination under rule of law enforced through international treaties, World Trade Organization, the International Monetary Fund, and others, while maintaining a level of control of domestic policies of states through economic pressure and sanctions. Rules and policies for conduct set by the institutions are now enforced by the institutions but carried out by the same colonial powers. Under the guise of democratic development, the weak-powerful dynamic continues. However, it is no longer an open colonial relationship but rather disguised as institutional equality. These institutional developments of the postwar period are in effect a continuation of the interwar technologies that Anghie identifies as techniques that gave the dynamic difference to the character of the Mandate System. "[I]n the case of the mandates, the conceptualization of sovereignty as something that could be created not only in its juridical form but also in sociological form, provoked the development of series of techniques including the fusion of law with administration and all its trappings."[58] These developments and techniques refer back to the institutionalization in international law and the transformation of the wealthy and powerful nations to those responsible for empowering the institutions for civilizing the uncivilized nations. From the categorization of resource states, in A, B, and C categories under the Mandate System. the development of the post-WWII institutional period defined these states in terms of their danger to peace and security to other nations.

On a societal level, the sanctions process that became popular in the 1990s has had significant influence on the conscious of the people. As the sanctions position is ultimately for a more pragmatic influence on the administration of the state, their enforcement and impact on the everyday life of the individual (in lack of basic foodstuff, medicine, etc.) attacks the psychology of the population. These sanctions are in effect thought by the sender to be changing the backward policies of the target and yet they are felt internally by the target as a way of manipulating self-governance and maintaining control. During the interwar period as colonialism continued, "the imposition of sanctions following any failure of the natives to meet universally posited standards no longer takes the form of punishment alone; rather, the application of new and formidable disciplines of management seeks to transform, not the body, but the soul of the native."[59] Now, with the UN's institutional control and backing, as the former colonies struggle to break away from the cyclical colonial relations, sanctions return the states back to the exact position as they were prior to colonization. The correlation between the former colonies and the currently sanctioned states is explained in Table 6.1. This table demonstrates that majority of states which have been exposed to UN sanctions after WWII were under some form of colonial control throughout their history. The Mandate System is shown as a form of advancing colonial power which was handed to the UN and later manifested as an independent control system in the form of economic sanctions over the same former colonial states. To further expose the close relationship between currently sanctioned states and the former colonial territories, Figure 6.2 maps the connection of former colonies, currently sanctioned states, to their colonizer.

The only way to move forward with the sanction debate in any meaningful manner is to step back and reanalyze the previous twenty years of sanctions. Taking this step backwards and unveiling the social significance and the consequences, negative or positive, opens a way to not walk in the same tracks as the former colonial period.

Thus to move away from the continuation of the same policies, archaic methods must be re-evaluated and include provisions beyond the UNSC's distribution of veto power between the power five (the UK, the US, France, Russia, and China). In order to hold the power five accountable and give a more substantial voice to other member states, a unanimous majority shall be able to overturn a decision. A unanimous majority would need to be determined by a vote of fifty-one percent against the proposed sanction or decision that has not been vetoed by one of the five members. Such a power structure would increase the active voice of other member states and lead to a unanimous decision with respect to sanctions. Furthermore it would enforce compliance as member states would have an active voice, thus, leading

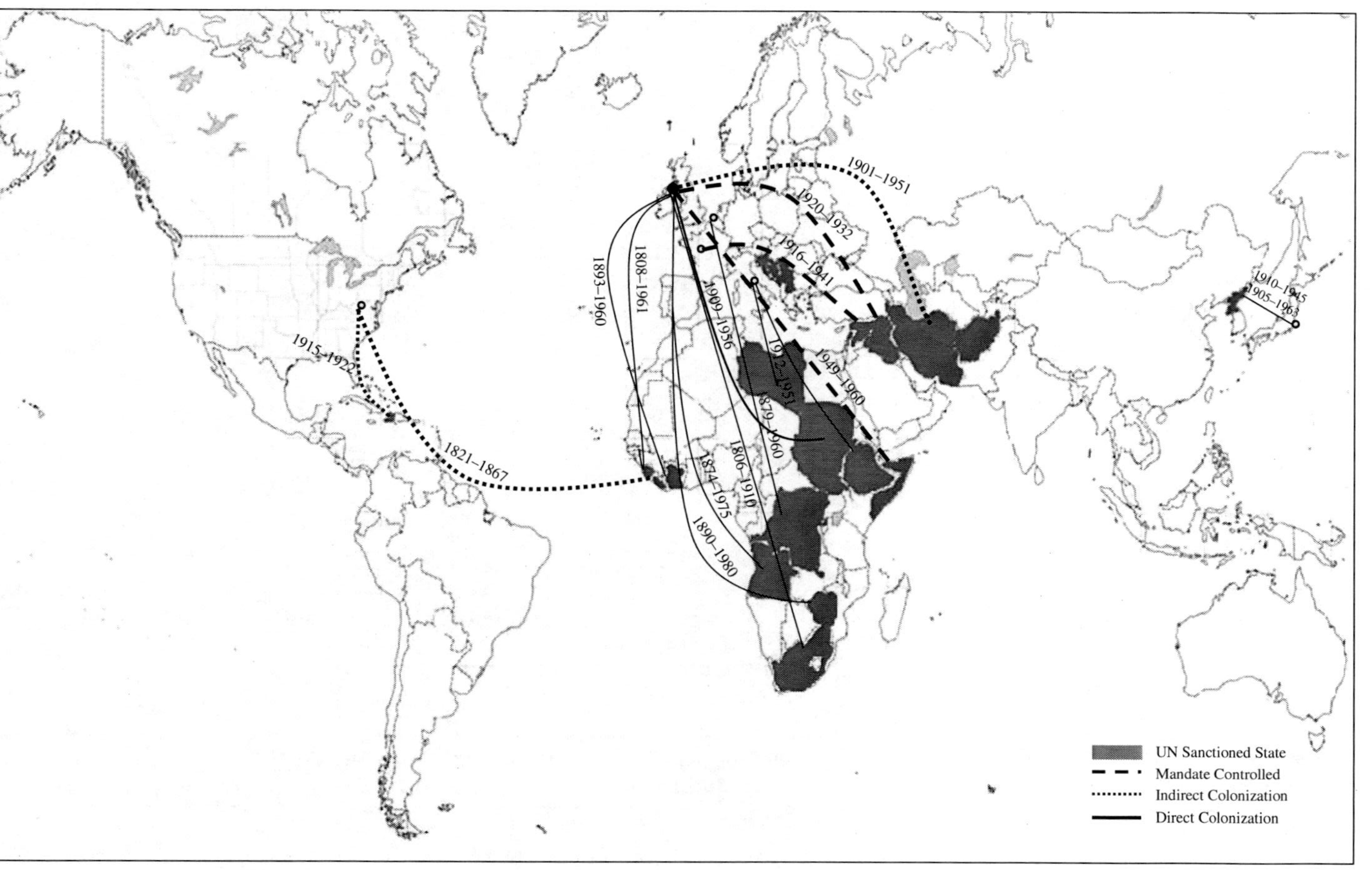

Figure 6.2 Mapping of Sanctions as Neocolonial Policies

Table 6.1 Catalogue of Sanctions State's Colonial History

Name of Colonial Region	Country Name	Duration	Colonizing Country	Part of the Mandate System	Comments	Sanctioned Period
American Society for Colonizing the Free People of Color of United States	Liberia	1821–1847	American Colonizer Society Not a government representative	No	Determination of colonization in the Liberia case is based on the Treaty between American Colonization Society and African Kings which was signed on May 11, 1825.	1992-partial sanctions cont.
Parte Françoise De S' Dominguez	Haiti	1697–1804	France	No	Haiti was a French Colony from 1697 to 1804, mainly used by the French to grow sugar. (Haiti declared independence on Jan 01, 1804). In November 1915 Republic of Haiti signed an agreement with the United States of America, which gave control of customs collection and Haitian finance the US. (See The Seizure of Haiti by the United States: A Report on the Military Occupation of the Republic of Haiti and the History of the Treaty Forced Upon Her, Foreign Policy Association, The National Popular Government League, April 1922)	1993–1994

Deutsch-Ostafrika till 1918 followed by Ruanda-Urundi	Rwanda	1894–1918	Germany	Yes: Level B Mandate. Belgian Admin 1924–1942 Under UN trusteeship 1942–1962	The 1924 League of Nations mandate assigned administration of Rwanda to Belgium. Thus from 1925 Ruanda-Urundi was linked with Belgian Congo. Congo was administered out of Belgium, Ruanda-Urundi was left to Tutsi aristocracy.	1994–1995
Anglo-Egyptian Sudan	Sudan	1899–1955	Britain	No	1896 Belgian control of Southern Sudan, turned to Britain in 1909–1956. Sudan was administered under Anglo-Egyptian control until 1956. The British-Egyptian agreement which was signed in 1953 gave Sudan independence on February 1, 1956. During this the Anglo-Egyptian ruling, the ruling party of Sudan was to be recommended by the British Government.	1996–2001 New targeted sanctions in 2005/2012-
Freetown/Sierra Leone	Sierra Leone	1808–1961	Britain	No-Continuation of the colony	Sierra Leone was first colonized by Britain in 1808: however, the native people revolted against the occupying powers multiple times. One of these revolts, the Hut Tax War of 1898, which ended organized movements against colonial powers.	1997–

(Continued)

Table 6.1 (Continued)

Name of Colonial Region	Country Name	Duration	Colonizing Country	Part of the Mandate System	Comments	Sanctioned Period
Abyssinia/Eritrea	Ethiopia and Eritrea	1936–1941	Belgium/Italy	No	Annexation of Ethiopia given by League of Nation in 1936 gave control of Ethiopia to Mussolini in Italy, until May 5, 1941 when Emperor Haile Selassie returned to throne.	2000–2001
Belgian Congo	Democratic Republic of Congo	1879–1960	Belgium	No-Continuation of the colony	In 1879 King Leopold II of Belgium established a joint stock company in Congo basin. His acquisition was affirmed at the Berlin Conference in 1884.	2003–
French West Africa	Cote d'Ivoire	1893–1960	French	No-Continuation of the colony	Cote d'Ivoire became a French colony in 1893 under Binger as the governor. During this Binger's governance, Malinke Chief Samori Ture fought against the French occupation for five years.	2004–
Syria Vilayet	Syria	1516–1914	Turkish (Ottoman Empire)	Yes	The division of post-WWI Syria was agreed upon secretly by François Georges-Picot and Mark Sykes. The Sykes-Picot Agreement was signed in 1916. League of Nations mandate was for French control of Syria from 1920 to 1941.	2005–

Korea	North Korea	1910–1963	Japan	No-Continuation of the colony	Annexation Treaty: Japan 1910 to 1945; Also the after the Russo-Japanese War, Eulsa treaty 1905 until 1963. The treaty on Basic Relations between Japan and the Republic of Korea signed in 1965 established that all prior treaties including Eulsa treaty (Japan-Korea Treaty of 1905), were null and void. Thus Korea was no longer under the Japanese diplomatic control.	2006–
Orange Free State	Rhodesia	1890–1980	Britain	No-Continuation of the colony	The country was divided between Cecil John Rhodes and his South African Company and other colonial participants.	1966–1979
Cape Colony	South Africa	1795–1910	Britain: 1795 to 1803 Dutch: 1803 to 1806 Britain: 1806 to 1910	No	The fist British establishment in South Africa was in 1814 when the Cape colony was purchased from Dutch East India Company.	1977–1994
Vilayet of Mosul/ Vilayet of Baghdad/ Vilayet of Basra (Also Mesopotamia)	Iraq	1532–1917	Turkish (Ottoman Empire)	British Mandate--August 10, 1920 to October 3, 1932	All government departments were run by the British government in Iraq under the Mandate System. Britain also retained dominant role after Iraq achieved nominal independence in 1932. (See Martin Thoma, Bob Moore, L.J. Butler, Crises of Empire: Decolonization and Europe's Imperial States, 1918–1975, Hodder Education 2008).	1990–2003

(Continued)

Table 6.1 (*Continued*)

Name of Colonial Region	Country Name	Duration	Colonizing Country	Part of the Mandate System	Comments	Sanctioned Period
NA	Yugoslavia		NA	NA	NA	1991–1996
Italian Somalia & British Somaliland	Somalia	1840–1960	Britain: 1840 – 1960 (British East India Company) Italy: 1880 – 1941 (Italian Somaliland) British: 1941 to 1949	Trust territory of Somalia: British Control from 1949 to 1960	Italy controlled north-east of Somalia which became Italian East Africa, after the Italo-Abyssian War. The British Somaliland was conquered in 1940. All of this territory was lost in 1942 and became under British control as a UN trust from 1949 until 1960.	1992–2006
Tripoli	Libya	1912–1951	Italy	N-Continuation of the Colony	1912 to 1951--By 1912 Treaty of Lausanne	1992–
Persia	Iran	1901–1951	Not a direct colony. Exclusive control of Iranian oil from 1901 to 1951.	NA	The basis of this analysis is on Anglo-Persian treaty with formed the Anglo-Persian oil company (Now British Petroleum). This agreement would give Iran 16% of profits of the oil extracted.	2006–
NA	Afghanistan	NA	NA	NA	NA	1999–2002 Partial sanctions cont.

Angola	Angola	1884–1975	Portugal	No-Continuation of Colony	Angola was colonized by the Portuguese in 1570. The Berlin Conference 1884–1885 defined the territory of Angola as a territory of Portuguese. Angola was given independence by the Alvor Agreement in Jan 15, 1975 (effective November 11, 1975).	1993–2002

to a diminished absolute power of the power five states and a more fluid decision-making process.

6.2.4 The Problem of Failed States

Just as the former colonial structures continue to influence state relations, the historical economic trauma caused by colonialism, war, and continued depletion of resources resurfaces in the economic structure of states. Some critics stress the humanitarian cost of the sanctions, rather than pointing to discredited economic models. In the humanitarian analysis, economists incorrectly value the loss of potential, quality of life, and precipitous fall of living standards as a result of the sanctions when weighing the likely benefits to the economy of the sanctioned country. As the conventional sanction analysis focuses on the effect of the sanctions on the ruling elite, or the dominant economic players, it often ignores the reality that the core economic actors of most sanctioned states are the local farmers and merchants who the sanctions injure most. The conventional analysis also ignores the reality that ruling elites in quasi- or failed states lack the capacity to provide law order and economic strength or to ensure a functioning and transparent economy.[60] It is unrealistic to assume that sanctioning a failing state would result in added control by the state. Illustratively an arms embargo has been imposed on Somalia since 2007; in spite of this the state has remained number two in the list of countries where government lacks legitimacy and control.[61]

In the case that follows, it is demonstrated that of all UN-imposed sanctions since 1945, totaling to 19, 11 have been on postcolonial states, which were already considered failing states.

6.3 CASE STUDIES

6.3.1 African States/Postcolonial Dimension

A further reality of the current political scene is that sanctions will have unpredictable results when they are applied against failing or newly formed states as discussed above. The sanctions imposed on African states are telling in this regard. Jeffery Herbest explains the dynamic of the postcolonial period stating "As calls for military victory appear to be politically incorrect in the current age, the vocabulary of victory and defeat has been transferred to the more neutral and technocratic language of sanctions and restraints on the trade of natural resources." First, the themes echoed above by critical colonial scholars are especially pertinent here. Even at first blush, it becomes obvious that in Africa, sanctions are or have been in effect against each nation which has sought political independence from the previous political or colonial, order. Secondly, the sanctions in place or threatened against African states are not amenable to traditional economic analysis due to the lack of data, lack of stable core industries on which to base the sanctions, lack of clear mandates from the ruling elite, and worse still, the ever-present political reality of state-failure. The ongoing conflict in Darfur provides a clear understanding of this reality. The sanctions on Sudan are in the form of an arms embargo on the Janjaweed militia group. This group has been connected to mass killing of African Sudanese of the region. The embargo was enacted in 2004 by Resolution 1556 and broadened in 2005 by 1591 to include all parties of theNorth Djamena Ceasefire Agreement and any other belligerents in the states of Northern Darfur, Southern Darfur,and Western Darfur.[62] The Janjaweed's presence is mostly in the region bordering the Central Arab Republic, Chad, and South Sudan. Though the conflict has been tied to the Janjaweed, there have been several reports and testimonies, which provide support that the Sudanese government has armed the group, even though the Sudanese government has continued to deny these claims.

A four member panel of experts was also established to monitor the arms embargo for six months. Scholars are in near universal agreement that it is impossible to impose sanctions against Sudan for violence in the Darfur region, because the state is nonresponsive and any sanctions would result in unpredictable, but catastrophic humanitarian costs. Sanctions would have no, or little, effect upon the politically entrenched local elites.

As colonial ruling left many African countries divided, it also left them with a lack of proper infrastructural or technological capabilities to compete in the market with the use of their natural resources. It further left them dependent on the occupying countries for assistance with resource allocation and production. This dependence increased the amount of conflict stretch, and has spread over to more recent times. In the case of South African sanctions, the effects of continuous colonial power are evident as the reports of the Commission on South Africa reveal, first clearly analyzing the interests of United Kingdom, US, and France, and the effect of sanctions on their trade. Also, the reports state that it is clear that there are two reasons, apart from political considerations, that United States and Britain are opposed to sanctions.

> One is the existence of important business groups in these countries having considerable interests in South Africa; the other is the fear that if sanctions were not enforced simultaneously by other competing countries, like Germany and Japan these business groups would lose through sanctions without the objective of sanctions being achieved.[63]

The commission further analyzed that the imports from South Africa were small and were not to affect the US and UK economies tremendously. It therefore decided to impose sanctions, emphasizing that the both the UK and US had not considered apartheid a "threat to peace" in South Africa. The commission further emphasized that UK, the US, and France were to change the direction of their policies in regards to the South Africa question.[64]

Ultimately economic sanctions on African states are by virtue decisions made by exclusion of African states. The hierarchy of decision-making in international law takes place without consideration for the national value processes of the developing nations. These growing states are extremely fragile in the international relations dynamic. As former colonial states are slowly attempting to form their position in the international forum economic sanctions can immediately impact their economic growth.

Returning to the definition of peace as was discussed in Chapter two of this book, in order to maintain peace, there is a need for economic stability. Therefore the only mean for the development of peace in the former colonial societies would be to assist in their economic development. Professor Muna Ndulo of Cornell Law School defines challenges to peacekeeping missions as processes that can assist political structure, demobilize armed forces, establish rule of law, promote security, support disarmament, hold elections, and jump-start the economy.[65] If to establish a peaceful state, economic stability and economic growth are necessary, depriving a state of such advancements would lead to either status quo or even further conflict. Economic sanctions in effect act as barriers to economic development. States that are already in economic turmoil because of years of colonial control, suffer from a weak economy, thus sanctions deprive the state of any advancement towards stability or control of the state's status.

Measures have been established in more recent years to both boost involvement of African states and diminish threats to peace. The pact on security, stability, and development in the Great Lake region which followed the Dar-es-Salaam Declaration on Peace, Security, Democracy, and Development (2004), was established in 2006 to give a legal framework to the declaration and was signed by Angola, Burundi, Central African Republic, Kenya, Republic of Congo, Rwanda, Sudan, Tanzania, Uganda, and Zambia. The ten protocols of the pact are:

- The Protocol on Non-aggression and Mutual Defence in the Great Lakes Region 2006;
- The Protocol on Democracy and Good Governance 2006;
- The Protocol on Judicial Cooperation 2006;
- The Protocol for the Prevention and the Punishment of the Crime of Genocide, War Crimes and Crimes against Humanity and all forms of Discrimination 2006;
- The Protocol Against the Illegal Exploitation of Natural Resources 2006;
- The Protocol on the Specific Reconstruction and Development Zone 2006;

- The Protocol on the Prevention and Suppression of Sexual Violence Against Women and Children 2006;
- The Protocol on the Protection and Assistance to Internally Displaced Persons;
- The Protocol on Property Rights of Returning Persons 2006;
- The Protocol on the Management of Information and Communication 2006.[66]

Despite these protocols, little has actually been done to implement them. Looting of extractable resources (especially easily concealed and valuable commodities, like diamonds) has continued and international monitoring groups and NGOs continue to see the same levels of violence. Cases brought to the ICJ involving Congo and Rwanda in regards to armed conflict in 1999,[67] the establishment of the International Criminal Tribunal for Rwanda (ICTR), and massive humanitarian aid missions have not abated the escalating levels of economic uncertainty in the region. Moreover, sanctions are still in place against Congo (arms embargo). It is questionable how this is so, in light of this newly formed treaty; the stated countries are still under international sanctions. Should the treaty be seen as a sign of sanction success or are there further proofs of relationship needed to measure success? It is axiomatic, however, that if conflict arises in any of the above countries, success no longer holds valid. Therefore, yet again there is more ambiguity in measuring the success of economic sanctions, especially since the pact cannot be directly correlated to UN-imposed sanctions.

6.3.2 Humanitarian Considerations/Third Parties

Further criticism against existing sanctions regimes oppose the ways in which the sanctions are implemented, rather than the underlying analysis of the reason for the sanctions in the first place, or the theoretical effectiveness of sanctions more generally. The sanctions against Iraq throughout the 1990s provide a good illustration of sanctioned countries' abilities to circumvent the sanction states. Iraq, for example, was able to subvert the UN sanctions scheme through the now-notorious Oil-for-Food (OFF) program. According to Richard Garfield,

> Oil sales from the first five six-month rounds of the OFF programme generated US $7.7bn for humanitarian goods. However, goods actually purchased with these funds amounted to a little over half of this total (53 per cent of all funds generated are destined for supplies; the rest go towards UN administration, reparations etc). This represents US $394 per capita in the centre and south of Iraq and US $480 per capita in the north (the latter being a mainly Kurdish area and UN administered). Even though far more goods are being imported to Iraq under OFF than

> at any time since the initiation of the embargo, the US $3–$4 worth of food and medicines distributed per capita per month represent only a fraction of the estimated US $12 imported per capita per month during 1988–1989.[68]

The OFF scandal shows the high enforcement costs which the UN or other sanctioning bodies must bear if they are to successfully monitor a sanctioned country's conduct, restrict trade, and take the related measures necessary to enforce the sanctions. Relatedly, it highlights the disproportionate effect of the sanctions on the poorest segments of the population, rather than the ruling elite who are the supposed target of the sanctions.

A second type of humanitarian cost associated with sanctions is the existence of side effects to sanctions. As the sanctions (such as ban on arms trade) take effect, the rogue parties in thirst of driving their agenda go through secondary sources to supply their corruption. For, finding ways to purchase these supplies, mostly arms, they resort to exploiting the resource-rich areas. This leads to further abuse of human rights. The Pulitzer Center on Crisis Reporting accounts that in East Democratic Republic of Congo children are left to mine for colton, cassiterite and gold which pays for much of the civil war that has killed over 4 million people in the region.[69] In the same report, Mvemba Phezo Dizolele, a policy analyst, states that where minerals were found, the negative "Mai Mai" forces were present, yet the real profiteers are the multinational corporations. The Mai Mai forces are militia groups in the southern DRC and are led by warlords and resistance fighters. This issue of multinationals will be addressed further in Chapter seven.

6.3.3 Unintended Consequences/Entrenchment

An important observed but clearly unintended consequence of trade sanctions is the development of local economic elites that are able to circumvent the sanctions schemes while simultaneously benefiting from the collapse of the intended domestic industry. It may be the divide between the wealthy and the poor in developing countries and their approach to acting as domestic investors; studies have shown that wealthy individuals in developing countries are less concerned with acting as investors in the economic development of the state.[70] Especially in cases where the sanctioning country's government is entrenched militarily, local economic elites seem to emerge to conduct the necessary trade, especially in goods necessary for the survival of the armed services. Yet aside from acting as important conduits for the flow of illicit goods, these individuals do not reinvest in the local industries, leading to additional capital flight. Thus, despite creating economic pressure on domestic industries, the sanctions in these cases do not create enough social pressure that would lead to change, while contemporaneously enabling local economic elites.

The increase in the number of economic elites that are consequently intertwined with the ruling elites or recruited by the ruling elites has a reverse effect on the economy but a direct effect on the level of control they hold. As Justman and Gradstein (1999) argue, economic growth dilutes the power of the elite by broadening political participation and reducing inequality.[71] And since economic sanctions are a form of stopping economic growth, it is then evidently the strengthening of the economic and ruling elite that is the direct consequence of economic sanctions.

Furthermore, elite plurality, in which the political and economic elites are separate, explains the adoption of a political franchise and industrialization in Western Europe, while 19th-century Eastern Europe, where unity among the elites was strong, did not adopt growth-enhancing institutions, since its elites held on to their wealth and power.[72] Thus an imperative fact in a sanctioned country remains the power of the ruling class. As a democratic process creates free competition among the would-be leaders, it is the democracy level of the target that will ultimately lead to success or failure rather than the power of the ruling class.[73] Astonishingly though, economic sanctions are in many cases imposed mostly on those who are not conventionally democratic.[74] Therefore, the ruling class has much more control over the masses and the society is left with the continuous ruling of those with the most power.[75]

6.3.4 Sanctions Evasion

Sanction-dodging and evasion also make measurement of the effectiveness of sanctions significantly more difficult. International border crossings are notoriously difficult to control. To demonstrate, while crossing a border between Russia and Kazakhstan in the summer of 2009, I witnessed the ease with which organized crime and other individuals can bypass international security checkpoints. For one hundred dollars, a full bus can pass through a border point without any inspection (all of the passengers went through passport control, but a small bribe allowed more than forty passengers to avoid customs controls). Charles Taylor's blatant disregard for UN sanctions against Sierra Leone and announcing that he would continue to trade with Sierra Leone is a more evident example of sanctions evasions. If corruption is so endemic, how can it be expected that a UN resolution will guarantee that officials will implement the sanctions? Respect for law, from ordinary citizens to officials, is what divides countries into ranks. This respect for the rule of law, indeed, is one criteria in Freedom House and other development indexes.

According to internal US Treasury reports, the US has developed computer software that can search electronic transactions for financial operations by named individuals or companies suspected of violation of federal sanctions legislation. Furthermore, since moving money around the world is difficult without passing through the banking system of a major financial center in the West these transactions would be even more difficult when initiated by sanctioned countries. However, secondary transactions can go through secondary persons or countries as "transactions partners"; therefore, it would mean that all possible partner countries would have to be sanctioned and all possible trading partners should also be targeted, making true control of sanctions virtually impossible. Such a comprehensive sanctioning process would be highly costly to international trade and thus impossible to implement.

6.3.5 Free Riders/Profiteers

When a country imposes unilateral sanctions against a targeted country, others may benefit tremendously from the sanctions. They can act as middle-men, trading on behalf of the sanctioned country, acting as a trading hub, and facilitating currency and commodity exchange between countries. Or they can exploit antagonism between two agents by increasing price points. I refer to this phenomenon as the free-rider problem.

In the case of UN multilateral sanctions, the free-rider problem creates a black market as is seen in many cases of arms embargos; an example of such is the *US v. Jasin* case, where Jasin was found to be conspiring to transfer $300-$500 million worth of military weapons to South Africa which was then to be sold to China. This was in fact during the time that sanctions were in place against the apartheid regime.[76] This case is representative of the ease with which companies are able to create a front line company to bypass sanctions and become profiteers of a sanction regime.

6.3.6 Problems of Measuring Data (Unquantifiable Data)

Another critique made of success/failure measurements is their reliance on unreliable or questionable data. Indeed, the reliability of economic indicators (data) in the sanctions context is one of the most vexing problems for economists. Though the following factors may be quantifiable in developed societies (those with well-built infrastructure, which allows for quantitative monitoring of resource flows/allocation), in traditional target states, these factors are not amenable to quantification based on a lack of data, massive population transfers (internal displacement, as in the case of the refugees fleeing war zones in Rwanda and elsewhere), and nonexistent or destroyed infrastructure. They include:

The factors listed in Table 6.2 not only pose a question of the measure of success, they also add to the side effects of the sanctions imposed. The human rights community has had great influence in bringing the side effects of sanctions to international attention. The work of NGOs such as International Red Cross, National Lawyers Guild, and others is extremely relevant to this debate. Nevertheless, as long as sanctions are imposed, these side effects will be present.

Table 6.2 The Impact of Economic Sanctions on Health and Wellbeing (by Richard Garfield)

Public Health	
Infant Mortality	Increase in infant deaths as reported by hospitals and in vital events recording systems
Hospital and Medical	Decrease in numbers of operations and X-rays performed
System Capacity	Diminished availability of vaccines; Reduced number of visits to health system
Low Birth Weight	Rise in reported percentage of low weight infants; Rise in number of pregnant women with low weight gain
Access to Safe Drinking Water	Decline in percentage of population receiving pumped water; Breakdowns in the availability of chlorine
Economic Level	
Conditions	Changes in income distribution across different social classes
Development (as measured income groupsby GDP/capita)	Declining availability/rising market prices of core commodities (necessaries)
Import/Export	Dependence on imports; Price of foodstuffs; Prices of exports; Declining availability/rising price of pharmaceuticals
Form of Economic Specialization	Change in urban/rural population mix
Migration	Presence of refugee camps; Increase in involuntary migration and populations of displaced persons; Start of new migratory population flows; Creation or rapid expansion of refugee camps and/or concentrations of internally displaced persons (IDPs)
Governance Status of Civil Society	Changes in government budgetary allocations; Increases in crime and civil unrest in society; Decline in number of independent civic organizations; Degree of political freedom; suppression of political parties; Decline in number of independent media outlets; Increasing number of political arrests[1]

(Continued)

Table 6.2 (*Continued*)

Public Health	
Level of Humanitarian Activity	Change in ratio of people served by aid; Activities programs relative to the people making demands on those services; Decline in the ability of humanitarian agencies to perform service

Source: Richard Garfield, The Impact of Economic Sanctions on Health and Wellbeing, RRN Network Paper, November 1999.

[1] I am especially suspect of these factors as variables in economic analysis because of the inherent subjective nature of the rights at issue and the notorious politicization of the indices which are used to measure or report on the status of these rights, such as the Freedom House Index, and related studies. This table provides a representation of the factors presented in Minera et al. found in The Impact of Economic Sanctions on Health and Wellbeing. The original table divided these factors into baseline and change indicators as recommended minimum monitoring indicators for sanctions.

6.4 NEW PARADIGM FOR DETERMINING EFFECTIVENESS OF SANCTIONS

6.4.1 Application / Rationality

Attempts at setting standards for economic measures of success/failure rely on the assumption that states are rational actors. The rationality principle despite being a bedrock principle undermining many economic theories, is of doubtful validity in political processes.[77] Rationality is central to sanctions deliberations.[78] Throughout much of the 20th century, the rationality principle was the main separating line between sociology (which admitted, and indeed studied, irrational group behavior) and the social interactions of rational economic agents, which was the purview of economists.[79] Advances in economic method mean that economics now also recognize and study irrational behavior.[80] For instance, the single most important contribution that law and economics has made to the study of law is the use of coherent theory of "rational choice theory" to examine how people are likely to respond to legal rules,[81] including accounting for microirrationalities, culture, customs and other mores.

Sanctions debates implicitly assume rationality on behalf of the sending body.[82] There is also an implicit assumption that the target will respond as a rational actor. This means that from the standpoint of the UNSC there is an assumption that sanctions deliberations will proceed logically towards an objective goal. The rationality assumption is grounded on several related assumptions pertaining to economic agents. These include self-interest, rational choice, expected utility, and others. Within expected utility theory, rationality is associated with several subthemes, each of which relates to sanctions deliberations: 1) subjective probability, 2) Bayesian learning[83], and, 3) maximization of expected utility. Bergeijk and Marrewijk use the expected utility to show the relationship between the length of time sanctions are imposed and the potential success. In their analysis they depend on the Bayesian updating to show that targets make changes in their choices based on past outcome.[84] More modern interpretations of rationalism also include the flexible standard of the typical behavioral patterns of capitalism, giving predictive potential to seemingly irrational economic trends based on empirical observation and/or statistical analysis.[85] The response to the strict rationality assumption has been the development of bounded rationality, as a dynamic model for selection among multiple equilibria.[86]

However, not all sanctions are enacted for economic reasons or are enacted as a manifestation of economic self-interest. Irrational factors such as anger, envy, sympathy, and honor may influence policymakers to adopt sanctions which would be a net negative economic result to them individually, or to their given country, or business concern. Relatedly, states routinely obey norms, which are not necessarily Pareto-improvements.[87]

At the first stage of sanctions deliberations, the rationality assumption is further suspect because of the large number of actors involved. In other words, we have to look not only at the rational choices of the sanctioning body. Traditional economic analysis also requires that we assume (to some degree) the rationality of the sanctioned country and its rulers. This assumption is similar to the assumption underlying the Nash theorem, that is, assuming rationality not only of individual players, but also a common knowledge of rationality between all agents.

The rationality assumption is more or less superfluous to current sanctions deliberations, which end at the first level. This is because states imposing sanctions for human rights or other irrational considerations are unlikely to be making these decisions based on economic principles; rather, the sanctions decision is more likely to result in an open-ended, politically motivated sanctions scheme. The decision of whether or not to sanction a country for "irrational" reasons generally turns on the level of economic ties between the sanctioned country and the sanctioning body. In the UN context, of course, there are no economic ties between the UNSC and the target but rather between the different member states and the target. More often than not, the first level cases involve situations where there is a small or nonexistent economic link between the two. As a result, the sanctioning country will determine whether or not to sanction based on the likely economic harm to *itself*. In the case of UN sanctions, multiple states are independently evaluating economic harm to themselves, but there is no global economic impact assessment. Each state analyzes net economic benefit/loss from its own perspective (and possibly taking into account the effect on the target state's economy). Because there are few trade connections to sever, and the likely negative impact of the sanctions on the sanctioning country will be small, the first level cases may result in indefinite and prolonged sanctions schemes, as in the example of North Korea.

Recently, there has been a move to begin evaluating international law from an economic perspective.[88] At the bottom of this trend is a belief that state action can be reduced to rational choice and that states can be equated as utility maximizing agents in an otherwise anarchic world. Alan Sykes summarizes this phenomenon well,

> Goldsmith and Posner argue that convergence in state practice occurs for reasons of pure national self-interest, albeit not the same reason every time. They further suggest that continued adherence to customary practice happens because the self-interested reasons for convergence remain in place, not because of any independent sense of legal obligation. *Opinio juris*, they suggest, is a fiction and what legal scholars refer to as customary law, is really no more than a descriptive account of certain regularities in the behavior of states.[89]

Until this point, the question of whether the effects of the sanctions outweigh the likely benefits is usually approached on normative, subjective grounds, often by liberal-leaning scholars.[90] Attempts to conceptualize economic sanctions as economic actions were usually limited to game-theoretic attempts. But a more realistic perspective must accommodate an irrational target, sender, and third state environment. The chaotic world of states (both target and sender) and the politicized, hidden agendas underlying sanctions deliberations mean that the actions of the involved actors are less driven by rational behavior. If they are actual rational thoughts these thoughts are bounded by the limited information that each actor obtains.

Aside from irrational actors, there are also illogical and unpredictable constraints on state action and decision makers. A nonlogical influence is any influence acting upon the decision-maker of which he is unaware and which he would not consider a legitimate influence upon his decision if he were aware of it.[91] Scholars suggest that the influence of illogical factors will be inhibited if the decision-maker has a great deal of information about the event in question, if he has a high level of skill in international affairs, if he believes he has influence on the event, and if he is in some way responsible for the consequences of whatever decision he makes. In addition, if the decision is specific, detailed, and made within a group context in which the decision-maker's biases are canceled out by countervailing biases, the chances for objectivity increases.[92] In the words of David Baldwin,

> From the standpoint of the logic of choice, the neglect of costs is unfortunate; but it is even worse to give the impression that one has taken them into account when one has not. Such confusion arises when assessments of economic sanctions use the terms 'effectiveness,' 'efficiency,'

and 'utility' interchangeably. In the context of the logic of choice, the concept of efficiency implies something about the relationship between inputs, that is, between costs and effectiveness. And the concept of the utility of a course of actions implies something about its net value. References to the 'utility' or 'efficiency' of sanctions imply that costs have been taken into consideration.[93]

If the UNSC has maximum information about the political situation in the target state and is under the assumption that sanctions should influence target state action, then the UNSC should be responsible for the decisions they make. The lack of information (not simply complete information, but basic data regarding target state trade, import-export, extent of unofficial black market trade, and so forth) makes the possibility of applying strict economic models to sanctions deliberations problematic. It is axiomatic that a model is only as good as the data fed into it.

Having surveyed the difficulty in current implementation regimes, and the problems in measuring success/failure, it becomes obvious that the fundamental problem with current sanctions deliberations, implementation, and measurement of success/failure rests in incomplete information. It is to this issue that the book turns to next. Specifically, is it possible to tailor sanctions schemes in such a way as to maximize likely effect (actually impact behavior of the target), while minimizing the effects on third parties (and innocent civilians), all while providing policymakers with predictable measures of success/failure?

6.4.2 Traditional Analysis for Imposing Sanctions (Costs)

Multiple economic factors exist in the *initial* decision of whether or not to sanction a country. These factors may be envisioned as barrier costs, or initial market entry costs. One of the major factors that goes into the economic decision-making is whether in enacting trade sanctions, the total cost of the sanctions will be more than the cost of direct means of achieving the stated objective, such as increased diplomacy. Commentators have observed in a wide variety of cases that unless directly involved as the victim of an alleged aggression, states have sought the minimum obligation that would entail a fixed cost to themselves.[94] Thus one of the factors militating success of sanctions is the impact of the sanctions on existing trade relationships. States have a demonstrated reluctance to upset existing markets, trading patterns, and other bilateral relations in order to undertake a sanction scheme.[95] Therefore in measuring success, this economic path dependence, where the sanction implementers are more inclined to continue its trade relationship rather than sever ties in the hope of influencing domestic policy, must be taken into consideration as an additional cost.[96]

Another feature in the sanctions decision in the expectation that the government will be forced into fear of economic breakdown and bring about changes that would be more in line with international law. There exist too many hurdles to really show the true effects of sanctions. Whether they are successful or not in the long-term remains a vague question which is being more and more influenced by external factors.[97] One such external factor is the actual cost for the enactment of sanctions, which includes the costs of the initial analysis (the costs of the process of sanctions deliberations). This cost is significant, as the analysis is usually performed over a prolonged time period and involves numerous agents. Moreover, international agencies clearly lack the organizational and constitutional capacities to correlate international offenses with punishments.[98]

Likewise, geography and implementation costs play decisive roles in the decision as to whether or not to sanction and ultimately the measures of success or failure. The geography of a country is an influential factor in determining the success of economic sanctions. The proximity and relationship with neighboring countries and their position on the stated sanction creates a channel for black market trading which can take place either through the native government or despite the native government. Iraq and its relationship with Jordan throughout the 1990s is a good illustration where geographic proximity was a factor allowing the sanctioned country to dodge the US sanctions efforts. As noted by Paul Conlon, the head of the UN Security Council Sanctions Committee in the 1990s, Jordan was able to provide small but critically important "Leakage" for Iraq.[99] Therefore Saddam Hussein was able to dodge sanctions through this geographic proximity.

As the decision-makers move forward in the sanctions process, they must consider their decisions in the spectrum of possible future rate of success rather than effectiveness and take into account the multiple uncontrollable costs associated with imposing sanctions. The new measurements of success must expose the challenges faced by institutions and seek to establish authority and to enforce international law and maintain positive movement in international relations. In evaluating the current form of international relations, the economic impact of the UN resolution would make it possible to analyze sanctions success/failure. Although these economic impacts can determine possible actions of states, the decision maker must also consider the rationality of actors (as discussed in 5.6.1) as they react to a sanctions regime.

As has been shown throughout this book, though UN sanctions cannot be considered sound economic decisions as they have a different impact on the multiple actors involved, balancing the competing interest of states and third parties could classify these sanctions as efficient. The first step in this process would be an economic analysis that shows informed understanding of the past and current economic situation of the country to be sanctioned. Thus the effectiveness of the proposed economic sanctions must be seen through examination of the internal economic situation of both the sender and the target is necessary. The sender of the economic sanctions must have

not only the motivation to sanction the target country but also a complete understanding of the target's identity, motives, and likely response. Additionally the sender must accept an economic loss. This method is more complicated in analysis of international sanctions, as the universe of variables is substantially large and goals and objectives are much more complex to define than in cases of unilateral sanctions. The question of whether measurement of costs for multilateral sanctions is feasible remains.

Conceptualizing the imposition of economic sanctions as transactions opens the possibility to make predictions regarding likely state actions. Such predictions must include the state's position, historical review of state action, and the state's economic needs and expectations. However because of the multidimensional nature of UN sanctions and the institutional involvement in the decision, evaluating sanctions from the perspective of one actor leaves sanctions analysis and ultimately implementation exposed to failure. In comparing institutional alternatives, for example, it should be asked what it is that would cause the most change in behavior of both the target country and also the sender institution itself. If UN sanctions imposed for a long period of time are not effective and do not impact the governing bodies of countries, alternatives need to be found, but there is a cost associated to this search of alternatives; it is this institutional cost that would affect the UN directly. Assuming that rational choice guides institutions, the product of impact of change will eventually affect the evolutionary path of change. Actual evaluation of institutional costs, institutional path-dependence, and no central institutional profitability are endogenous to a traditional economic success or failure; measures are seldom considered in UN decisions to sanction a state.

6.4.3 New Measurement of Success

Much like the revisions of measurements of success in the current US War on Terror, new measurements of success for sanctions must take into account a wide variety of data. This requires a fundamental reassessment of sources, perspectives, and goals. Can we develop a systematic measurement model? Ultimately, I think not. But we can greatly improve upon the current model.

The new war success measurements being formulated by the White House, for instance, increasingly focus on the way *opponents* view the US.[100] Whereas, before, the US focused on the number of enemy combatants killed in action, or the notorious "rat rate" (the measure of good tips about the location of insurgents or the planting of bombs, versus misleading tips), now the methodology looks to public opinion polls.[101] Polls, it is predicted, will provide a much more scientific understanding of the degree to which Afghan citizens view the US, or view local police corruption, performance, etc. Such measures of success may also apply to sanctions and more specifically to the UN sanctions regime. It is questionable

whether a sanction that was meant to have negative impact on the country would lead to any approval from the target country's point of view. And, if it is an arms embargo, then the general population would not have much awareness of such activities. However, as the sanctions have evolved to include targeted and financial sanctions, it is necessary to envision creative methods of determining sanctions success beyond economic or political analysis. Chapter seven will survey the evolution of so-called "smart" targeted sanctions, offering proposals for making information flows even more transparent and complete for enforcement of traditional trade sanctions.

7 Policy Recommendations

> What is at stake is not so much to analyze the actions of the Security Council with a view to assessing the legality of a particular conduct, but to integrate Security Council decision-making into a larger framework encompassing economic law in order to establish the legitimacy and legality of Security Council decisions. What emerges from the analysis of current practice is that this integration occurs in an *ad hoc* manner, and benefits from grey areas and exceptional regimes granted by instruments of international economic law.
>
> —Laurence Boisson de Chazournes[1]

The above analysis (Chapters four, five, and six) and the accompanying case studies amply illustrate the inefficiency of the current sanctions scheme. To use an American metaphor, the conventional international trade sanctions scheme is akin to using a shotgun to swat a mosquito. A more directly targeted, second-generation scheme would be more effective at achieving the goals of the sanctioning party in a global economy, while also protecting ordinary citizens' and third parties' rights. As Rose Gottemoeller, US Assistant Secretary of State for Verifications, Compliance, and Implementation, concluded in early 2008, smart sanctions "had been honed through the 'the war on terror', and sanctions are hitting their targets among corrupt elites more often."[2] Though this positive outlook may give some indication of the success of sanctions, the problem still remains unresolved with respect to the potential for long-term success. In addition, such an outlook may be more realistic with respect to unilateral sanctions than UN international sanctions regimes. In particular, as the strength of sanctions increases because of the noncompliance of target states, the sanctions move closer to the original comprehensive sanctions regimes. Thus with respect to the UN, a mere shift in sanction policies may not be the final solution; rather, as de Chazournes identifies, there is a gap between Security Council decision-making and economic law, which would need to be addressed for a more rational sanctions practice.[3] This gap, which is a result of an ambiguous process, can be tightened by rethinking the structure of the institution, as will be discussed in this chapter.

There have been many calls to reform the UN to make it more responsive to threats to peace. The Brahimi report and An Agenda for Peace, for example, were introduced with recommendations for wide-ranging reforms to strengthen peace-building operations. In the domain of sanctions, in 2006, the UN convened an informal working group on the general issues of sanctions. The report of this working group outlined important institutional and substantive changes for improving sanctions design, implementation, evaluation, and follow-up. The report outlines, in very general and ambiguous terms, changes that must be implemented to make sanctions more effective. This chapter addresses these suggestions and explains that, even if implemented, these changes do not represent any substantive changes in the dominant UN sanctions paradigm and other more specific alternative policy recommendations are needed to actually change the current process.

Of the three main types of sanctions—import /export sanctions, financial sanctions, and diplomatic sanctions—the analysis above has demonstrated the relative inefficiency of trade sanctions (import and export), touching briefly on problems of financial sanctions as the likely and much more used successful form of economic sanctions in the recent times. An example of the failure of financial sanctions was the US sanctions regime against Iran in the wake of the 1979 hostage crisis. In response, to the Iranian actions, the US froze the assets of the Iranian government in the US, established the US-Iran Claims Tribunal, and set up a reparations scheme to compensate US companies and individuals for losses incurred as a result of the Islamic Revolution in Iran. Though these sanctions may seem a success from one perspective, they would not be a possible option on an international level, as they would give rise to possible illegitimate financial claims against the target from member states.

Following the post-Cold War period, the 1990s were distinguished as the sanctions decade. Since 2001, similar financial sanctions, which seem narrowly defined compared to trade sanctions, have become the more popular form of combating conflict situations without any military interference. Financial sanctions restrict the sanctioned country's government, firms, and individuals from easily moving capital; therefore, theoretically minimizing harm to the general population. Furthermore, the negative economic consequences of sanctions are avoided, as small firms and small producers in the targeted country are still able to operate, putting economic control of the target state in the hands of a disperse number of actors, and allowing for the development of stronger local markets, higher local production, and not restricting opportunity costs for individuals within countries that are under sanction. Financial sanctions, therefore, are thought more likely to actually drive the population of a country to enforce change within their political and legal arena. The second possible outcome is to actually drive the change within the policymaking powers to bring about change within their political and legal structure.

Financial sanctions are seen to be better suited for a modern global economy than trade sanctions for the following reasons. First, financial sanctions target only the rogue-party's assets, or the assets of a given organization whose policies are inconsistent with international norms. Secondly, financial sanctions are, in theory, easier to enforce than traditional trade sanctions, which call for blockades, massive enforcement costs, monitoring costs, etc. In addition, sanctions aimed at delaying/denying credit, or monetary grants to targets are theoretically much easier to monitor. The studies conducted on the success of financial sanctions including a study done by Hufbauer find that these sanctions show more instances of success than comprehensive sanctions. It should not be overlooked that the specificity and the confined nature of financial sanctions may be the reason for the cases of success. When these financial sanctions target large institutional pillars of a country, the result can be similar to their older counterparts, even comprehensive sanctions. For example, sanctions imposed on the Central Bank of Iran are much more comprehensive than sanctions that target the financial resources of the ruling elite. Another example is the sanctions regime of 2010 by the US on Iran, which was followed by the EU imposing similar sanctions. These sanctions led to an eighty percent decrease in the value of the currency in less than one year. Even prior to the rapid devaluation of the currency, CNN reported in 2010 that the sanctions on the Iranian Central Bank had led to a fifty percent increase in the price of basic necessities such as meat and milk, making life unaffordable for the general population.

Thus, financial sanctions may give rise to the very same unintended consequences of trade sanctions. Though no documented cases are presented thus far, financial sanctions could lead to other consequences. By depriving leaders of their cash in foreign bank accounts, sanctioning countries may create situations where brutal dictators will exert even heavier duties and taxes from their populations in order to recoup the losses they incurred as a result of their assets being frozen, or they may resort to theft and the control of natural resources. Additionally, the dictator may resort to violence or brutality in retaliation for actions of the sanctioning body or will simply exact rents from ordinary citizens. On a broader level, the unpredictability of banking deposits may make dictators more prone to invest in underground or unregulated banks, giving rise to the same black market problems addressed in section 6.3.6 with respect to trade sanctions. Such ambiguities in the movement of capital may also create instability in the world financial sector, as investors' security interests in targeted countries' bonds, for instance, may be undermined.

Returning to the etymology of the word "sanction" discussed in Chapter two, we can explore a yet more efficient sanction scheme, which state parties or international bodies may employ in dealing with rogue or noncooperative global actors. This is the evolution of so-called "positive" sanctions, "smart" sanctions, "targeted" sanctions, "financial" sanctions, and similar euphemisms for sanctions. These sanctions alternatives are explored in the sections that follow in this chapter and additional, more specific proposals to make sanctions effective are analyzed.

7.1 FINANCIAL SANCTIONS AND THE EVOLUTION OF "SMART SANCTIONS"

Financial sanctions are any multilateral sanctions whose mode of enforcement calls for the freeze of assets and bank accounts held in domestic banks within the implementing countries of individuals or firms who are listed on the resolution authorizing sanctions.[4] These sanctions are seen as more rational than previous ambiguous trade sanctions, because the new "smart" sanctions are clearly defined: they identify specific, concrete individuals, firms, bank account numbers, etc. However, they still lack subject matter specification and time limits. The advantages of smart sanctions over traditional trade sanctions are: 1) financial sanctions do not have catastrophic humanitarian consequences;[5] 2) the number of targets is finite, leading to easier implementation monitoring costs;[6] and 3) there is near universal consensus among NGOs, the foreign policy and intelligence community, international lawyers, development experts, and scholars that financial sanctions are worthwhile enforcement mechanisms, though nearly everybody relies on anecdotal evidence to support the case for such assertions. The shift in sanction policies towards the Taliban regime pursuant to Resolution 1390 (2002) provides clear evidence of UN Sanctions enforcement on a finite target. This shift directed the sanctions from the Afghan regime to individual leaders and members of Al-Qaeda. The mechanisms for this shift were to be carried out by the UN Sanctions Enforcement Support Team. Several recent developments that have brought smart sanctions even greater acceptance; the Bush administration's position on the "War on Terror" highlighted overwhelmingly successful strategies for reducing threats through applying strategic sanctions on terrorist networks' financial resources. The shift in the sanctions regime in Afghanistan was a direct influence of "War on Terror" policies and the overthrow of the Taliban government in 2001. In addition, increased transparency in the banking sector brought about by new regulations passed in the wake of the 2008–2009 financial crisis has unveiled that in the enforcement of financial sanctions, sanctions-dodging has become more difficult.[7] Are smart sanctions any more immune to the criticism outlined in Chapter six (concerning measurements of success/failure) than traditional sanctions?

Changes in international financial regulation following the 2008–2009 financial crisis include: 1) increased reporting standards,[8] 2) greater transparency, and 3) increased international monitoring of capital flows and interbank settlements. Financial regulations are often perceived as narrowly tailored, meaning they only affect the states, firms, and individuals who are deemed to be violating international law. As they do not restrict trade, they are seen as more flexible and humanitarian (in that they allow import/export of foodstuffs, medicine, etc.).[9] While narrowly targeted financial sanctions (i.e., freezing the assets of political and military leaders held outside the country) cause little collateral damage, they are nevertheless inconvenient in that they are difficult to apply and not sufficiently damaging to the targeted individuals if these persons are able to otherwise appropriate financial resources. When targeting individuals or firms, sanctions may also raise new issues in terms of the rights of individuals or corporations. This is particularly true in relation to decisions by the UN Sanctions Committees to list or delist natural and corporate persons targeted by sanctions. There is growing concern about respect for the due process of law in the absence of an effective remedy for individuals or entities wrongly listed to challenge such decisions.[10] In the more recent years, the UNSC has in fact introduced new delisting procedures for individuals who believe they are wrongfully accused. Financial sanctions have their own dark sides and unintended consequences, as shall be seen in section 7.3.

7.2 POSITIVE SANCTIONS

Many forms of sanctions present some kind of retaliation from the sanctioned state in response or in the form of nationalist response. Such a response can be diminished if sanctions provide an incentive for changed action, rather than depriving the target of rights and benefits they received previously. This type of incentive for change is also known as positive sanctions. Positive sanctions present an alternative to economic sanctions, which threaten to take away certain economic freedoms to achieve stated changes. Positive sanctions amount to "carrots" that pull the sanctioned country towards the policy goal of the sanctioning body, rather than punish the sanctioned country for failure to live up to those goals. There are many forms of positive sanctions, such as financial aid and technological and military cooperation, and many belong to the existing practice and constant flow of international interactions among nations.[11]

The traditional form of sanctions used, negative sanctions, in essence allude that if the sanctioned country makes certain changes, they would then be given back their freedom. This means that if the country is able to function without certain economic freedoms or is able to find a way around them, the effect of the negative sanction has been neutralized. Positive sanctions, on the other hand, would extend an offer to the nation that would bring certain added benefits to the economy if the sanctioned country is able to comply or make the given changes.[12] From the viewpoint of third party countries, which have to implement sanctions, there may not be much difference between the two approaches, but there are qualitative differences between the two.

Positive sanctions can also be imagined as a variant of aid or development treaties. An example of such a sanction is the African Growth Opportunity Act (AGOA), which was signed into law in 2000 by President Clinton. The execution of this act resulted in the creation of more jobs, the establishment of factories, and an increase in exports (mostly in the textile industry).[13] The AGOA is clearly an example of a case in which positive relations led to economic growth. But, to be more effective, it is necessary that the international community recognize positive sanctions as a method of approaching conflict. The legislation of the AGOA authorized the US president to determine which sub-Saharan African countries would be eligible for AGOA (currently forty-one eligible countries), of course to move towards a market-based system and free trade. It should be noted that in regards to positive sanctions, just as in any other form of sanctions, the target's rationality, as defined in section 6.4.6 is of question. The target's reaction to positive or negative sanctions is unpredictable as the target's rational motives might be increased power, or the target may be driven by irrational motives, such as hatred for a particular group or faction. This fact is further compounded since in both types of sanctions, the target experiences economic consequences at a time much later than when the sanctions are imposed.

7.3 SANCTIONS ON INDIVIDUALS / CORPORATIONS: MONITORING FINANCIAL TRANSACTIONS

Though targeted sanctions may focus on a particular industry as positive or negative sanctions, the targets could also be individuals or specific corporations. In their modern, post-Iraq, form targeted sanctions have been centered on freezing of financial assets or restrictions of the banking industry of a target. With the meteoric development of international banking and proposals for international banking regulation stemming from the 2008–2009 financial crisis, the 2010s have seen the imposition of greater control over traditionally private banking functions. This is a positive development from the viewpoint of sanctions enforcement. International financial institutions are already beginning to develop and implement sanctions against individuals and firms. In 2004, for instance, the World Bank uncovered a massive fraud in relation to the World Bank administered "Emergency School Readiness Project" (ESRP) in Timor-Leste (East Timor).[14] The World Bank immediately responded by imposing sanctions against the firms and individuals involved in the fraud.[15] The World Bank's sanctions committee, charged with blacklisting individuals and firms guilty of fraud or mismanagement of international aid funds, has provided a meaningful framework for more targeted sanctions of an international character.[16] Consequently, through bank practice, these individuals and firms are also blacklisted from working across the International Financial Institutions sector and with conducting development work in national banks.

Similar to the veil-lifting doctrine attaching responsibility for corporate malfeasance on individual board members of executives, there is a growing push to "lift the corporate veil" in the international sphere.[17] Corporations are known to be a factor in influencing domestic and international sanctions policy, especially in cases when the corporation is in dire need of a natural resource available in a country under economic sanctions. Illustrative of this phenomenon is a corporation's need for raw material and resources from a sanctioned state. This is especially evident in today's consumer electronics industry. One of the needed components in the industry's production is columbite–tantalite (colton), a metallic ore, which is minded mostly in East DRC and Rwanda.[18]

Despite the conflict in the DRC and multilateral sanctions against the region, the exploitation of colton in the area has continued. To date, eighty percent of the industry's colton comes from East DRC, notwithstanding that profits from colton exploitation have been used for rebel group funding in the area.[19] But corporations, because they are not subjects under international law, enjoy practical immunity for these actions. Thus, there is the need for a centralized control mechanism that would streamline the role of corporations and monitor their activities in conflict-infected areas. Section 7.5 discusses the possibility of preemptive evaluation in regards to conflict prevention.

7.3.1 Legal Problems with Sanctions Against Individuals

With the increasing attention and implementation of "smart solutions" international law must develop new substantive and procedural protections for individual's rights. A case arising out of Sweden in late 2001 is illustrative of this need. In this case, three Swedish citizens were listed as terrorist entities under America's antiterrorism laws, an Executive Order 13224 (2001).[20] The US Office of Foreign Asset Control (OFAC) promptly requested that the UN Taliban Sanctions Committee issue an order to freeze assets belonging to the individuals and two firms. The individuals immediately protested the accusations of connections with international terrorism, but without avail, since there were no judicial or administrative procedures for individuals to challenge the UN Sanctions Committee's decrees.[21] The individuals therefore appealed to the Swedish government, which in turn appealed to the Taliban Sanctions Committee, requesting further evidence showing that the Swedish citizens had connections with terrorism. Upon receipt of the information, the Swedish Security Police issued a report stating that nothing in the documentation presented showed that the individuals or organizations were connected to international terrorism.[22]

The case then proceeded to the UN Security Council, where despite the request of the Swedish government, the US, the UK, and Russia objected to the removal of the individuals from the list of sanctioned entities. Although the request to the UNSC proved unsuccessful, the Swedish critique led to the Sanctions Committee issuing a statement on delisting procedures. Two of the individuals immediately provided additional information to the US OFAC, and within two days the US government requested that the Sanctions Committee remove the individuals from the list of subjects whose assets should be frozen. The third individual provided information one month later but the US OFAC denied the petition for re-examination, effectively making delisting by the UNSC Taliban Sanctions Committee impossible.[23] In response to this case, the UNSC adopted Resolution 1452, which allows an implementing state to grant a humanitarian exception in exacting the prescribed financial freeze sanctions.[24] It remains to be seen how the exception will be implemented by other states.

With respect to the substantive defense of individuals' rights, it remains very much left to the domain of bilateral negotiation. Thus had Sweden not intervened on behalf of its citizens, it is likely that they would not have been delisted from the terrorist list. Cramer emphatically stresses the lack of procedural safeguards as well,

> [...] It should be underlined that none of the three, during these procedures, have been given the possibility to directly defend themselves against the accusations posed against them. The delisting procedure does not constitute an instrument for *individual review*, and it is, moreover, not directly available to the targeted individual.[25]

Cramer continues his analysis by evaluating the possibility of the legal review of implementation measures. One such option is review by the European Court of Justice (ECJ) or other tribunals. The individuals in question did file petitions with the Court of First Instance of the EC. Additionally, they had the option of petitioning under Swedish law for a review from the UNSC order at the ECJ.[26] There is currently no consensus on what national or regional courts will do (or what standard of review, procedural rules, or evidentiary rules they would apply) when confronted with a challenge to UNSC resolutions by an individual whose international human rights have been violated by UNSC action.

7.3.2 Existing OFAC Financial Oversight Capacity

Currently, the US Department of Treasury monitors a wide range of financial transactions involving foreign trade and foreign entities. For example, the Office of Foreign Asset Controls monitors the following transactions:

a. *Securities Data*, such as US transactions in long-term securities—monthly; covers US and foreign securities; Monthly monitoring of foreign holders of Treasuries; data on foreign securities; Annual monitoring of holdings of US securities and foreign securities (both long-term & short-term securities);

b. *Banking Data*—monthly liabilities to, and claims on, foreign residents (includes short-term securities);
c. *Derivatives Contracts*—quarterly holdings and net cash settlements with foreign residents;
d. *Nonbanking Data*—quarterly liabilities to, and claims on, unaffiliated foreign residents;
e. *Quarterly Data* on US Gross External Debt.[27]

Efficient financial oversight leads to more possibilities in regards to control of assets, not only of individuals but to create a more transparent and controlled multinational trade.

7.4 LACK OF ALTERNATIVES

As has been discussed in the previous chapters, there are many problems associated with sanctions. These can be grouped into four categories: (1) lack of a specific, concrete quantifiable objective; (2) lack of institutional practice within the UN with implementation of sanctions; (3) a large number of countervailing factors militating against sanctions enforcement; and (4) the lack of any workable success/failure measurement strategy. Assuming that a given sanction scheme is not a military strategy for weakening a state before armed conflict (the issue discussed in section 5.1.3, *infra* that sanctions are often a preparatory stage before war), if the UNSC is genuinely interested in preventing, for instance, arms from reaching a given conflict zone, is there a way to make current sanctions regimes more effective in practice? More generally, aside from financial sanctions, are there ways to make existing multilateral trade sanctions more effective? This section will demonstrate that the answer to this question is in the affirmative. It could be that the answer lies with a more aggressive, innovative, and technologically savvy way of regulating or simply monitoring trade and the activities of multinational corporations (MNCs).[28] MNCs hold a strong position in the international political sphere because of their ability to move capital. Thus with respect to MNCs and movement of capital, many state boundaries and borders have dissolved. The liquidity of the movement of capital and goods between states has made MNCs veritable actors in the international arena. This is not a new development, either. Coca-Cola, for instance, continued its presence in South Africa during the ten years of sanctions. Since, MNCs have received their raw resources from sanctioned countries; as globalization has continued and MNCs have gained even greater positions of power and influence in the international community, it is imperative that they are looked at as quasistate actors. Therefore, a more thorough analysis of these MNCs is in order. The MNCs' role could be positive in a state's transition after sanctions. After the sanctions were removed from South Africa, Nelson Mandela thanked some of the multinational firms that defied sanctions and stayed in South Africa to do what they could to help bring about change. Such defiance against sanctions would be contrary to what the sanctions aim to achieve and could extend the period of time sanctions are in place.

Preemptive measures should, theoretically, start before conflict has risen. As demonstrated in Chapter four, evaluation is by far the most influential tactic to ensure conflict prevention. To take preemptive measures, a more evolved view on trade, resources, and the new actors in world economic trade would be necessary. This of course means an acknowledgement of the basic realities of 21st century trade and technology and the role of non-state economic actors, such as MNCs.

7.4.1 Preemptive Measures and Extending the Evaluation Process

Before delving into dealing with MNCs, an analysis of possible preemptive measures is necessary. Realist observations reveal that the vicious cycles of conflict start from the availability of financing, weapons, and other tools of conflict trade. A preemptive measure would require a broader, more global approach on monitoring the sources of funding for rogue states, the presence of natural resources, etc. To put this squarely, this requires greater oversight and monitoring of international shipping.

One way to achieve this goal would be to for states to monitor their natural resources in an attempt to fight against nuclear proliferation. While some states have been developing nuclear technology peacefully there are those who have gone beyond peaceful technology in order to stay politically competitive. Since the passing of the Nuclear Non-Proliferation Treaty (NNPT) in 1970, four countries have been able to develop a nuclear weapon. The NNPT is a subject of much scholarly debate. The four states that have not signed the treaty: India, Pakistan, North Korea and potentially Israel (Israel has kept an ambiguous policy position in regards to their advancement in nuclear weapons technology) are confirmed holders of nuclear warheads. These states did not sign the treaty, arguing that the NNPT created a club of "nuclear haves" and a larger group of "nuclear have-nots." To sanction a country for developing nuclear technology is useless unless the sources of the resources of this technology are discovered. One way to address this issue is to analyze countries that are providers of the natural resources needed for nuclear technology (in this case uranium). Further, it is necessary to monitor the trade relationships of these states with states in pursuit of nuclear weapons. This would mean a rigorous evaluation of countries holding such resources, such as Uzbekistan, Jordan, Tajikistan, Australia, South Africa, etc. Current technology allows for this control. Advances in real-time satellite imagery, GPS technology, shipping lane monitoring, and tracking now mean that it is possible to observe, from a command center, the activities of large container ships (from smaller cargo carriers to single container-size truck deliveries) in the countries under sanction. The UNSC, as the supposed center of peace keeping and conflict prevention, is logically entitled to take advantage of such technology for peaceful purposes. A possible command center within the UNSC apparatus, or within individual UNSC Sanctions Committees, which would be equipped to monitor and alert the UN of large ships and cargo shipments arriving in ports of entry in target states could work as a possible hub of streamlining information. In other words, it is possible to make the UNSC a viable watchdog against, arms shipments into countries like the DRC or Sierra Leone. As this entails an encroachment on individual, firm, and state sovereignty and ancillary legal issues, the rationales for this innovative sanctions management proposal are addressed in the remaining sections of this chapter.

7.4.2 The Role of MNCs in Conflict

The following section introduces and elaborates on ways that more control can be carried out to both the *ex ante* and *ex post* control of conflict situations. As will be demonstrated such controls can be through MNC regulation, possible global taxation, and regulation of foreign direct investment.

First, what is meant by MNCs and why is it imperative to regulate the conduct of corporations on the international plane? Several defining features of MNCs are: (1) the movement of large amounts of capital between states; (2) the ability to rapidly obtain, develop, and apply new technologies; and (3) mobility across territorial boundaries of states.[29] MNCs are essentially large corporations who conduct business in states other than their state of "nationality" or incorporation.

Global industrial and financial firms have long been the targets of controversy from both the right as well as political left. Due to their size, they command the ability to obtain swift and favorable financing; because of scale, they are able to procure and apply raw materials and technologies in ways that drive out competition. Thus from the right, MNCs are suspect because they have the capacity to develop into monopolies and to stifle competition.[30] From the left, MNCs are attacked for enjoying virtual impunity for misdeeds committed in weak states as a lack of an external oversight body, which removes any check on corruption.

Though corporations have a robust influence on international transactions and they carry an independent personality under domestic law, they are, both traditionally and under current mainstream interpretations, not envisioned as subjects under international law.[31] Historically, in cases of state-chartered or state-owned corporations such as the Dutch and British East India Companies, these corporations were and are seen as extensions of the state. In the 20th century, attempts by corporations to willingly subject themselves as subjects of international law have also been rebuffed. An example of which is the famous *Barcelona Traction* case before the International Court of Justice (ICJ).[32] In this case Belgian stockholders of an MNC incorporated in Canada sought to sue the government of Spain for the infringement of their rights under international law; the court held that only the state (in this case, Canada) could sue in the ICJ on behalf of the corporation, not the corporation itself. This example illustrates that there remains a gap between state and corporate influence.

The concept of "subjects" of international law has been under question since the initial years of UN formation. Traditionally, international law was deemed to apply exclusively to nations (sovereign states), so only nations were deemed "subject."[33] Although some commentators have crafted innovative arguments for why MNCs involuntarily become subjects under customary international law, it is uncontroversial that MNCs are *not* subjects of international law. MNCs are not contemplated or held accountable for their actions by the UN Charter or any other international convention, and there is little state practice or *opinio juris* imposing responsibility on MNCs for violations of either international human rights or other international law norms. Thus, despite their growing size and influence, MNCs remain outside of conventional international law. Notwithstanding that MNCs now routinely enter into negotiations and agreements with foreign states, their legal status and rights in these transactions are akin to the rights of an individual (i.e., the rules of private international law). MNCs presumably carry the nationality of their state of incorporation; however, unlike ships (which also must fly the flag of one nation when in international waters), MNCs have the right to "forum shop," claiming nationality in warmer regulatory climates through subsidiaries, spin-offs, and reincorporation. Therefore their state of origination or incorporation cannot be held accountable for their actions and there is a need to maintain a form of responsibility for the MNCs under international law.

7.4.3 History of UN Reform Concerning MNCs

In the 1970s, several attempts were made to regulate the activities of MNCs at the UN level. High-level projects and conventions were drafted to regulate the activities of MNCs but these were not adopted by the UN save for a recommendation of good practice and the development of *voluntary corporate social responsibility* norms (CSR). The UN's Centre on Transnational Corporations and the separate Commission on Transnational Corporations were closed down by Secretary General Boutros-Ghali in 1992; in 1992–1993, they were collapsed into the broader Department for Economic and Social Development, and in 1993, the Programme on Transnational

Corporations was transferred to the United Nations Conference on Trade and Development (UNCTAD) in Geneva. The UNCTAD's Division on Investment, Technology and Enterprise Development currently implements this program.

Independently from the UN, the Organization for Economic Cooperation and Development (OECD) in 1976 adopted the first OECD Guidelines for Multinational Enterprises.[34] Since then, voluntary Corporate Social Responsibility "guidelines" have proliferated under the auspices of the OECD, G7, and other bodies.[35] Importantly, none of the UN, OECD, or other organizations provides a programmatic enforcement mechanism.[36]

The need to move away from amorphous goals like corporate responsibility for human rights violations towards a more strategic, concrete form of oversight means that we must select specific substantive areas, where oversight will be welcomed by the international community, *as well as* agreeable to the MNCs themselves.[37] Seeking to "impose" outside regulation on MNCs without the corporate lobby's prior input and assent is doomed to failure from the outset. Thus, the UN must adopt a conservative strategy of selecting relatively neutral regulatory spheres and imposing light regulatory measures, initially. Three such spheres to be evaluated are 1) the regulation of global trade, particularly shipping, 2) the regulation of global financial transactions, and 3) the regulation of foreign direct investment.

Current enforcement is confined to litigation grounded in a loose web of mostly domestic regulations.[38] Statutes like the Alien Tort Claims Act (US) allow aggrieved plaintiffs to sue MNCs for violations of international standards in the home state of the corporation.

Looking further at international trade, most influence on trade and the unintentional growing dependence of multinationals is due to the expansion of Foreign Direct Investment. If we have made the decision to influence the world economic order through regulation or sanctions, then the best alternative maybe to total control trade, which would create complete transparency and absolute control and would extend the control of all international transactions. Consequently, more control would be a transparent trade system that would allow for less *off the record* activities. Because of the influence and power of the UNSC, the regulatory spheres discussed in this section would only be executed correctly if the task falls under the control of UNSC.

7.5 REGULATION OF GLOBAL TRADE

A second area in which the immediate UNSC regulation of MNCs is possible concerns global shipping. Whereas technological barriers previously made regulation of global shipping difficult, as mentioned in section 7.4.1, recent advances in GPS and other tracking technologies make the regulation of global trade possible and advisable. Moreover, the current pirate attacks in international waters (not only in Somalia but also in the South China Sea and the infamous Malacca Strait) heighten the need for a coordinated international approach to regulating maritime trade. Although it is likely to be opposed by maritime organizations and shipping companies, the recent pirate attacks make regulation in this sphere less controversial.

The possible creation of an international organ, under the aegis of the UNSC, capable of monitoring all large ocean-going commercial vessels (such as oil tankers, container ships, etc.) would change the dynamic of UNSC's current process. The total number of such vessels is relatively small. According to the CIA Factbook, the total number of world merchant ships of 1,000 gross register tons or over was 30,936. By comparison, a proposed International Maritime Tracking Agency would monitor approximately 5,000 of the largest of these ships. All large vessels of this type are already equipped with GPS and other sophisticated tracking systems. The new monitoring agency (tentatively called IMTA—International Maritime Tracking Agency) would be charged with licensing ocean-going vessels. Such activities can be financed by contribution and license fees, which are pooled to fund environmental damage and accident response efforts.

7.5.1 Regulations of Foreign Direct Investment [FDI]

One of the areas of trade that remains minimally regulated and monitored by the UN is foreign direct investment (FDI). Of the three substantive fields discussed in this section, the regulation of FDI is the most complex mainly because of the breadth of the problem as well as the complexity of the financial, trade, and the labor standards involved.

Recent discussions of UN regulation over FDI seem to start and end with a debate over *holders*—primarily *stake*- versus *share*holders. Shareholders are the actual shareowners of a given MNC; whereas, stakeholders are conceived as individuals and groups who are directly affected by the MNCs' conduct.

However effective previous CSR campaigns have been, as demonstrated in section 7.3, MNCs' profit motive can override their corporate responsibility. As Milton Friedman famously wrote in a 1970 *New York Times* article, a corporation's sole corporate social responsibility is to make a profit.[39] This mantra remains dominant today. Not only that, but profit incentives have pushed MNCs to take on high-risk positions in the FDI in order to reach a higher return in terms of increased potential losses for shareholders and the economy as a whole. Through the ease of moving capital, MNCs have gained effective influence over the domestic policies of a target state. The ramifications of the current financial crisis on the FDI have been stark. Russia, for instance, lost close to $150 billion in FDI from September 2008 to February 2009 as a result of the crisis.[40] The financial crisis has brought home the need to either set regulations concerning the global financial "architecture" (which is highly unlikely) or alternatively distribute the regulatory responsibility to an international body through taxation (as opposed to legal regulation of operations and methods).

Like shipping regulations discussed above, the proposals concerning the FDI have been around for over thirty years in response to a multitude of different conditions.[41] Prof. Stenzel argues the need for a Tobin tax that would be collected on crossborder currency transactions and the funds could be used for environmental protection; in 1996, a number of UN development staff members proposed a similar international tax on currency transactions. The global tax issue was also discussed by UN Secretary General Kofi Annan in December 2000 and has been brought up by the UN Department of Economic and Social Affairs. To this date a true international system of taxation has not yet been implemented.[42] The creation of a debt arbitration mechanism and a currency tax transaction would also represent a step forward in the democratization of the UN because many crucial mechanisms of power in the global political economy are based on economic dependency on an investor nation or investor MNC.[43]

7.5.2 Global Taxation/Restructuring UN Funding

For the purpose of establishing a sustainable regulatory framework, the funding of the UN needs to shift from dependence on country contribution to self-sufficiency. Within the structure of the UNSC, there have been years of restructuring proposals in order to create a more democratic representative or parliamentary system, whether by an increase in the number of representative countries or changing the veto power and procedure. The UN has looked into funding sources, such as taxation as an alternative source of funding, but the details of Security Council deliberations on this issue have not been published or discussed publicly.[44] The UN's interest in taxation as a funding source was faced with a funds use restriction by the US. The US use restriction on UN dues, "prohibited the UN from using any of funds paid by the US for the 'promulgation of enforcement of any treaty, resolution, or regulation authorizing the United Nations . . .to tax any aspect of the Internet or international currency transactions.' "[45]

From the previous section, we can see that UN restructuring and FDI regulation go hand in hand. The UN is unable to aggressively target corporate abusers while its own funding is dependent on contributions from the industrialized wealthy states home to the largest MNCs.

7.5.3 Theoretical Roadblocks to Taxation

Contrary to regulating MNCs, shipping, and the FDI, which provide possibilities for confronting conflict and rogue states, global taxation would provide a preparatory position for the UN and UNSC both internally and externally. Global taxation is neither a new concept nor a fringe concept. It has been analyzed and defended by such esteemed international law scholars as Thomas Franck.[46] Tax treaties have also been discussed as a means for long-term financing for poor countries.[47] Corporate and foreign investment taxation by the United Nations must overcome the following obstacles:

a. *Investment Freeze* (taxation may limit free flow of capital (it has been convincingly argued that double-taxation would limit the flow of capital);
b. *Sovereignty*;
c. *Institution-building/Bureaucracy* (who takes the responsibility for reporting and collection?)
d. *Enforcement* (what institutions should be involved in the enforcement aspect of tax collection?)

The recent financial crises have shown that economies that were least affected by the financial crises were those whose economies were inward-oriented such as India.[48] Put another way, India had strong regulatory and legal institutions in place to protect investor confidence, while at the same time, having domestic economic and financial institutions that reduced the reliance on foreign capital, and hence exposure to the current credit crunch.

The ability of the UN to maintain a separate financial fund would make it less impacted by the volatility of the world financial markets. One possible mean of gaining such financial independence could be taxation of foreign direct investment. The taxation of corporations involved in foreign direct investment sets tangible controls on investment and encourages internal development onward. The taxation of foreign investments may also lead to more internal controls by the recipient states. As many states which may have removed barriers for FDI are still seen as high risk, the taxation of FDIs will lead to an adjustment of risk factors in accordance to political risk. This would discourage investors from engaging in highly risky investments and keep them conscious of true profits versus artificial profits. Furthermore, once the MNC has invested in the target country, taxation would slow disruptive rapid capital flight (such as in Russia, but more important for smaller developing nations without a large reserve fund like Russia).

It could be argued that such taxation would reverse continuous efforts to decrease the barriers of foreign direct investment (FDI); however, taxation here is not introduced as a barrier but rather an incentive for true return on investment (ROI) analysis, especially in industries such as energy, telecommunications, transport, and retail (all industries requiring long lead time of five to ten years to recover profit).

7.5.4 Programmatic Proposal

The detailed scope of my proposed UN corporate taxation scheme on foreign direct investment and international trade shipments is described in this section. These taxes, "nationally applied and internationally coordinated," have as their goal the provision of revenue to the UNSC, allowing the UN apparatus to take on agendas less directly linked to the benefits of strong permanent members. The proposal is as follows:

1. Applicable taxes are primarily on investment in the form of capital, transport of goods and services, as well as income of foreign executives. All income on capital that is earned through foreign direct investment is not subject to taxation. Contracting states or political subsidiaries are also not subject to taxation under the UN FDI tax.

   a. FDI is defined by the flow of financial capital, the value of *stock* accumulated by investing firms, the investment position, and the income flows from an investment.
   b. Applicable tax rate is equal to one and a quarter percent of the transaction cost.[49] This rate is meant to keep the tax high enough to make a real difference in firm behavior rather than act as a symbolic, perfunctory, or negligible license scheme (as in the case of the shipping proposal above). This is similar to the Tobin tax, which was proposed with an adjustment for today's more volatile market.

2. Any gain from sales of land and property that will be used by a foreign entity is also subject to taxation; salary of employees is *not* subject to taxation.

   a. The funds from all taxation will be transferred to a new emergency funding unit of the UN, to be created pursuant to this program;
   b. The UN FDI tax shall be separate from any existing bilateral treaties and is meant to be complimentary (not substitute) to such treaties.

This proposal may seem a radical departure from the existing UN framework. The next sections of this chapter assess viability of these proposals and outline precedents for such proposals in legal, political science, and economics scholarship.

7.5.5 UN FDI Tax and Alternative Developments

In 2003, French President Jacques Chirac commissioned a report from a working group to develop innovative proposals for global taxation in the service of alternative globalization.[50] Headed by Jean-Pierre Landau—then inspector-general of the Banque de France—the report advanced a pragmatic and realistic approach. The Landau Report recommended working *within* the existing international system, where only sovereign states have the power to tax. Consequently, the development funding mechanism would have to be built on their explicit consent. The Landau Report does not discuss any proposed institutional structure, and does not refer to the UN as an institutional mechanism for implementing international taxes or even as a forum for considering an international tax. The current proposal is more radical in scope as it calls for the establishment of a direct taxing authority to be administered at the UN level. Following the Landau Report and similar initiatives, global taxation has become one of the most contested issues in international law, the development arena, and in national policy circles.[51]

Proponents and opponents of international taxes clearly see their creation as part of a bigger project: the creation of new forms of global governance that international taxation would help to promote and consolidate.[52] Such forms of taxation because of profit shifting in multinational firms, and crossborder shopping has been addressed in particular with respect to the tax harmonization of the EU. This form of tax policy would lead to coordination in different areas of tax policy with emphasis on regional tax harmonization in the EU.[53] Unlike the Landau Report, the proposal here explicitly sets out the goal of international taxation. A similar perspective was adopted by the Zedillo Commission on development finance, which calls for a world council of Heads of State and Government to promote better global governance.[54] The Commission also recommends the creation of a world tax organization to study, among other things, the technical feasibility of an international tax. The proposal for an FDI tax outlined here is a very ambitious approach, but one that would ultimately create the most robust precedent for international taxation, and in turn, improve monitoring and implementation capacity for new generation sanctions regimes. Related policy proposals to ensure a more democratic decision-making body includes the expansion of the UNSC.

7.6 UNSC EXPANSION: FORM AND SUBSTANCE

UNSC expansion has as its goal an increase in the number of permanent members within the Security Council and for a more democratic apportionment of power within the UNSC. Contrary to skeptics, who feel the proposal is the agenda of small, undeveloped but ambitious states, there are some large UN members who have pushed for UNSC expansion. Canada, for instance, has voiced its support for a stronger UN since 1992. This was first brought to the UN through a letter sent to the Secretary General by the Canadian Prime Minister Brian Mulroney.[55] Prime Minister Mulroney's concern in regards to the UN's capability to intervene effectively in Bosnia and Herzegovina led him to propose a stronger and more influential UN. He also urged for a needed increase in the number of UN and Russian peacekeeping troops and changes within domestic legal restriction on troops deployed by other sovereign states.

The discussion of UN enlargement is a complex topic that has received much attention both in academic as well as popular press.[56] The rule of "Great Power Unanimity," nine votes including concurring vote of all five permanent members of the Security Council is not a true representation of world legal ideology as there is no African permanent member and no Middle Eastern permanent member. UNSC expansion is also directly linked to the questions of sanctions as under the current structure; inevitably sanctions will continually be posed on the same targets. The US representative to the UN has also addressed the expansion of the UN. According to John Bolton, the US believes membership as it stands reflects the world of 1945. The US' position is to add Japan to the permanent members of the UN to depoliticize UNSC. Japan has been looked at as a possible option because of its financial contribution to the UNSC. Japan's has been a strong financial contributor to the UN at nineteen and a half percent compared to the leading financial assistance from the US at twenty-two percent of total annual contributions.[57]

In 1963, the UN General Assembly (UNGA) passed a resolution (Resolution 1990) with the goal of enlarging the General Committee of the UNGA,

> *Taking into account* the considerable increase in the membership of the United Nations,
>
> *Taking also into account that* the General Committee of the General Assembly should be so constituted as to ensure its representative character on the basis of a balanced geographical distribution among its members,
>
> *Believing that* for those reasons it is desirable to enlarge the composition of the General Committee [. . .][58]

Consequent to Resolution 1990 the UN Charter, Articles 31 and 38 were amended to increase the number of individuals representing unrepresented countries, which included representatives from African and Asian states, Eastern European states, Latin America, and Western Europe.

However since 1968, despite an increase in member states, there have been no added amendments in order to increase the number of permanent representatives. In 1992, the break of the Soviet Union led to an increase in the number of UN member states. In 1968, the UN had a total of 108 member states; in 2008, the number of UN member states had increased to 192. This increase is particularly important with respect to UNSC decisions. It should be noted that disagreement among current permanent members is what has kept the UNSC from expanding the number of its representatives. There is no consensus from states on which new states should be added. One of the proposals which called for adding Japan as a permanent member state has been blocked by China.

The proposal of this book is to increase the number of permanent UN members from five to seven. China, as the sole representative of the Asian continent, lacks representation of extreme cultural, legal, and ideological differences of Western Asia; in addition, including India as a permanent member to the UNSC may be most logical. India, as one of the most populous countries in the Asian continent, connects the Western Asian continent to the East and has a religious and population diversity that is representative of the region. Additionally to minimize power dispersion, there needs to be an African country added as a permanent member to the UNSC; which African country to be added as a permanent member is a subject of further discussion as current conflict in many of the states creates my biased opinion towards them.

7.7 FEASIBILITY AND OUTLOOK (2015–2025)

The restructuring of the UN and the UNSC is a debated concept, which has been in both scholarly and policy attention for over fifteen years. There are however more pragmatic restructuring possibilities that could benefit the international world order with less delay. As discussed in Chapter five and proposed in this work MNCs are central to the future of international conflict prevention. The organizational structure to regulate MNCs has been established before and the same structure can be relied upon for proposing future regulatory control.

From 1973 to 1992, the UN's Centre for Transnational Corporations served as a focal point, within the United Nations system, for all matters related to MNCs and foreign direct investment (FDI). In its seventeen years, the Centre for Transnational Corporations was composed of three divisions: information analysis, policy analysis, and advisory services.

To apply the changes recommended in this chapter, the best approach would be to re-establish the Centre for Transnational Corporations as a standalone organ of the UN to implement the policy proposals set out above. It is important that this organ does not follow the same permanent member framework as the UN and UNSC, in order for its activities to be completely objective with no political incentives. Additionally, as it was demonstrated in this chapter, some form of taxation for increased accountability of MNCs, thus a regulatory division charged with administering the licensing of such taxation schemes would be one viable option.

Paramount in this effort is the systematic inclusion of the corporate lobby in these deliberations. It is clear that MNCs will seek to avoid interference in their businesses through taxation or regulation by the UN or any other international body. The proposals set out above seek to present a workable structure that has sufficient flexibility to encourage full compliance and participation. Lacking cooperation it is imperative to advance the program above by democratic international means.

8 Conclusion

The growing interest in the use of sanctions by the UN has seen a corresponding growth in a number of analyses of economic sanctions produced by scholars from all conceivable social science disciplines, law, economics, political science, international relations, business, etc. However, the diversity of methodological approaches to sanctions has served to cloud rather than clarify the underlying issues. The contribution of the present book to the sanctions conversation has been to reorient scholarly attention to the big issues, primarily to the *purpose* of sanctions. Without clearly identifying objectives for imposing sanctions schemes, it is impossible to measure success or failure, or to properly and effectively implement said sanctions.

Sanctions practice is not a recent phenomenon. Just as the formation of nation states, borders, and political divisions has become the basis of an international order, global economic relations have expanded and borders of trade have dissolved. Multilateral trade agreements (WTO), the expanded reach of multinational corporations, and ease of trade have led to ambiguities in the sanction phenomenon. What was once used as a form of punishing rogue states is now used as a top weapon against individuals in the War on Terror. Today as in yesteryears, the same politically charged ideologies apply. Sanctions are political phenomena, first and foremost. Contemporary policymakers face new challenges and opportunities with respect to sanctions: globalization and advances in economic relationships, counterideologies from multiple cultural backgrounds, advancements in technology and science, all play a crucial part in world trade and international relations. Just as it would be unreasonable to downplay the effect of new nonstate actors in the international arena, it would be unwise to defer to old methods and methodologies in approaching new sanctions schemes.

Although the effectiveness, implementation, and costs of sanctions continue to trouble analysts, there is every indication that economic sanctions are here to stay. Even if they are ambiguous or an overbroad policy-making weapon, the reality is that they provoke *some* response in the target country (though, as has been shown, this response may be worse off for the global community than the initial conditions).[1] Yet the fact that UN-imposed economic sanctions are increasingly used in response to alleged threats to peace or security does not *eo ipso* mean that they are the most effective tool in the UN decision-makers' arsenal. Secretary General Ki-Moon's statement that their increased use attests to their effectiveness may be wrong. Increased resort to armed combat in the 16th and 17th centuries between colonial powers did not attest to the fact that armed conflict was the most effective conflict dispute mechanism. Perhaps, sanctions short of war are the worst foreign policy tool. It may be that Kofi Annan's approach to peace making is not only more reasonable or humane-sounding, but also more strategically sound and more effective,

> "Unless the government and people of a given country are genuinely willing to confront the problems that may cause conflict, there is not much that even the best informed and most benevolent outsiders can do."

As I have shown above, multilateral economic sanctions are problematic based on a number of factors:

a. They have been shown to be imposed for *nonrational* and *ambiguous* reasons;
b. It is *impossible* to evaluate and measure success or failure of sanctions under current paradigms;
c. Implementation is challenged by the target and *sanctions evasion* is difficult to monitor

The goals of this book have been to bring to attention numerous problems that international sanctions face and propose alternatives. My intuition and research have led me to believe that the problems of multilateral sanctions do not reside in the implementation, evaluation, or effectiveness of sanctions. The core problem with current sanctions is that they are impossible to measure as they extend to historical policies. Yet each of these factors is only used as a tool to methodically analyze the current situation; the more important question we must ask is why sanctions are even used in the first place? If it is the matter of continuing the tradition of sanctions as a measure of dealing with conflict, then maybe it is time to stop, take a few steps back, and realize that the world has evolved and it may be that an alternative to sanctions is possible in dealing with conflict situations.

With consideration to the difficulty of measuring the success of sanctions, it is still vital to the international community to have specific measures for dealing with conflict situations. Special theoretical and practical attention must be devoted to nonstate actors. Over the past two decades, and with increased globalization, multinational corporations have not simply redefined international trade, they have also entered the conflict scene. Blackwater,

Inc. is as much an international actor as the US Marines. Google, Inc. has as much access to satellite imagery, if not more, than many of the world's governments. Taking for granted that conflict prevention will not necessarily be resolved by sanctions, in order to close the gap between scholarly and policy arguments, we have to accept the reality of sanctions and find more innovative ways of applying them. My policy proposal has sought to demonstrate how these technologies may be used to monitor financial transactions just as they can be used to spot (within a margin of error of one meter) the location of cargo ships delivering weapons to a distant port.

We are faced with establishing guidelines for more specific and context driven process in dealing with sanctions. The "carrot and stick" system may be the best foreign policy tool when dealing with unilateral issues, but in preventing international conflict it lies short of being anything but a political game enticing and in situations inflating the issue for a longer period of time. I attempted to give a more advanced cooperative and controlled approach in dealing with sanctions only to bring even more attention to the lack of consensus in their application.

In the early 1990s Hufbauer wrote that the United Nations should not necessarily eschew sanctions, but they should realize that effective multilateral sanctions are likely to remain a rare event.[2] All of the complexities and failures of sanctions are not reason to avoid responding, in a multilateral manner, to a conflict situation. But when we face a problem with a dull knife that slowly scrapes at the problematic organ, we are not healing but just letting the organ slowly rot internally. If the present book has been successful at showing one thing, I hope it is that sanctions are far from a precise remedy. It may be time to change a losing strategy and experiment with other options.

Notes

NOTES TO CHAPTER 1

1. Jay Solomon, "Iran's Banks Face Increasing Pressure from the West," *Wall Street Journal*, February 18, 2012, http://online.wsj.com/article/SB1000142405297020405980457722902398982959 2.html.
2. Glenn Greenwald, "Iran Sanctions Now Causing Food Insecurity, Mass Suffering" *The Guardian*, UK edition, Sunday, October 7, 2012.
3. Ibid., (question by Blake Hounsehll, editor of *Foreign Policy* magazine).
4. David M. Malone, ed., *The UN Security Council: From the Cold War to the 21st Century* (Boulder: Lynne Rienner Publishers, 2004), 174.
5. "North Korea Threatens to Retaliate Against UN Sanctions," *Voice of America-News*, November 2, 2009, http://www.voanews.com/content/a-13–2009–07–26-voa7–68804437/362309.html; Edith M. Lederer—Associated Press Writer, "U.S. Upbeat on NKorea Sanctions Enforcement," *The Associated Press*, July 30, 2009, http://www.newsday.com/us-upbeat-on-nkorea-sanctions-enforcement-1.1338849.
6. Edith M. Lederer, "U.S. Upbeat on NKorea Sanctions Enforcement"
7. David E. Sanger, "U.S. Weighs Iran Sanctions if Talks Are Rejected," *New York Times*, August 2, 2009, http://www.nytimes.com/2009/08/03/world/middleeast/03nuke.html?_r=0.
8. "U.S. Threatens Eritrea with Sanctions," *Aljazeera*, Last modified on July 29, 2009, http://www.aljazeera.com/news/americas/2009/07/2009729173824992324.html. (Since 2011, the number on UN members has increased to 193 with the addition of South Sudan.)
9. Sharon Otterman, "U.S. Opens Way to Ease Sanctions Against Syria," *New York Times*, July 28, 2009, http://www.nytimes.com/2009/07/29/world/middleeast/29syria.html.
10. "U.S. Envoy Says Sudan Sanctions Should Be Eased," *Reuters*, July 30, 2009, http://www.reuters.com/article/2009/07/30/us-sudan-darfur-sanctions-idUSTRE56T6CV20090730.
11. Secretary-General Ban Ki-moon, UN Headquarters, UN News Centre, "Speech to the Symposium on Enhancing the Implementation of Security Council Sanction," April 30, 2007, https://www.un.org/apps/news/infocus/sgspeeches/statments_full.asp?statID=81; United Nations Security Council (SC), Informal Working Group on General Issues of Sanctions, Best Practices and Recommendations for Improving the Effectiveness of United Nations Sanctions, 2006.
12. Gary C. Hufbauer and Barbara Oegg, "Economic Sanctions: Public Goals and Private Compensation," *Chicago Journal of International Law* 4, no. 2 (2003): 328.

13. John Bolton, House Committee Hearing on Status of U.N. Investigations, Washington, DC, Thursday, March 16, 2006.
14. Ibid.
15. Paul Conlon United Nations Sanction Papers, 1991–1995, The University of Iowa Libraries, Iowa City, Iowa.
16. Steven Myers and Jane Perles, "No Movement on Major Disputes as Clinton Meets with Chinese leaders," *New York Times*, September 6, 2012.
17. Paul Conlon United Nations Sanction Papers, 1991–1995, The University of Iowa Libraries, Iowa City, Iowa. I am very grateful to Denise K. Anderson at the University of Iowa Library for her support in duplicating the manuscripts and papers of Paul Conlon.
18. Steven R. Ratner and Anne-Marie Slaughter, *The Methods of International Law* (Washington, D.C.: American Society of International Law, 2004), 3.
19. Hans Morgenthau, "Positivism, Functionalism, and International Law," *American Journal of International Law* 34, no. 2 (1940): 260, 284. I glean my definition of positivism from Hans Morgenthau's seminal article.
20. Bruno Simma and Andreas L. Paulus, "*The Responsibility of Individuals for Human Rights Abuses in Internal Conflicts: A Positivist View*," in *The Methods of International Law,* eds., Steven R. Ratner and Anne-Marie Slaughter (Washington, D.C.: American Society of International Law, 2004), 26–7.
21. Ibid., citing South West Africa (*Eth. v. S. Afr.*; *Liber. v. S. Afr.*), Second Phase, Judgment, 1966 ICJ Rep. 6, 34, ¶ 49 (July 18).
22. Jean Combacau, *Sanctions*, in Rudolf Bernhardt, Rudolf L. Bindschedler, and Peter Macalister-Smith (eds.) *Encyclopedia of Public International Law Vol. 4,* (Amsterdam [etc.]: Elsevier, 2000): 311–3.
23. Ibid.
24. Martti Koskenniemi, *Letter to the Editors of the Symposium*, in Ratner and Slaughter, eds., *The Methods of International Law* (Washington, D.C.: American Society of International Law, 2004), 114 (emphasis added).
25. Ibid.
26. Secretary General Ban Ki-moon, UN Headquarters, UN News Centre, "Speech to the Symposium on Enhancing the Implementation of Security Council Sanction," April 30, 2007; UN Development Program, Executive Board of the United Nations Development Programme and of the United Nations Population Fund, "Draft Country Programme Document for Somalia (2008–2009)," UN Doc. DP/DCP/SOM/1/Rev.1, July 2, 2007.
27. Koskenniemi, "Letter to the Editors of the Symposium," 117.
28. Nicholas Mercuro, *Law and Economics: Recent Economic Thought* (Boston: Kluwer Academic, 1989), 61.
29. Koskenniemi, "Letter to the Editors of the Symposium," 124.
30. Kenneth W. Abbott, "Modern International Relations Theory: a Prospectus for International Lawyers," *Yale Journal of International Law* 14, no. 2 (1989): 335; Kenneth W. Abbott, and Duncan Snidal, "Why States Act through Formal International Organizations," *Journal of Conflict Resolution* 42, no. 1 (1998): 3, 12–18.
31. Vera Gowlland-Debbas, Mariano Garcia Rubio, and Hassiba Hadj-Sahraoui, *United Nations Sanctions and International Law* (The Hague: Kluwer Law International, 2001): 4; For a great review of the state of the art and Vera Gowlland-Debbas, see "Book Review: UN Sanctions in International Law," *American Journal of International Law*, 96 (April, 2002): 506.
32. Amnesty International, "Death Penalty Facts," last modified May 2012, http://www.amnestyusa.org/pdfs/DeathPenaltyFactsMay2012.pdf.

33. R.T. Naylor, *Economic Warfare: Sanctions, Embargo Busting, and Their Human Cost* (Boston: Northeastern University Press, 1999).
34. Myres S. McDougal, "Harold Dwight Lasswell 1902–1978" (1979), Faculty Scholarship Series, Paper 2663, http://digitalcommons.law.yale.edu/fss_papers/2663.
35. Anne-Marie Slaughter, "International Law and International Relations Theory: A Dual Agenda," *American Journal of International Law* 87 (1993): 205–39.
36. United States, UN, *Sanctions After Oil-for-Food: Still a Viable Diplomatic Tool?: Hearing Before the Subcommittee on National Security, Emerging Threats, and International Relations of the Committee on Government Reform, House of Representatives, One Hundred Ninth Congress, Second Session, May 2, 2006* (Washington: U.S. G.P.O., 2006), Serial No. 109–75.
37. Peter Wallensteen, ed., *International Sanctions: Theory and Practice: Proceedings of the Nordic Conference on Sanction Research* (Sigtuna, Sweden, April 27–28, 1968); Richard N. Haass, ed., *Economic Sanctions and American Diplomacy* (New York: Council on Foreign Relations, 1998), 1–17.
38. Wallensteen, *International Sanctions: Theory and Practice.*
39. Ugo Mattei, *Comparative Law and Economics* (Ann Arbor: University of Michigan Press, 1997), 14–15.
40. David M. Trubek, and Alvaro Santos eds., *The New Law and Economic Development: A Critical Appraisal* (New York: Cambridge University Press, 2006): 174–81 (emphasis on introduction).
41. Received wisdom dictates that U.N. sanctions are presumptively legal due to the broad mandate given by Chapter VII of the UN Charter.
42. Cassandra LaRae-Perez, "Economic Sanctions As A Use of Force, Re-Evaluating the Legality of Sanctions from an Effects-Based Perspective," *Boston University International Law Journal* 20, no. 161 (2002): 162.
43. Ibid.
44. Christopher C. Joyner, "United Nations Sanctions After Iraq: Looking Back to See Ahead," *Chicago Journal of International Law* 4 (2003): 344–5; *see also* Christopher C. Joyner, *International Law in the 21st Century: Rules for Global Governance* (Lanham, Md: Rowman & Littlefield, 2005): 184–8.
45. Joyner, *International Law in the 21st Century.*
46. *See* Military and Paramilitary Activities (Nicaragua v. U.S.), 1986 I.C.J. 14, June 27, 1986 (finding *opinio juris* and state practice for binding customary international law principle of nonintervention in another state's political, economic, social, and cultural systems).
47. Adam Benforado and Jon Hanson, *The Costs of Dispositionism: The Premature Demise of Situationist Law and Economics* (Baltimore: University of Maryland, 2005), 84 in *Ideals, Beliefs, Attitudes, and the Law: Private Law Perspectives on a Public Law Problem*, ed., Guido Calabresi (Syracuse, N.Y.: Syracuse University Press, 1985).
48. Peter Wallensteen and Carina Staibano, eds., *International Sanctions: Between Words and Wars in the Global System* (London: Frank Cass, 2005), 120–6, 170.
49. Robert A. Dahl, *Modern Political Analysis* (Englewood Cliffs, N.J.: Prentice-Hall, 1963), 18; David A. Baldwin, *Economic Statecraft* (Princeton, N.J.: Princeton University Press, 1985).
50. Myres S. McDougal, "Some Basic Theoretical Concepts About International Law: A Policy-oriented Framework of Inquiry," *Journal of Conflict Resolution* 4, no. 3 (1960): 337–54.

NOTES TO CHAPTER 2

1. David A. Baldwin, "The Sanctions Debate and the Logic of Choice," *International Security* 24, no. 3 (1999): 80.
2. Ernst B. Haas, *When Knowledge Is Power: Three Models of Change in International Organizations* (Berkeley: University of California Press, 1990), 16–18.
3. Ian Brownlie, *International Law at the Fiftieth Anniversary of the United Nations General Course on Public International Law* (Leiden, the Netherlands: Martinus Nijhoff, 1995); D. W. Bowett, *Bowett's Law of International Institutions* (London: Sweet & Maxwell, 2001); Thomas M. Franck, *The Power of Legitimacy Among Nations* (New York: Oxford University Press, 1990).
4. Oona Anne Hathaway and Harold Hongju Koh, *Foundations of International Law and Politics* (New York: Foundation Press, 2005): 68–9 (discussing Andrew Guzman's compliance-based theory of international law and efficient breach to justify state violations of international obligations)
5. Ibid.
6. Joy K. Fausey, "Does the United Nations' Use of Collective Sanctions to Protect Human Rights Violate its Own Human Rights Standards?" *Connecticut Journal of International Law* 10, no.1 (1994): 193, 196.
7. Anton M. van Kalmthout, *Sanctions Systems in the Member States of the Council of Europe 1, Deprivation of Liberty, Community Service and Other Substitutes* (Deventer: Kluwer, 1988): 440–72.
8. Georges Abi-Saab, "The Concept of Sanctions in International Law," in *United Nations Sanctions and International Law,* eds. Vera Gowlland-Debbas, Mariano Garcia Rubio, and Hassiba Hadj-Sahraoui (The Hague: Kluwer Law International, 2001): 39.
9. *Webster's Collegiate Dictionary*, 9th ed., "sanction."; *Black's Law Dictionary*, 9th ed., "sanctions."
10. Fausey, "Does the United Nations' Use of Collective Sanctions to Protect Human Rights Violate its Own Human Rights Standards?" 196.
11. *Webster's Unabridged Dictionary*, 2nd ed., "sanctions."
12. Fernando R Tesón, *Humanitarian Intervention: An Inquiry into Law and Morality* (Ardsley, N.Y.: Transnational Publishers, 2005): 28.
13. Ibid., 115.
14. Thihan Myo Nyun, "Feeling Good or Doing Good: Inefficacy of the U.S. Unilateral Sanctions Against the Military," *Washington University Global Studies Law Review* 7, no. 3 (2008): 458.
15. M. Codsi Goubran, *Le problème des sanctions dans l'évolution de l'arbitrage international* (Paris: E. Sagot, 1923).
16. United Nations Security Council (SC), 1340th Meeting, Resolution 232 (1966) of 16 December 1966, S/RES/232, http://www.unhcr.org/refworld/docid/3b00f23414.html.
17. *World Encyclopedia of Peace*, 2nd edition, "UN Economic Sanctions."
18. David A Baldwin, *Economic Statecraft* (Princeton, N.J.: Princeton University Press, 1985), 189.
19. Hossein Askari, et al., *Economic Sanctions: Examining Their Philosophy and Efficacy* (Westport, Conn.: Praeger, 2003), 44.
20. Preston Brown, *The Kuwait/Iraq Sanctions: U.S. Regulations in an International Setting* (New York: Practising Law Institute, 1991), 22.
21. Ibid., 34–61.
22. Benjamin B. Ferencz, *New Legal Foundations for Global Survival: Security Through the Security Council* (New York: Oceana, 1994).

23. Jonathan Kirsher, "The Microfoundations of Economic Sanctions" *Security Studies* 6, no. 3 (1997): 36–40, quoted in Terry L. Deibel, *Foreign Affairs Strategy: Logic for American Statecraft* (New York: Cambridge University Press, 2007), 260.
24. Jean Combacau, "Sanctions," in *Encyclopedia of Public International Law Vol. 4*, eds., Rudolf Bernhardt, Rudolf L. Bindschedler, and Peter Macalister-Smith, (Amsterdam [etc.]: Elsevier, 2000), 313.
25. United Nations General Assembly, "A More Secure World: Our Shared Responsibility, Report of the High-Level Panel on Threats, Challenges and Change," UN Doc. A/59/565, 8 (2004), http://www.un.org/secureworld/report.pdf.
26. Laura Picchio Forlati, and Linos-Alexandre Sicilianos, *Les Sanctions économiques en droit international=Economic sanctions in international law* (Leiden [etc.]: Martinus Nijhoff, 2004), 167–174.
27. United Nations, "Enhancing the Implementation of United Nations Security Sanctions: A Symposium," Sponsored by the Permanent Mission of Greece to the United Nations, April 30, 2007, http://www.watsoninstitute.org/pub/UNSC-Enhancing_Implementation_Sanctions.pdf (remarks of Greek Ambassador to the UN, Ambassador Vassilakis).
28. David Cortright, and George A. Lopez, *Sanctions and the Search for Security: Challenges to UN Action* (Boulder: Lynne Rienner, 2002), 13.
29. Vera Gowlland-Debbas, Mariano Garcia Rubio, and Hassiba Hadj-Sahraoui, *United Nations Sanctions and International Law* (The Hague: Kluwer Law International, 2001), 96 (referring to Article 16 of the OAS Charter of 1948 and Article 19 in the 1967 version).
30. UN Charter, Article 55.
31. [*transl.*, V.A. Vasilenko, Sanctions Under International Law (Kiev: Higher School 1982).]; Royal Institute of International Affairs, *International Sanctions; A Report by a Group of Members of the Royal Institute of International Affairs* (London: Oxford University Press, 1938).
32. Vera Gowlland-Debbas, ed., United *Nations Sanctions and International Law*, 96.
33. United Nations, "Report of the Sub-Commission on the Promotion and Protection of Human Rights: The Adverse Consequences of Economic Sanctions on the Enjoyment of Human Rights," U.N. Doc. E/CN.41/Sub.2/2000/33 (1999): 19–20.
34. Report of the Sub-Commission on the Promotion and Protection of Human Rights; The Adverse Consequences of Economic Sanctions on the Enjoyment of Human Rights, U.N. Doc. E/CN.41/Sub.2/2000/33, at 19–20 (1999).
35. Laurence Boisson de Chazournes, "Collective Security and The Economic Interventionism of the UN—The Need for a Coherent and Integrated Approach," *Journal of International Economic Law* 10, no. 1 (2007): 51, 58–59.
36. Jeremy Matam Farrall, *United Nations Sanctions and the Rule of Law* (Cambridge: Cambridge University Press, 2007), 1–23.
37. Thomas George Weiss, David Cortright, George A. Lopez, and Larry Minear, *Political Gain and Civilian Pain: Humanitarian Impacts of Economic Sanctions* (Lanham: Rowman & Littlefield, 1997) 58–64.
38. Ibid.
39. John R. Crook, "United States Imposes New Economic Sanctions on Several Countries," *American Journal of International Law* 102, no. 1 (2008): 174–6.
40. James M. Murphy, *Sanctions in Transition* (London: The David Davies Memorial Institute of International Studies, 2000), 8.

41. August Reinisch, "Developing Human Rights and Humanitarian Law Accountability of the Security Council for the Imposition of Economic Sanctions," *American Journal of International Law* 95, no. 4 (2001): 851–72.
42. Peter Wallensteen, and Carina Staibano, *International Sanctions: Between Words and Wars in the Global System* (London: Frank Cass, 2005), 1, 229.
43. Ibid.
44. Report to the Ranking Member, Subcommittee on National Security and Foreign Affairs, "Iran Sanctions: Impact in Furthering U.S. Objectives is Unclear and Should be Reviewed," Government Accountability Office (2007).
45. Ibid., 17.
46. Ibid., 20–22.
47. Kayhan News, 28 Shahrivar 1388 (September 18, 2009) Issue 19466.
48. Iranian Official State News Agency, Keyhan News (February 10–21, 2007).
49. Ibid.
50. William H. Kaempfer, and Anton D. Lowenberg, "Unilateral Versus Multilateral International Sanctions: A Public Choice Perspective," *International Studies Quarterly* 43, no. 1 (1999): 37–58.
51. Makio Miyagawa, *Do Economic Sanctions Work?* (Basingstoke: Macmillan, 1992), 221–3.
52. Shao Jie, "Washington Expected to Shift Policies Toward Sudan," *Xinhua News Agency*, August 27, 2009, http://news.xinhuanet.com/english/2009–08/27/content_11955484.htm.
53. Failed State Index 2012, The eighth annual collaboration between Foreign Policy and Fund for Peace, http://www.foreignpolicy.com/failed_states_index_2012_interactive.
54. Weiss et al., *Political Gain and Civilian Pain: Humanitarian Impacts of Economic Sanctions*, 78.
55. Ibid.
56. David Cortright, George A. Lopez, and Linda Gerber, *Sanctions and the Search for Security: Challenges to UN Action* (Boulder: Lynne Rienner Publishers, 2002), 11.
57. Ibid., Appendix A—List of all countries currently sanctioned by U.S.
58. "When High Oil Prices are a Taxing Issue," Investment Adviser, *Financial Times*, April 21, 2008; John D. Mckinnon, "US Raises Ire Over Chavez, Weighs Actions," *Wall Street Journal*, (March 13, 2008): A5.
59. Geoffrey Leslie Simons, *Imposing Economic Sanctions: Legal Remedy or Genocidal Tool?* (London: Pluto Press, 1999), 2.
60. Stuart E. Eizenstat, *Do Economic Sanctions Work? Lessons from ILSA & Other U.S. Sanctions Regimes*, Occasional Paper, (2004), http://www.acus.org/files/publication_pdfs/65/2004–02-Economic_Sanctions.pdf.
61. David Cortright, "Humanitarian Sanctions? The Moral and Political Issues," Human Rights Brief 3, no. 1, Center for Human Rights and Humanitarian Law; David Cortright, George A. Lopez, and Linda Gerber, *Sanctions and the Search for Security: Challenges to UN Action* (Boulder: Lynne Rienner Publishers, 2002), 1–6; Thomas George Weiss, David Cortright, et al., eds. *Political Gain and Civilian Pain* (Lanham: Rowman & Littlefield, 1997), 43–78.
62. Max Hilaire, *United Nations Law and the Security Council* (Burlington, Vermont: Ashgate, 2005), 87.
63. Richard Haass, *Economic Sanctions and American Diplomacy* (New York: Council on Foreign Relations, 1998), 57; Paul Conlon, *United Nations Sanctions Management: A Case Study of the Iraq Sanctions Committee, 1990–1994* (Ardsley, N.Y.: Transnational Publishers, 2000), 165.

64. "Historical Note on the Security Council's Disputed Right to Ban Supplies of Foodstuffs to a State Under Sanction," in Paul Conlon United Nations Sanction Papers, 1991–1995, The University of Iowa Libraries, Iowa City, Iowa.
65. Haass, *Economic Sanctions and American Diplomacy,* 205–206.

NOTES TO CHAPTER 3

1. Kenneth W. Abbott, "International Relations Theory, International Law, and the Regime Governing Atrocities in Internal Conflicts," *American Journal of International Law* 93, no. 2 (1999): 361–79.
2. United Nations General Assembly, "A More Secure World: Our Shared Responsibility, Report of the High-Level Panel on Threats, Challenges and Change," UN Doc. A/59/565 (2004): 8, http://www.un.org/secureworld/report.pdf.
3. Herbert G. Nicholas, *The United Nations as a Political Institution* (London: Oxford University Press, 1975), 76.
4. Ibid.
5. Michael J. Matheson, *Council Unbound: The Growth of UN Decision Making on Conflict and Postconflict Issues after the Cold War* (Washington, D.C.: US Institute of Peace Press, 2006), 34; see also the text of the UN Charter, Article 52 to 54.
6. United Nations, Declaration on Essentials of Peace, G.A. Res. 290 (IV), at 10, U.N. GAOR, 4th Sess., 261st plen. Mtg., U.N. Doc A/Res/4/290 (Dec. 1, 1949).
7. Karel Wellens, "The UN Security Council and new Threats to the Peace: back to the Future," *Journal of Conflict & Security Law* 8, no. 1 (2003): 21.
8. Natasha Balendra, "Defining Armed Conflict" (2007). New York University Public Law and Legal Theory Working Papers, Paper 63, http://lsr.nellco.org/nyu_plltwp/63. Natasha T. Balendra, "Defining Armed Conflict," *Cardozo Law Review*, 29 (2008): 2475 (discussing the inability of international humanitarian law, the Geneva conventions, and customary law to provide a dispositive definition of armed conflict).
9. Reuters, "Russia says attacking Iran would be 'disastrous,': Ifax," *Chicago Tribune News*, September 6, 2012, http://articles.chicagotribune.com/2012–09–06/news/sns-rt-us-nuclaer-iran-russia-attackbre88509w-20120905_1_ifax-interfax-nuclear-program.
10. Reuters, "Russia Says Attacking Iran Would Be 'Disastrous,': Ifax," *Chicago Tribune News*, September 6, 2012, http://articles.chicagotribune.com/2012–09–06/news/sns-rt-us-nuclaer-iran-russia-attackbre88509w-20120905_1_ifax-interfax-nuclear-program; Vera Gowlland-Debbas, Mariano Garcia Rubio, and Hassiba Hadj-Sahraoui, *United Nations Sanctions and International Law* (The Hague: Kluwer Law International, 2001), 8.
11. Anthony R. Reeves, "Sexual Identity as a Fundamental Human Right," *Buffalo Human Rights Law Review* 15 (2009): 219.
12. His Holiness, The 14th Dalai Lama of Tibet, The 14th Dalai Lama Nobel Lecture, December 11, 1989, http://www.dalailama.com/messages/acceptance-speeches/nobel-peace-prize/nobel-lecture.
13. Dictionary.com, Unabridged, Random House Inc., "peace," http://dictionary.reference.com/browse/peace.
14. *Webster's Third New International Dictionary*, Unabridged, "peace," (1993), 1660.

15. Daniel W. Abbott, "The United Nations and Intrastate Conflict: A Legislative History of Article 39 of the United Nations Charter," *University of California at Davis Journal of International Law and Policy* (Spring 2002): 282 quoted in Kristen E. Boon, "Coining a New Jurisdiction: the Security Council as Economic Peacekeeper," *Vanderbilt Journal of Transnational Law* 41, no. 4 (2008):1020.
16. Ibid.
17. Inger Österdahl, *Threat to the Peace: The Interpretation by the Security Council of Article 39 of the UN Charter* (Uppsala: Iustus, 1998). An excellent analysis of peace under international law and "threats to peace"; Daniel Pickard, "When Does Crime Become a Threat to International Peace and Security?" *Florida Journal of International Law* 12, no. 1 (1998): 8–9.
18. Hans Kelsen, *Recent Trends in the Law of the United Nations* (London: Stevens & Sons, Ltd., 1951), 930.
19. The Secretary General, Report of the Secretary General on the Question of Uganda, delivered to the Security Council and the General Assembly, U.N. Doc. S/2005/770 (Jan. 26, 2006).
20. UN Charter.
21. Michael Howard, The Invention of Peace and the Reinvention of War (London: Profile, 2002): 2 quoted in Kristen E. Boon, "Coining a New Jurisdiction: the Security Council as Economic Peacekeeper," 1017–1018 (emphasis added).
22. Gowlland-Debbas, *United Nations Sanctions and International Law*, 8.
23. Philippe Sands, Pierre Klein, and D.W. Bowett, *Bowett's Law of International Institutions* (London: Sweet & Maxwell, 2001): 52, 2.054 quoted in Karel Wellens, "The UN Security Council and New Threats to the Peace: Back to the Future," *Journal of Conflict & Security Law* 8, no. 1 (2003): 21 ("the problem may be one of acquiring accurate factual knowledge of events, rather than one of legal definition").
24. Hans Kelsen, *The Law of the United Nations: A Critical Analysis of its Fundamental Problems* (New York: F.A. Praeger, 1951); Gowlland-Debbas, *United Nations Sanctions and International Law*, 8–11; Indar Jit Rikhye, and Kjell Skjelsbaek, *The United Nations and Peacekeeping: Results, Limitations, and Prospects: the Lessons of 40 Years of Experience* (New York: St. Martin's Press, 1990); Indar Jit Rikhye, *The Theory & Practice of Peacekeeping* (New York: Published for the International Peace Academy by St. Martin's Press, 1984), 132; Jean Combacau, "Sanctions," in Rudolf Bernhardt, Rudolf L. Bindschedler, and Peter Macalister-Smith *Encyclopedia of Public International Law Vol. 4,* (Amsterdam [etc.]: Elsevier, 2000), 312 (discussing sanctions and liability for wrongful acts committed under international law or failure to respect an international obligation).
25. Kelsen, *The Law of United Nations*, 123.
26. *UN Security Council Extends Mission in Sierra Leone for Six Months,* 2003 WLNR 581763 (September 19, 2003), retrieved from Westlaw. ("In adopting the resolution, the 15-member body welcomed the increasing security in Sierra Leone and encouraged 'further progress towards strengthening the capacity of the Sierra Leone Police and armed forces to maintain security and stability independently.' ")
27. Kelsen, *The Law of United Nations*, 369.
28. Ibid.
29. "Use of Force," UN Charter, Article 2 in Edmund Jan Osmańczyk, and Anthony Mango, *Encyclopedia of the United Nations and International Agreements* (New York: Routledge, 2003), 2571.

30. Louis Henkin, "Conceptualizing Violence: Present and Future Developments in International Law," *Albany Law Review.* 60, no. 3 (1997): 571–8.
31. Although it can be argued from Article 39 of the UN Charter that breach of peace is equivalent to prohibition of any threats to peace.
32. Gowlland-Debbas, *United Nations Sanctions and International Law*, 8.
33. Michael R. Fowler, and Jessica Fryrear "Collective Security and the Fighting in the Balkans," *Northern Kentucky Law Review* 30, no. 3 (2003): 325–6.
34. (S/24137, 22 June 1992).
35. Ibid.
36. David A Baldwin, *Economic Statecraft* (Princeton, N.J.: Princeton University Press, 1985), 347.
37. United Nations General Assembly, "A More Secure World: Our Shared Responsibility, Report of the High-Level Panel on Threats, Challenges and Change," UN Doc. A/59/565, at 8 (2004).
38. Anne-Marie Slaughter, "Security, Solidarity, and Sovereignty: the Grand Themes of UN Reform," *American Journal of International Law* 99, no. 3 (2005): 622–3.
39. United Nations, Charter of the United Nations, October 24, 1945, 1 UNTS XVI, http://www.unhcr.org/refworld/docid/3ae6b3930.html.
40. James H. Lebovic, "Uniting for Peace? Democracies and United Nations Peace Operations after the Cold War," *The Journal of Conflict Resolution: a Quarterly for Research Related to War and Peace* 48, no. 6 (2004): 910–915 (examining liberal conflict theory and whether the role of democracy inclines nations towards greater participation in post-Cold War peace operations).
41. "Historical Note on Relations with NGOs and the Public" in Paul Conlon United Nations Sanction Papers, 1991–1995, The University of Iowa Libraries, Iowa City, Iowa.
42. Seyed Mohammad Bagher, Masbahzadeh, Farajam va Aghaze Jonbeshhaye Siyasi dar Afghanistan (Shah Mohammad, Sherkate Ketan, 1374) [Seyed Mohammad Bagher Msbahzadeh, *The Rise and Fall of the Political Movement in Afghanistan* (Sherkateh Ketab, 2005): 392 (Author's translation from *Farsi*)]
43. Ibid.
44. Kelsen, *The Law of the United Nations,* 359.
45. One-hundred and three members of the United Nations participated in the Convention on Privileges and Immunities of the United Nations.
46. *Nicole v. United Nations Mission in Liberia*, 2009 WL 2370179, (2 E.D.Pa. (citing *Emmanuel v. United States*, 253 F.3d 755, 756 (1st Cir. 2001)).
47. Convention on Privileges and Immunities of the United Nations, Apr. 29, 1970, T.I.A.S. No. 6900, 21 U.S.T. 1418, 1970 WL 104387 (U.S. Treaty).
48. Paul Conlon, *United Nations Sanctions Management: A Case Study of the Iraq Sanctions Committee, 1990–1994* (Ardsley, NY: Transnational Publishers, 2000), 122.
49. "Historical Note on Relations with NGOs and the Public" in Paul Conlon United Nations Sanction Papers, 1991–1995, The University of Iowa Libraries, Iowa City, Iowa.
50. Oscar Schachter, "United Nations Law," *American Journal of International Law* 88, no. 1 (1994): 8.
51. Baldwin, *Economic Statecraft*, 104–5 (referring to Henry Bienen and Robert Gilpin and noting that use of economic sanctions "has a detrimental impact on foreign perception of the United States").
52. Schachter, "United Nations Law," 18 (Referring to the central importance of the veto in the Security Council. "The veto power or principle of unanimity,

is a legal rule embodied in the Charter for political reasons and used (or, some would say, abused) by the permanent members primarily in their national interests.").

53. Ibid.
54. Timothy Hillier, *Sourcebook on Public International Law* (London: Cavendish, 1998), 568.
55. "The Limits of Another Form of Supervision: Political Control by the General Assembly," in Mohammed Bedjaoui, *The New World Order and the Security Council: Testing the Legality of Its Acts* (Dordrecht: M. Nijhoff Publishers, 1993), 119–26.
56. Schachter, "United Nations Law," 2. Oscar Schachter was the director of the UN general legal division, where since 1953 he worked in framing the legal foundation of the UN. He was also a Professor of Law at Columbia University.
57. Ibid., 3.
58. Ibid., 7.
59. Gary C. Hufbauer and Barbara Oegg, "Economic Sanctions: Public Goals and Private Compensation," 307 (giving examples of Somalia, Liberia, and Rwanda).
60. UN Charter.
61. Ibid.
62. Thomas George Weiss, "Sanctions as a Foreign Policy Tool: Weighing Humanitarian Impulses," *Journal of Peace Research*. 36, no. 5 (1999): 500.
63. Ibid., 309.
64. Chronology of Reporting on Events Concerning the Conflict in Darfur, Sudan, Coalition for International Justice, February 2006, 336.
65. United Nations General Assembly, Security Council, Report of the panel on United Nations Peace Operations, United Nations, A/55/305-S/2000/809, 21 August 2000.
66. I borrow this metaphor from Gray L. Dorsey. The *status quo* and *inertia* arguments can be applied with equal force, no pun intended, to the reaction of the target elites and target mass population. Gray L. Dorsey, *Beyond the United Nations: Changing Discourse in International Politics and Law* (Lanham: University Press of America, 1986).
67. Ibid., note 72, page 67.
68. Margaret P. Doxey, *Economic Sanctions and International Enforcement* (London: published for the Royal Institute of International Affairs, by Oxford University Press, 1980), 14.

NOTES TO CHAPTER 4

1. "Historical Note on the Issue of Oil Belonging to the Kuwait Petroleum Company in Aden," in Paul Conlon United Nations Sanction Papers, 1991–1995, The University of Iowa Libraries, Iowa City, Iowa.
2. Indar Jit Rikhye and Kjell Skjelsbaek, *The United Nations and Peacekeeping: Results, Limitations and Prospects: the Lessons of 40 Years of Experience* (Basingstoke: Macmillan in association with the International Peace Academy, 1990): 33–4.
3. Jutta Brunnee, "The Security Council and Self-Defence: Which Way to Global Security?" *Legal Aspects of International Organization, 44* in eds., Niels Blokker, and Nico Schrijver (Leiden: Martinus Nijhoff Publishers, 2005), 107.

4. Edmund Jan Osmańczyk, *The Encyclopedia of the United Nations and International Agreements* (Philadelphia: Taylor and Francis, 1985), 1018–22.
5. "The Paul Conlon Historical Note on Iraqi Frozen or Impounded Assets, Control of Iraqi Frozen or Impounded Assets and Historical Note on Control of Iraqi Shipping," in Paul Conlon United Nations Sanction Papers, 1991–1995, The University of Iowa Libraries, Iowa City, Iowa.
6. S.C.O.R., The Situation between Iraq and Kuwait: Report of the Secretary-General on the implementation of Paragraph 5 of Security Council Resolution 687 (1991), U.N. Doc. S/22454 (April 3, 1991).
7. Paul Conlon United Nations Sanction Papers, 1991–1995, The University of Iowa Libraries, Iowa City, Iowa.
8. Erika de Wet, "The Role of Human Rights in Limiting the Enforcement Power of the Security Council: A Principled View," in *Review of the Security Council by Member States* (2003), 147–159.
9. Mark Landler and David Sanger, "U.S. Presses China for Tough Response to North Korea," *New York Times,* May 28, 2009, http://www.nytimes.com/2009/05/29/world/asia/29diplo.html?_r=1&ref=global-home.
10. Letter from Comoros, Mauritius, Seychelles, Zambia and Zimbabwe to the committee, October 15, 1990, U.N. DOC. S/AC.25/1990/COMM.50, in *1990 Comms Log* 27.
11. United Nations Security Council (SC), Ad hoc Committee, Letter dated November 15, 1990 from the Committee to Comoros, Mauritius, Seychelles, Zambia and Zimbabwe, U.N. DOC. S/AC.25/1990/NOTE/49, in 1990 Notes Log 26.
12. Paul Conlon, United Nations Sanction Papers, 1991–1995, The University of Iowa Libraries, Iowa City, Iowa.
13. UN Charter, Article 25.
14. "Use and Effect of Unilateral Sanctions," Hearing Before the Subcommittee on Trade, 106th Congress, Serial 106–68 (May 7, 1999) (GPO, Washington 2000).
15. S/24034, May 29, 1992.
16. Per Cramer, "Recent Swedish Experience With Targeted UN Sanctions: The Erosion of Trust in the Security Council," in Erika De Wet, André Nollkaemper, and Petra Dijkstra, *Review of the Security Council by Member States* (Antwerp: Intersentia, 2003): 94–98; *see also* the discussion in § 7.3.1.
17. Security Council, Letter Dated 19 June 1992 from the Minister for Foreign Affairs of the Republic of Slovenia Addressed to the Secretary General, U.N. Doc. S/24120 (June 19, 1992).
18. United Nations Documents, Security Council 47th Year Plenary Meetings (1992), S/24121; S/24122 to S/24127; S/24128–24129; S/24130 to S/24138 [microfiche].
19. Joseph A Klein, *Global Deception: The UN's Stealth Assault on America's Freedoms* (Los Angeles: World Ahead Publishing, Inc, 2005), 183.
20. Ibid.
21. Ibid.
22. Glenn H. Kaminsky and Charles G. Wall, *Destined for Terror: Coping With the Most Restrictive of U.S. Export Controls*, Practicing Law Institute, 910 PLI/Comm 227 (2008).
23. Foreign Operations, Export Financing and Related Programs Appropriations Act of 1997, Public Law 105–277, 112 Stat. 2681–176, Div. A, § 101(d) (September 30, 1997).
24. 22 USC. §2377 (United States Code, 2010).

25. Kenneth Katzman, The Iran-Libya Sanctions Act (ILSA), CRS Report for Congress, April 19, 2005.
26. Ibid.
27. H.R. 2347—CRS Report for Congress, The Iran Sanctions Act, Kenneth Katzman, Specialist in Middle Eastern Affairs, Foreign Affairs, Defense, and Trade Division, October 12, 2007.
28. International Security and Development Cooperation Act of 1985.
29. 50 US Code Annotated §§ 1701–1707 (1977).
30. Weekly Compilation of Presidential Documents Volume 29, Number 28 (Monday, July 19, 1993), 1326 available at http://www.gpo.gov/fdsys/pkg/WCPD-1993–07–19/html/WCPD-1993–07–19-Pg1325.htm.
31. Cuban Liberty and Democratic Solidarity (Libertad) Act of 1996, (Codified in Title 22, Sections 6021–6091 of the U.S. Code), P.L. 104–14, One Hundred Fourth Congress of the United States of America. Section 101.
32. Morris H. Morley, and Chris McGillion, *Unfinished Business: America and Cuba After the Cold War, 1989–2001* (Cambridge: Cambridge University Press, 2002) quoted in Steven Lee Myers, "Clinton Troubleshooter Discovers Big Trouble from Allies on Cuba," *New York Times*, October 23, 1996, p. 1, 52.
33. 50 U.S.C.A. § 1707 (1977).
34. Ibid., 114.
35. Ibid., 114.
36. The Antiterrorism and Effective Death Penalty Act, PUBLIC LAW 104-132-APR. 24, 1996.
37. Raj Bhala, "Fighting Bad Guys with International Trade Law," *U.C. Davis Law Review.* 31, no. 1 (1997): 114–116.
38. Ibid.
39. Glenn H. Kaminsky and Charles G. Wall, *Destined for Terror: Coping With the Most Restrictive of U.S. Export Controls*, Practicing Law Institute, 910 PLI/Comm 227 (2008).
40. Ibid.
41. Australian Government, Department of Foreign Affairs & Trade, UN Security Council Sanctions (Somalia), http://www.dfat.gov.au/un/unsc_sanctions/somalia.html (list of changes made in Australian legislation in implementing UN sanctions against Somalia).
42. "Persons and entities subject to UN Security Council financial sanctions," [MS Excel file], http://www.dfat.gov.au/icat/regulation8_consolidated.xls.
43. "Charter of the United Nations Act 1945, Act No. 32 of 1945 as amended," http://www.comlaw.gov.au/comlaw/Legislation/ActCompilation1.nsf/0/08329E7217BC1D72CA257412001173A9?OpenDocument.
44. Australian Government, Department of Foreign Affairs and Trade, "How are UN Sanctions Implemented in Australia?" http://www.dfat.gov.au/un/unsc_sanctions/unsc_sanctions_how.html.
45. Charter of the United Nations (Sanctions—Democratic People's Republic of Korea) Regulations 2008, Legislative Instrument Compilation (current)—F2009C00624, SLI 2008 No. 30 (July 31, 2009).
46. Vera Gowlland-Debbas, "The Domestic Implementation of UN Sanctions," in *Review of the Security Council by Member States. The Domestic Implementation of UN Sanctions*, eds., Erika de Wet & Andre Nollkaemper (Antwerp: Intersentia, 2003), 70.
47. Mehrdad Payandeh and Heiko Sauer, "European Union: UN Sanctions and EU Fundamental Rights," *International Journal of Constitutional Law* 7, no. 2 (2009): 311.

48. Ibid., 308, 310–5.
49. Council Regulation (EC) No 337/2000 (14 February 2000) (targeted financial sanctions against Afghan faction which also calls itself the Islamic Emirate of Afghanistan to implement sanctions imposed by UNSC Resolution 1267 (1999)); Report by the European Union to the Committee Established Under Paragraph 6 of Resolution 1373 (2001), Adopted by the UNSC at its 4385th Meeting on 28 September 2001, http://ec.europa.eu/external_relations/organisations/un/docs/eu1373_en.pdf.
50. This text is the same in EC regulations implementing sanctions against Sierra Leone, and others, http://eur-lex.europa.eu/LexUriServ/LexUriServ.do?uri=OJ:L:2000:043:0001:0011:EN:PDF; Council Regulation (EC) No 467/2001 of 6 March 2001 (EC) No 337/2000, Official Journal L 67, 09/03/2001 p. 1.
51. Guidelines on Implementation and Evaluation of Restrictive Measures (Sanctions) in the Framework of the EU Common Foreign and Security Policy, Council of The European Union, 17464/09, Brussels, December 15, 2009.
52. Horace Virgil Harrison, *The Role of Theory in International Relations* (Princeton, N.J.: Van Nostrand, 1964). Harold Lasswell calls this phenomenon a developmental construct.
53. United Nations, *Basic Facts about the United Nations* (United Nations Department of Public Information, 2000), 70..
54. Raimo Väyrynen, "Towards Effective Conflict Prevention: A Comparison of Different Instruments," *The International Journal of Peace Studies* 2, no.1 (1997).
55. United Nations, *Basic Facts about the United Nations* (United Nations Department of Public Information, 2000), 70.

NOTES TO CHAPTER 5

1. Alexander DeConde, Richard Dean Burns, and Louise Bilebof Ketz, *Encyclopedia of American Foreign Policy Vol. 2, E-N*, Encyclopedia of American Foreign Policy (New York, N.Y., [etc.]: Scribner, 2002), 39.
2. Ibid; *see also* Christopher C. Joyner, *International Law in the 21st Century: Rules for Global Governance* (Lanham, Md: Rowman & Littlefield, 2005); Margaret P. Doxey, *International Sanctions in Contemporary Perspective* (New York: Macmillan, 1996); Gary Clyde Hufbauer, Jeffrey J. Schott, and Kimberly Ann Elliott, *Economic Sanctions Reconsidered* (Washington, DC: Institute for International Economics, 1990); Daniel W. Drezner, *The Sanctions Paradox: Economic Statecraft and International Relations* (Cambridge [England]: Cambridge University Press, 1999); David A. Baldwin, "The Sanctions Debate and the Logic of Choice," *International Security* 24, no. 3 (1999).
3. Gary C. Hufbauer, "Economic Sanctions: America's Folly," in *Economic Casualties: How U.S. Foreign Policy Undermines Trade, Growth, and Liberty*, Solveig Singleton and Daniel T. Griswold (Washington, D.C.: Cato Institute, 1999), 91–92.
4. Kenneth W. Abbott, "Toward a Richer Institutionalism for International Law and Policy," *Journal of International Law and International Relations* 9, no. 1–2 (2005): 12.
5. Edward Mcwhinney, *United Nations Law Making: Cultural and Ideological Relativism and International Law Making for an Era of Transition* (New York: Holmes & Meier Pub, Inc., 1984): 9.

6. Ibid.
7. Oscar Schachter, "United Nations Law," *American Journal of International Law* 88, no. 1 (1994): note 2.
8. Roger Fisher, *Points of Choice*, International Crisis and the Role of the Law (Oxford: Oxford University Press, 1978): 22–37.
9. Ibid.
10. Peter A.G. van Bergeijk, and Charles van Marrewijk, "Why Do Sanctions Need Time to Work? Adjustment, Learning and Anticipation," *Economic Modeling* 12, no. 2 (1995): 75–86.
11. Gary Clyde Hufbauer, Jeffrey J. Schott, and Kimberly Ann Elliott, *Economic Sanctions Reconsidered: Supplemental Case Histories* (Washington, D.C.: Institute for International Economics, 1990).
12. Vik Kanwar, "Two Crisis of Confidence: Security Non-Proliferation and the Rule of Law Through Security Council Resolutions," *Ohio Northern University Law Review* 35, no. 1 (2009): 213.
13. Asif Efrat, "*A Theory of Internationally Regulated Goods*," Fordham International Law Journal 32, no. 5 (2009).
14. Jonathan Schell, *The Seventh Decade: The New Shape of Nuclear Danger* (New York: Metropolitan Books, 2007): 95–100; Stockholm International Peace Research Institute, *SIPRI Yearbook 2007: Armaments, Disarmament and International Security* (Oxford: Oxford University Press, 2007).
15. Georges Abi-Saab, *The United Nations Operation in the Congo, 1960–1964*, (Oxford: Oxford University Press, 1978), 198.
16. Gary C. Hufbauer, Jeffrey J. Schott, Kimberly Ann Elliott, *Economic Sanctions Reconsidered: History and Current Policy* (Washington, D.C.: Institute for International Economics, 1990), 98–9.
17. Ibid., 100.
18. Margaret P. Doxey, *Economic Sanctions and International Enforcement* (London: Macmillan for the Royal Institute of International Affairs, 1980), 106.
19. Security Council, Letter Dated 27 May 1992 from the Minister For Foreign Affairs of Bosnia and Herzegovina Addressed to the President of the Security Council, U.N. Doc. S/24024 (May 27, 1992) (letter dated 27 May 1992, Haris Silajdzic).
20. Security Council, Letter Dated 22 June 1992 From the Minister for Foreign Affairs of the Republic of Bosnia and Herzegovina addressed to the President of the Security Council, U.N. Doc. S/24137 (June 22, 1992).
21. General Assembly, 46th Sess. Review of the Implementation of the Declaration of the Strengthening of International Security, U.N. Doc. A/46/936, S/24074 (June 6, 1992).
22. Secretary General, Identical Letters Dated 6 June 1992 From the President of the Presidency of Bosnia-Herzegovina Addressed Respectively to the Secretary General and the President of the Security Council, U.N. Doc. S/24081 (June 10, 1992).
23. John Norris, "Getting It Right: What the United States Can Do To Prevent Genocide and Crimes Against Humanity in the Twenty-First Century," *Yale Law & Policy Review* 27, no. 2 (2009).
24. Robert L. Rothstein, *Planning, Prediction, and Policymaking in Foreign Affairs; Theory and Practice* (Boston: Little, Brown, 1972); Orville G. Brim, Jr., *Personality and Decision Process*, Studies in the Psychology of Thinking (Stanford, Calif.: Stanford University Press, 1962).
25. "Mugabe's Peers Guilty," *Daily Mail*, June 26, 2008 (for a summary of Robert Mugabe's political election and civil war in Congo); "DR Congo: President Brutally Represses Opposition," *News Press*, November 26, 2008;

Charles Onyango-Obbo, "Will Election Cap a Dismal Year for Africa, or Show The Way?" *East African,* December 25, 2007.

26. S.C.O.R., Security Council Resolutions, U.N. Doc. S/RES/1493 (July 28, 2003).
27. Report from Yoweri Kaguta Museveni, President of Uganda, S/2005/770, 26 Jan 2006, letter was dated 7 December 2005, Distributed on 26 Jan 2006 in regards to Ugandan observations of November 4–11, 2005.
28. Ibid., 12.
29. U.N. Security Council, 6625th Meting. "Resolution 1896 (2009) [On previous topic]" (S/RES/1896). November 30, 2009.
30. U.N. Security Council, 6432nd Meeting, "Resolution 1952 (2010) [on extension of measures on arms, transport, financial and travel against the Democratic Republic of the Congo imposed by resolution 1807 (2008) and expansion of the mandate of the Committee established pursuant to resolution 1533 (2004)]" (S/RES/1952), November 29, 2010.
31. U.N. Security Council, 5861st Meeting. "Resolution 1807 (2008) [on renewal of measures on arms embargo against all non-governmental entities and individuals operating in the Democratic Republic of the Congo]" (S/RES/1807) March 31, 2008.
32. U.N. Security Council Committee Established Pursuant to Resolution 1533 (2004) Concerning the Democratic Republic of Congo. (S/AC.42/2012/NOTE26) November 27, 2012.
33. Paul Conlon, *United Nations Sanctions Management: A Case Study of the Iraq Sanctions Committee, 1990–1994* (Ardsley, N.Y.: Transnational Publishers, 2000).
34. Peter A.G. van Bergeijk and Charles van Marrewijk, "Why Do Sanctions Need Time to Work? Adjustment, Learning and Anticipation," *Economic Modeling* 12, no. 2 (1995): 75–86.
35. Ibid.
36. Paul A. Volcker, Richard J. Goldstone, and Mark Pieth, *The Management of the United Nations Oil-For-Food Programme* (Independent Inquiry Committee into The United Nations Oil-For-Food Programme, 2004), http://www.iic-offp.org/documents/Sept05/Mgmt_V1.pdf.
37. Ibid.
38. *Karim v. AWB Ltd.* 2008 WL 4450265, 1 (S.D.N.Y.) (S.D.N.Y., 2008).
39. David Malone, *The UN Security Council: From the Cold War to the 21st Century* (Boulder: Lynne Rienner Publishers, 2004): 167.
40. David Cortright, George A. Lopez, and Linda Gerber, *Sanctions and the Search for Security: Challenges to UN Action.* (Boulder: Lynne Rienner Publishers, 2002): 136–8.
41. Peter A.G. van Bergeijk, and Charles van Marrewijk, "Why Do Sanctions Need Time to Work? Adjustment, Learning and Anticipation," *Economic Modeling* 12, no. 2 (1995): 76.
42. Fiona McGillivray, Allan C. Stam, "Political Institutions, Coercive Diplomacy, and the Duration of Economic Sanctions," *Journal of Conflict Resolution* 48, no. 2 (2004): 154–172.
43. Ibid.
44. Christopher C. Joyner, "United Nations Sanctions After Iraq: Looking Back to See Ahead," *Chicago Journal of International Law* 4 (2003): 344–345; *see also* Christopher C. Joyner, *International Law in the 21st Century: Rules for Global Governance* (Lanham, Md.: Rowman & Littlefield, 2005).
45. Ibid., United Nations Sanctions After Iraq.
46. McGillivray and Stam, "Political Institutions, Coercive Diplomacy, and the Duration of Economic Sanctions," 155.

47. Laurence Boisson de Chazournes, "Collective Security & The Economic Interventionism of the UN—The Need for a Coherent and Integrated Approach," *Journal of International Economic Law* 10, no. 1 (2007): 51, 58–59.
48. Anthony Arnove, "Iraq Under Siege: The Deadly Impact of Sanctions and War," *Suffolk Transnational Law Review* 25, (2001): 279.
49. Amira Howeidy, "Death for Oil: An Interview with Dennis Halliday, Ex-UN Secretary-General Heading the UN Humanitarian Mission in Iraq," *Al-Ahram Weekly*, July 19, 2000, Cairo, Egypt.
50. Laurence Boisson de Chazournes, "Collective Security and the Economic Interventionism of the UN: The Need for a Coherent and Integrated Approach." *Journal of International Economic Law* 10, no. 1 (2007): 51–86.
51. "Historical Note on the Security Council's Disputed Right to Ban Supplies of Foodstuffs to a State under Sanction," in Paul Conlon United Nations Sanction Papers, 1991–1995, The University of Iowa Libraries, Iowa City, Iowa.
52. Paul Conlon, "The UN Needs More Than New Leadership," *Swiss Review of World Affairs,* no. 4 (1997) (arguing for UN reform based on emphasis on broad structural conditions).
53. Solomon Major and Anthony J. McGann, "Caught in the Crossfire: 'Innocent Bystanders' As Optimal Targets of Economic Sanctions," *The Journal of Conflict Resolution: a Quarterly for Research Related to War and Peace* 49, no. 3 (2005): 337–59.
54. Ibid., 339.
55. Ibid.
56. Thomas George Weiss, David Cortright, George A. Lopez, and Larry Minear, *Political Gain and Civilian Pain: Humanitarian Impacts of Economic Sanctions* (Lanham, Md.: Rowman & Littlefield, 1997), 78.
57. Sumon Dantiki, "Power Through Process: An Administrative Law Framework for United Nations Legislative Resolutions," *Georgetown Journal of International Law* 40, no. 2: 655–702 citing Kim Lane Scheppele, "Other People's Patriot Acts: Europe's Response to September 11," *Loyola Law Review* 50, no. 1 (2004): 112–3.
58. Ibid.
59. Security Council, Letter Dated 19 June 1992 from the Minister for Foreign Affairs of the Republic of Slovenia Addressed to the Secretary General, U.N. Doc. S/24120 (June 19, 1992).
60. UN Charter, Art. 50 (emphasis added).
61. Laurence Boisson de Chazournes, "Collective Security and The Economic Interventionism of the UN—The Need for a Coherent and Integrated Approach," *Journal of International Economic Law* 10, no. 1 (2007): 51, 59–60.
62. Historical Note on the Issue of Oil Belonging to the Kuwait Petroleum Company in Aden. The letter presented to Mauritius, Seychelles, Zambia, and Zimbabwe to the Committee, October 15, 1990, U.N. Doc. S/AC.25/1990/COMM.50, in 1990 Comms Log 27.
63. Ibid.
64. Ibid citing Djacoba Liva Tehindrazanarivelo, *Les sanctions des Nations unies et leurs effets secondaires: assistance aux victimes et voies juridiques de prévention* (Paris: Presses universitaires de France, 2005): 88; Strategic Planning Unit, Executive Office of the Secretary General, UN Sanctions : How effective ? How Necessary ? (United Nations, New York, March 2009).
65. UN Charter, Article 49.
66. UN Charter, Article 50 (emphasis added).

67. Laurence Boisson de Chazournes, "Collective Security & The Economic Interventionism of the UN—The Need for a Coherent and Integrated Approach," *Journal of International Economic Law* 10, no. 1 (2007): 60.
68. UN Charter, Article 50.
69. Ibid.
70. Laurence Boisson de Chazournes, "Collective Security & The Economic Interventionism of the UN—The Need for a Coherent and Integrated Approach," *Journal of International Economic Law* 10, no. 1 (2007): 51, 58–59; Laurence Boisson de Chazournes, "Collective Security and The Economic Interventionism of the UN—The Need for a Coherent and Integrated Approach," *Journal of International Economic Law* 10, no. 1 (2007): note 33 citing Margaret Doxey, "United Sanctions: Lessons of Experience," in 2nd Interlaken Seminar on Targeting United Nations Financial Sanctions, 29–31 March 1999, Swiss Federal Office for Foreign Economic Affairs, in cooperation with the UN Secretariat, 207–19), http://archive-ouverte.unige.ch/downloader/vital/pdf/tmp/92dcp2bjv5hqhv8inj9ge833i4/out.pdf.
71. Ibid; *see also Implementation of provisions of the Charter related to assistance to third States affected by the application of sanctions*, Report of the Secretary General, A/53/312 fs (27 August 1998).
72. Ibid; Leonard T. Kapungu, *The United Nations and Economic Sanctions against Rhodesia* (Lexington, Mass.: Lexington Books, 1973), 83.
73. Historical Note on Personalities Participating in the Work of the 661 Committee (discussing the poor state of legal affairs despite participation of top international law scholars such as Peter Hohenfellner, Colin Keating, Phillipe Kirsch, Robert Rosenstock, Francis Delon, Helmut Freudenschuss, Anthony Aust, and Martti Koskenniemi).
74. Paul Conlon, "The UN Needs More Than New Leadership," *Swiss Review of World Affairs,* no. 4 (1997).
75. Joseph Klein, "The UN's Gravy Train to Iran," *Front Page Magazine*, June 17, 2008, http://frontpagemag.com/readArticle.aspx?ARTID=31337.
76. Ibid.
77. "Historical Note on the Jan Falk Engineering Case," in Paul Conlon, United Nations Sanction Papers, 1991–1995, The University of Iowa Libraries, Iowa City, Iowa.
78. Ibid.
79. Gary C. Hufbauer, Jeffrey J. Schott, and Kimberly Ann Elliott, *Economic Sanctions Reconsidered: History and Current Policy*, 2nd ed. (Washington, DC: Institute for International Economics, 1990): 118.
80. Margaret P. Doxey, *International Sanctions in Contemporary Perspective,* 107.
81. Ibid; *see also* "N Korea 'Presses South Over Pay,' " BBC News, Last updated June 11, 2009, http://news.bbc.co.uk/2/hi/asia-pacific/8094437.stm.
82. Joseph Klein, "The UN's Gravy Train to Iran," *Front Page Magazine*, June 17, 2008, http://frontpagemag.com/readArticle.aspx?ARTID=31337 (citing Islamic Republic of Iran United Nations Development Assistance Framework (UNDAF) 2005–2009, September 15, 2004); Military Industries in the Islamic Republic of Iran: An Assessment of the Defense Industries Organization (DIO), prepared for the United States Air Force Wright-Patterson AFB, Ohio (May 1996).
83. United Nations Security Council (SC), Letter Dated 5 June 5 1992 from the Representative of the United States of America to the United Nations, Addressed to the Secretary General, U.N. Doc. S/24069, June 5, 1992.

84. United Nations Security Council, Letter from Edward J. Perkins, S.C.O.R, 47th Sess., Report of the Security Council, U.N. Doc. A/47/2 (Supp), January 25, 1994.
85. United Nations, G.A.O.R., 46th Session, Review of the Implementation of the Declaration on the Strengthening of International Security par. 12–15, U.N. Doc. A/46/932, S/24043, May 30, 1992.
86. Jose E. Alvarez, "The Security Council's War On Terrorism: Problems and Policy Options," in Erika De Wet, André Nollkaemper, and Petra Dijkstra, *Review of the Security Council by Member States* (Antwerp: Intersentia, 2003), 142.
87. Ibid.
88. Walter Menta and Kevin Kelley, "Somalia: Eritrea Furious with UN Stance," *Daily Nation*, December 6, 2011, http://www.nation.co.ke/News/politics/Eritrea-furious-with-UN-stance/-/1064/1285022/-/13upwv0z/-/index.html.
89. Paul Conlon, *United Nations Sanctions Management: A Case Study of the Iraq Sanctions Committee, 1990–1994* (Ardsley, N.Y.: Transnational Publishers, 2000): 166.
90. Robin Renwick, *Economic Sanctions* (Cambridge, Mass.: Center for International Affairs, Harvard University, 1981): 16–20; *see also* Robert G.D. Laffan in Veronica Toynbee, *ed. Survey of International Affairs, 1938*. Vol. III. Royal Institute of International Affairs, (Oxford University Press, 1953): 235.
91. Paul Conlon, *United Nations Sanctions Management: A Case Study of the Iraq Sanctions Committee: 1990–1994* (Ardsley, N.Y.: Transnational Publishers, 2000): 168–9.
92. Amira Howeidy, "Death for Oil: An Interview with Dennis Halliday, Ex-UN Secretary-General Heading the UN Humanitarian Mission in Iraq," *Al-Ahram Weekly*, July 19, 2000, Cairo, Egypt.
93. Paul Conlon, *United Nations Sanctions Management: A Case Study of the Iraq Sanctions Committee, 1990–1994* (Ardsley, N.Y.: Transnational Publishers, 2000): 172–175.

NOTES TO CHAPTER 6

1. Thomas W. Lippman, "U.S. Rethinking Economic Sanctions," *Washington Post*, January 26, 1998, A6, quoted in Terry L. Diebel, *Foreign Affairs Strategy: Logic for American Statecraft* (New York: Cambridge University Press, 2007): 264.
2. David A. Baldwin, *Economic Statecraft* (Princeton, N.J.: Princeton University Press, 1985): 130–42.
3. Ibid., 133.
4. David A. Baldwin, *Economic Statecraft* (Princeton, N.J.: Princeton University Press, 1985): 130–138. For a review of the debate, see the classic analysis in David A. Baldwin's *Economic Statecraft*.
5. David R. Francis, "Economic Scene: Sanctions on Iran and Israel could defuse Middle East," *Christian Science Monitor*, August 5, 2009, http://www.csmonitor.com/Business/2009/0805/economic-scene-sanctions-on-iran-and-israel-could-defuse-middle-east.
6. Ibid.
7. Fiona McGillivray and Allan C. Stam, "Political Institutions, Coercive Diplomacy, and the Duration of Economic Sanctions." *The Journal of Conflict Resolution* 48 no. 2 (2004): 154–172.; Jaleh Dashti-Gibson, Patricia Davis,

and Benjamin Radcliff, "On the Determinants of the Success of Economic Sanctions: An Empirical Analysis," *American Journal of Political Science* 608 (1997): 41; Richard N. Haass, ed., *Economic Sanctions and American Diplomacy* (New York: Council on Foreign Relations, Inc., 1998), 1–12; Elizabeth Sara Rogers, "The Influence of Domestic Politics on United States Foreign Policy: Towards a Theory of Social Interests and Economic Sanctions Use," (PhD diss., Duke University, 1992).

8. Fiona McGillivray and Allan C. Stam, "Political Institutions, Coercive Diplomacy, and the Duration of Economic Sanctions." *The Journal of Conflict Resolution* 48 no. 2 (2004): 157.
9. Ibid.
10. David E. Sanger, Eric Schmitt, and Thom Shanker. "White House is Struggling to Measure Success in Afghanistan," *New York Times*, August 7, 2009, A4.
11. Peter A.G. van Bergeijk and Charles van Marrewijk, "Why Do Sanctions Need Time to Work? Adjustment, Learning and Anticipation," *Economic Modelling* 12, no. 2 (1995): 75.
12. Ibid.
13. The author is referring to the conflict between the Assad regime and the rebel groups in Syria that led to a large number of casualties during 2011–2012 and continues.
14. David A. Baldwin. "The Sanctions Debate and the Logic of Choice." *International Security* 24 (2000): 80–107.
15. Ibid.
16. Baldwin, "The Sanctions Debate," 87
17. J.P. Hayes, *Economic Effects of Sanctions on Southern Africa*, Thames Essay No. 53 (Aldershot, Hampshire, England: Gower, 1987): 2.
18. Ibid.
19. Hayes, *Economic Effects of Sanctions*, 8note 6, quoting Bull Hedley, "Economic Sanctions and Foreign Policy," *The World Economy* 7, no. 2 (1984): 218–222.
20. Gary C. Hufbauer, Jeffrey J. Schott, and Kimberly Ann Elliott, *Economic Sanctions Reconsidered: History and Current Policy*, 2nd ed., (Washington, DC: Institute for International Economics, 1990).
21. Hufbauer, Schott, and Elliott, *Economic Sanctions Reconsidered*, 92–93; Hufbauer, *et al.*, *Economic Sanctions Reconsidered*, 3rd ed. (Washington, D.C.: Institute for International Economics, 2007).
22. Ibid., 125.
23. Ibid., 125.
24. Robert P. O'Quinn, *A User's Guide to Economic Sanctions* (The Heritage Foundation, 1997), http://www.heritage.org/research/NationalSecurity/BG1126.cfm#2#2.
25. Ibid.
26. Ibid.
27. Ioana M. Petrescu, *Rethinking Economic Sanction Success: Sanctions as Deterrents* (Washington, DC: American Enterprise Institute, 2008), 6, http://www.aei.org/files/1969/12/31/111009sanctions.pdf.
28. T. Clifton Morgan and Valeria L. Schwebach. "Fools Suffer Gladly: The Use of Economic Sanctions in International Crises," *International Studies Quarterly* 41, no. 1 (1997), 42 (emphasis added).
29. Robert A. Pape, "Why Economic Sanctions Do Not Work," *International Security* 22, no. 2 (1997): 90–136.
30. Paul Conlon, *United Nations Sanctions Management: A Case Study of the Iraq Sanctions Committee, 1990–1994* (Ardsley, N.Y.: Transnational Publishers, 2000), 165.

31. Orde F. Kittrie, "Averting Catastrophe: Why the Nuclear Nonproliferation Treaty is Losing Its Deterrence Capacity and How to Restore It," *Michigan Journal of International Law* 28, no. 2 (2007): 337–400.
32. Peter Wallensteen, ed., *International Sanctions: Theory and Practice*, (Uppsala, Sweden: Department of Peace and Conflict Research, 1969), 56.
33. Ibid.
34. Robin Renwick, *Economic Sanctions,* (Cambridge, Mass.: Harvard University Center for International Affairs, 1981): 15.
35. E.H. Carr, *The Twenty Years Crisis, 1919–1939: an Introduction to the Study of International Relations*, (London: Macmillan, 1939, revised edition, 1946): 118–9.
36. M.S. Daoudi, and M.S. Dajani, *Economic Diplomacy: Embargo Leverage and World Politics* (Boulder: Westview Press, 1985). There is some correlation between incidents of sanctions and eventual war, but further research must be conducted on this issue.
37. Mark Mazetti, and Eric Schmitt, "U.S. Expands Its Drone War into Somalia," *New York Times*, July 1, 2011.
38. M.S. Daoudi and M.S. Dajani, *Economic Diplomacy: Embargo Leverage and World Politics* (Boulder: Westview Press, 1985).
39. Baldwin, "The Sanctions Debate," 80.
40. Daniel W. Drezner, "Bargaining, Enforcement and Multilateral Sanctions: When is Cooperation Counterproductive?" *International Organization*, 54 (2000): 73–102; Daniel W. Drezner, "On the Balance Between International Law and Democratic Sovereignty," *Chicago Journal of International Law*, 2 (2001): 321.
41. For details of the Iranian 2009 protests see Casey L. Addis, Iran's 2009 Presidential Elections, Congressional Research Service (June 22, 2009).
42. Peter Wallensteen, *A Century of Economic Sanctions: A Field Revisited*, Uppsala Peace Research Papers No. 1, (Uppsala University, Sweden: Department of Peace and Conflict Research, 2000): 5, www.pcr.uu.se/digitalAssets/18/18601_UPRP_No_1.pdf.
43. Baldwin, "The Sanctions Debate," 90.
44. James A. Gardner, *Legal Imperialism: American Lawyers and Foreign Aid in Latin America* (Madison, Wis.: University of Wisconsin Press, 1980); David. Kennedy, *The Dark Sides of Virtue: Reassessing International Humanitarianism (*Princeton, N.J.: Princeton University Press, 2004); Antony Anghie, *Imperialism, Sovereignty, and the Making of International Law* (Cambridge, UK: Cambridge University Press, 2005): 22–9.
45. Rohit Chopra, "Rethinking Globalism and Cultural Identity: Cultural Colonialism in the Global Economy," *University of California Journal of International Law & Policy* 14(2007):104
46. Ibid.
47. Ibid.
48. Antony Anghie,"Colonialism and the Birth of International Institutions: Sovereignty, Economy, and the Mandate System of the League of Nations," *New York University Journal of International Law and Politics* 34, no. 3 (2002): 518.
49. Duncan Kennedy, "Three Waves of Globalization," in eds., David M Trubek and Alvaro Santos, *The New Law and Economic Development: A Critical Appraisal* (Cambridge [u.a.]: Cambridge University Press, 2009).
50. Kennedy, "Three Waves of Globalization"; James A. Gardner, *Legal Imperialism: American Lawyers and Foreign Aid in Latin America* (Madison, Wis.: University of Wisconsin Press, 1980): 90.

51. Margaret Kohn and Keally D. McBride, *Political Theories of Decolonization: Postcolonialism and the Problem of Foundations* (New York: Oxford University Press, 2011), 7.
52. Ibid.
53. Margaret Kohn and Keally D. McBride, *Political Theories of Decolonization: Postcolonialism and the Problem of Foundations* (New York: Oxford University Press, 2011), 8.
54. Ibid., 17.
55. Anghie,"Colonialism and the Birth of International Institutions," 518.
56. Ibid.
57. Ibid.
58. Antony Anghie, *Imperialism, Sovereignty, and the Making of International Law* (Cambridge, UK: Cambridge University Press, 2005), 188.
59. Anghie,"Colonialism and the Birth of International Institutions," 621.
60. Robert H. Jackson, *Quasi-States: Sovereignty, International Relations, and the Third World*, Cambridge Studies in International Relations (Cambridge: Cambridge University Press, 1990); William Reno, *Warlord Politics and African States* (Boulder: Lynne Rienner Publishers, 1998).
61. Foreign Policy, "Failed States: An Eighth Annual Collaboration between Foreign Policy and Fund for Peace," 2012, http://www.foreignpolicy.com/failed_states_index_2012_interactive.
62. Darfur Peace and Accountability, Pub. L. 109–344, Oct. 13, 2006, 120 Stat. 1869.
63. Ronald Segal, *Sanctions against South Africa* (Harmondsworth: Penguin Books, 1964): 250 (Note that what the commission mentions here is the reports of a special committee formed on the policies of apartheid of the government of the Republic of South Africa).
64. Ronald Segal, *Sanctions against South Africa*, 270–1.
65. Muna Ndulo, "United Nations Peacekeeping Operations and Security and Reconstruction" *Akron Law Review* 44, no. 3 (2011): 769–808 (referring to U.N. Secretary General, Implementation of the Recommendations of the Special Committee on Peacekeeping Operations: Rep. of the Secretary General, 75, U.N. Doc. A/62/627 (December 28, 2007).
66. Chaloka Beyani, "Introductory note on the Pact on Security, Stability and Development in the Great Lakes region" [online] (London: LSE Research Online, 2007), Available at: http://eprints.lse.ac.uk/2429.
67. Case Concerning Armed Activities on the Territory of the Congo (New Application: 2002) (Democratic Republic of the Congo v. Rwanda) 2002 I.C.J. 219, 294 (Jul. 10, 2002); Benedict Kingsbury and J.H.H.Weiler, "Studying the Armed Activities Decision," *New York University Journal of International Law and Politics* 40 (2008): 7.
68. Richard Garfield, *The Impact of Economic Sanctions on Health and Wellbeing*, RRN Network Paper (Nov. 1999) *available at:* http://www.reliefweb.int/Library/documents/Networkpaper.pdf
69. Video: Mvemba Phezo Dizolele, Congo's Bloody Coltan, Pulitzer Center for Crisis Reporting, Featured in Foreign Exchange with Fareed Zakaria (Fall 2006).
70. Michael P. Todaro and Stephen C. Smith, *Economic Development* (Harlow [u.a.]: Addison-Wesley, 2004), 727.
71. John Higley and Michael G. Burton, "The Elite Variable in Democratic Transitions and Breakdowns," *American Sociological Review* 54, no. 1 (1989): 17–32.
72. Kenneth Joseph Arrow, Samuel Bowles, and Steven N. Durlauf, *Meritocracy and Economic Inequality* (Princeton, N.J.: Princeton University Press, 2000);

Daron Acemoglu, and James A. Robinson, "Persistence of Power, Elites, and Institutions," *The American Economic Review (Evanston)* 98, no. 1 (2008): 267–93.
73. Joseph Alois Schumpeter and Tom Bottomore, *Capitalism, Socialism and Democracy* (New York: Routledge, 1992), 285.
74. Elise S. Brezis and Peter Temin, "*Elites and Economic Outcome*," in *The New Palgrave Dictionary of Economics*, 2nd ed., Steven N. Durlauf and Lawrence Blume, eds. (Palgrave Macmillan, 2008), 814.
75. An example of this is the result of the recent Iranian elections where there is still debate on whether or not the elected party is the one chosen by the population.
76. *United States of America v. Thomas Jasin*, 280 F.3d 355, 357 (2002).
77. This is a common (although unrealistic) assumption in the relevant literature.
78. James Mayall, "To Sanction or Not to Sanction? Rationality and Realism in South African Politics," *London School of Economics Quarterly* 1, no. 4 (1987): 371–384; James Mayall, *Nationalism and International Society* (Cambridge, U.K.: Cambridge University Press, 1990).
79. Steven Durlauf, and Lawrence Blume, eds., *The New Palgrave Dictionary of Economics*, "Rationality" (2008), 895 (discussing rationality assumption in economics).
80. D. Wade Hands, *Reflection Without Rules: Economic Methodology and Contemporary Science Theory* (Cambridge: Cambridge University Press, 2001), 1–19, 81–82; Joel P. Trachtman, *The Economic Structure of International Law* (Cambridge, Mass.: Harvard University Press, 2008), 10 (discussing rationality in international law).
81. Thomas S. Ulen, "The Future of Law and Economics," in *Legal Orderings and Economic Institutions*, eds., Ugo Pagano, Fabrizio Cafaggi, and Antonio Nicita (London: Routledge, 2007).
82. George Tsebelis, "Are Sanctions Effective?: A Game-Theoretic Analysis," *Journal of Conflict Resolution* 34, no. 1 (1990): 4.
83. Bayesian learning assumes that players update their subjective probabilities in the face of inconsistencies through the use of Bayes rule until consistency is achieved.
84. Peter A.G. van Bergeijk and Charles van Marrewijk, "Why Do Sanctions Need Time to Work? Adjustment, Learning and Anticipation,"*Economic Modelling* 12, no. 2 (1995).
85. Ibid.
86. Herbert Alexander Simon, *Models of Bounded Rationality 3, Empirically Grounded Economic Reason* (Cambridge, Mass.: MIT Press, 1997).
87. Jon Elster and Aanund Hylland, *Foundations of Social Choice Theory* (Cambridge, Mass.: Cambridge University Press, 1989).
88. Joel P. Trachtman, *The Economic Structure of International Law* (Cambridge, Mass: Harvard University Press, 2008), 10 (discussing rationality in international law); Jack L. Goldsmith and Eric A. Posner, *The Limits of International Law* (Oxford: Oxford University Press, 2005), 10.
89. Alan O. Sykes, "International Law," in A. Mitchell Polinsky and Steven Shavell, *Handbook of Law and Economics* (Amsterdam: Elsevier, 2007), 764.
90. Thomas G. Weiss, "Sanctions as a Foreign Policy Tool: Weighing Humanitarian Impulses," *Journal of Peace Research* 36, no. 5 (1999): 499–509.
91. Sidney Verba, "Assumptions of Rationality and Non-Rationality in Models of the International System," *World Politics* 14, no. 1 (1961): 94.
92. Robert L. Rothstein, *Planning, Prediction, and Policymaking in Foreign Affairs* (Boston: Little Brown and Company, 1972): 179 citing Sidney Verba,

"Assumptions of Rationality and Non-Rationality in Models of the International System," *World Politics* 14, no. 1 (1961): 99–105.

93. David A. Baldwin, "The Sanctions Debate and the Logic of Choice," *International Security* 24, no. 3 (1999): 85.
94. C. Lloyd Brown-John, *Multilateral Sanctions in International Law: A Comparative Analysis* (New York: Praeger, 1975): 361.
95. Ibid.
96. Ibid.
97. Dean Lacy and Emerson M. S. Niou, "A Theory of Economic Sanctions and Issue Linkage: The Roles of Preferences, Information, and Threats," *The Journal of Politics*, Volume 66, Issue 01 (2004)
98. Paul Conlon, *United Nations Sanctions Management: A Case Study of the Iraq Sanctions Committee, 1990–1994* (Ardsley, N.Y.: Transnational Publishers, 2000): 78–85.
99. Ibid., 165.
100. David E. Sanger, "U.S. Weighs Iran Sanctions if Talks Are Rejected," *New York Times*, August 2, 2009, http://www.nytimes.com/2009/08/03/world/middleeast/03nuke.html?_r=0.
101. Ibid.

NOTES TO CHAPTER 7

1. Laurence Boisson de Chazournes, "Collective Security & The Economic Interventionism of the UN—The Need for a Coherent and Integrated Approach," *Journal of International Economic Law* 10, no. 1 (2007): 51.
2. Daniel W. Drezner, "The Power of Economics and Public Opinion," *Policy Review*, no. 172 (March 30th, 2012, http://www.hoover.org/publications/policy-review/article/111651.
3. Boisson de Chazournes, "Collective Security," 51.
4. David Malone, *The UN Security Council: From the Cold War to the 21st Century* (Boulder: Lynne Rienner Publishers, 2004), 173.
5. Ibid., 169.
6. Ibid.,173.
7. Damian Paletta and Alessandra Galloni, "Europe, US Spar On Cure for Banks," *Wall Street Journal* (September 23, 2009) *available at* http://online.wsj.com/article/SB125366282157932323.html
8. Lisa Jucca, "No Way to Hide for US Tax Cheats After UBS deal," Reuters (August 12, 2009), *available at* http://www.reuters.com/article/2009/08/12/us-ubs-tax-snapanalysis-sb-idUSTRE57B4AA20090812
9. Orde F. Kittrie, "New Sanctions for a New Century: Treasury's Innovative Use of Financial Sanctions," *University of Pennsylvania Journal of International Law* 30, no. 3 (2009): 789.
10. Laurence Boisson de Chazournes, *Journal of International Economics Law* 10 (2007):62 (*citing* Alec Van Vaerenbergh, *Due Process of Law in the Work of UN Security Council Sanctions Committees*, Master Thesis, GIIS, Geneva, October 2006; Thomas J. Biersteker, and Sue E. Eckert, *Strengthening Targeted Sanctions Through Fair and Clear Procedures White Paper* (Providence, R.I.: Watson Institute for International Studies, Brown University, 2006).
11. Peter A. G. van Bergeijk, *Economic Diplomacy, Trade and Commercial Policy: Positive and Negative Sanctions in a New World Order* (Aldershot: E. Elgar, 1994): 20.

12. Peter Wallensteen, and Carina Staibano, eds., *International Sanctions: Between Words and Wars in the Global System* (London: Frank Cass, 2005): 231–9.
13. One Hundred Sixth Congress of the United States of American, the Second Sessions, *African Growth Opportunity Act*, H.R. 434, May 18, 2000.
14. Edith Wilson, "Timor-Leste: World Bank Sanctions Companies in School Project," World Bank, November 22, 2004, http://web.worldbank.org/WBSITE/EXTERNAL/NEWS/0,,contentMDK:20284963~menuPK:34463~pagePK:64003015~piPK:64003012~theSitePK:4607,00.html
15. "World Bank Sanctions Firm, Its Owner for Fraudulent Practices Under Bank-Financed Projects In Senegal," US Fed News Service, Including US State News, *HighBeam Research,* 2008, http://www.highbeam.com/doc/1P3–1494129071.html.
16. The World Bank Sanctions Committee, Sanctions Committee, http://web.worldbank.org/WBSITE/EXTERNAL/PROJECTS/PROCUREMENT/0,,contentMDK:50002288~pagePK:84271~piPK:84287~theSitePK:84266,00.html.
17. Ignaz Seidl-Hohenveldern, *Corporations in and Under International Law* (Cambridge: Grotius, 1987), 27–51.
18. Aaron Ezekiel, "The Application of International Criminal Law to Resource Exploitation: Ituri, Democratic Republic of the Congo," *Natural Resources Journal.* 47, no. 1 (2007): 225–245.
19. Naomi Cahn, "Beyond Retribution and Impunity: Responding to War Crimes of Sexual Violence," *Stanford Journal of Civil Rights & Civil Liberties* 1 (2005): 223.
20. Per Cramér, "Recent Swedish Experiences with Targeted UN Sanctions: The Erosion of Trust in the Security Council," in *Review of the Security Council by Member States*, eds., Erika de Wet, and Andre Nollenkaemper (Antwerp, Oxford, New York, Intersentia, 2003), 94–8 (these individuals and organizations seated in Sweden were Barakaat International Foundation; Somali Network AB, Abdirisak Aden; Abdi Abdulaziz Ali and Ahmed Yusaf Ali).; for additional factual information and procedural case history before the European Council, *see* Council Regulation (EC) No 467/2001 of March 6, 2001, prohibiting the export of certain goods and services to Afghanistan, strengthening the flight ban and extending the freeze of funds and other financial resources in respect of the Taliban of Afghanistan, and repealing Regulation (EC) No 337/2000, Official Journal L 67, 09/03/2001, p. 1.
21. Per Cramer, "Recent Swedish Experiences of with Targeted UN Sanctions," 94–8.
22. Ibid 91.
23. Ibid 95.
24. United Nations Security Council, Resolution 1452, par. 1(a), U.N. Doc. SC/RES/1452, December 20, 2002, http://www.un.org/ga/search/view_doc.asp?symbol=S/RES/1452%282002%29.
25. Cramer, "Recent Swedish Experience With Targeted UN Sanctions," 96.
26. Erika De Wet, André Nollkaemper, and Petra Dijkstra, *Review of the Security Council by Member States* (Antwerp: Intersentia, 2003), 147–59 (listing cases to 2003).
27. U.S. Department of Treasury, Treasury International Capital (TIC) System, http://www.treas.gov/tic/; Federal Reserve Board, "Understanding U.S. Cross-Border Securities Data," Federal Reserve Bulletin, Last updated February 5, 2009, www.federalreserve.gov/pubs/bulletin/2006/crossbordersecurities/default.htm.

28. Dan Danielsen, "Corporate Power and Global Order," in Anne Orford, *International Law and Its Others* (Cambridge: Cambridge University Press, 2006), 2.
29. Cynthia A. Williams, "Corporate Social Responsibility in an Era of Economic Globalization," *University of California Davis Law Review* 35, (2002): 725–32 ("mobility" of MNCs means they can move operations to more favorable regulatory climates).
30. Official Journal of the European Union, Consolidated Version of the Treaty on European Union, Articles 81–83, December 29, 2006, http://eur-lex.europa.eu/LexUriServ/site/en/oj/2006/ce321/ce32120061229en00010331.pdf. The European Community's competition case law illustrates the threat from monopolies and the EU's efforts to combat corporate abuse. The Microsoft cases before the EC are good examples of this problem.
31. Hastings College of the Law (San Francisco, California, 2001), "18th Annual Symposium: Holding Multinational Corporations Responsible Under International Law," *Hastings International and Comparative Law Review* 24, no. 3 (2001).
32. Barcelona Traction Case (*Belgium v. Spain*), 1970, I.C.J. 3, 63.
33. West Publishing Company, *The Guide to American Law: Everyone's Legal Encyclopedia* (St. Paul, Minn.: West Publishing Company, 1984), 250.
34. OECD Guidelines for Multinational Enterprises (2011), http://www.oecd.org/document/28/0,2340,en_2649_34889_2397532_1_1_1_1,00.html.
35. The OECD issued revised norms in 1979, 1982, 1984, 1991, and 2000.
36. Sub-Commission on the Promotion and Protection of Human Rights, 55th Sess., Agenda Item 4, "Norms on the Responsibilities of Transnational Corporations and other Business Enterprises with regard to Human Rights," U.N. Doc. E/CN.4/Sub.2/2003/12/Rev.2 (2003).
37. Cynthia A. Williams, "Corporate Social Responsibility in an Era of Economic Globalization," 711–2.
38. Menno T. Kamminga, and Saman Zia-Zarifi, *Liability of multinational corporations under international law* (The Hague: Kluwer Law International, 2000); Ignaz Seidl-Hohenveldern, *Corporations in and Under International Law* (Cambridge: Grotius, 1987), 128–45 (examining problems concerning legal personality of corporations under international law).
39. Milton Friedman, "The Social Responsibility of Business Is to Increase Its Profits," *New York Times Magazine*, September 13, 1970.
40. Robert Jellinek, *Russia and the Global Meltdown: Domestic and Foreign Policy Responses to the International Financial Crisis* (Carnegie Moscow Center for International Peace, 2009).
41. The list of scholars, organizations, and NGOs writing for FDI regulation is deep. For a good bibliography, *see* the sources cited in, Paulette L. Stenzel, "Why and How the World Trade Organizations Must Promote Environmental Protection," *Duke Environmental Law and Policy Forum* 13, no. 17 (2002).
42. Vito Tanzi, "Is There a Need for a World Tax Organization?" in *The Economics of Globalization: Policy Perspectives from Public Economics*, eds. Assaf Razin, and Efraim Sadka (New York: Cambridge University Press, 1999).
43. Heikki Patomaki, "Rethinking Global Parliament: Beyond The Indeterminacy of International Law," *Widener Law Review* 13, no. 2 (2007).
44. Sabrina Haake, "U.N. Dues: Default Ruse," *Tulane Journal of International and Comparative Law* 17, no. 1 (2008): 46 (discussing the limited UN funding and the search for alternative sources).

45. Ibid.
46. Adesegun A. Akin-Olugbade, "Legal Aspects of the Cancellation of Sovereign Debt Obligations by Selected Multilateral Financial Institutions," *Banking and Finance Law Review* 23, no. 2 (2008): 289.
47. Alison D. Christians, "Tax Treaties for Investment and Aid to Sub-Saharan Africa: A Case Study," *Brooklyn Law Review* 71, no. 2 (2005): 644.
48. Aaditya Mattoo and Arvind Subramanian, "From Doha to the Next Bretton Woods: A New Multilateral Trade Agenda," *Foreign Affairs* 88, no. 1 (2009): 15–26.
49. David Spencer, "The United Nations: A Forum for Global Tax Issues?" *New Zealand Journal of Taxation and Policy* 12 (2006): 224.
50. There are several campaigns for a uniform Financial Transaction Tax also referred to as The Robin Tax. Over fifty organizations and NGOs support FTT.
51. Department of Economic and Social Affairs, *World Economic and Social Survey 2012: In Search of New Development Finance* (New York: United Nations, 2012).
52. Robin Boadway, "National Taxation, Fiscal Federalism and Global Taxation," in Anthony Barnes Atkinson, *New Sources of Development Finance* (Oxford: Oxford University Press, 2004), 210–6.
53. Andreas Haufler, *Taxation in a Global Economy: Theory and Evidence* (Cambridge: Cambridge University Press, 2008).
54. The commission is named after former Mexican President Ernesto Zedillo.
55. Letter from the Permanent Representative of Canada to the United Nations, to the Secretary General, par. 14, 24, May 26, 1992, U.N. GAOR, 46th Session, U.N. SCOR, 47th year 47, U.N. Doc. S/24011, A/47/929, May 27, 1992. This is a joint UNGA and UNSC letter.
56. United Nations, *Basic Facts about the United Nations* (United Nations Department of Public Information, 2000), 431.
57. John Bolton, Sanctions Hearing Committee.
58. United Nations, GAOR, 18th Session, Resolution 1990, Annexes par. 1, U.N. Doc A/5497, December 17, 1963.

NOTES TO CHAPTER 8

1. *See* Thomas Erdbrink, *Iran's Ahmadinejad to Address U.N. as Pressure Builds for Sanctions: Nation Must Respond to International Concerns*, Washington Post (August 31, 2009), available at http://www.washingtonpost.com/wp-dyn/content/article/2009/08/31/AR2009083102865.html?hpid=topnews.
2. Gary C. Hufbauer, Jeffrey J. Schott, and Kimberly Ann Elliott, *Economic Sanctions Reconsidered: History and Current Policy*, 2nd ed., (Washington, DC: Institute for International Economics, 1990)

Bibliography

BOOKS CONSULTED

Alexander, Kern. *Economic Sanctions: Law and Public Policy*. Basingstoke [England]: Palgrave Macmillan, 2009.

Annan, Kofi A. *The Question of Intervention: Statements by the Secretary-General*. New York: United Nations Dept. of Public Information, 1999.

Askari, Hossein. *Economic Sanctions: Examining Their Philosophy and Efficacy*. Westport, Conn.: Praeger, 2003.

Baderin, Mashood A., and Robert McCorquodale. *Economic, Social and Cultural Rights in Action*. Oxford: Oxford University Press, 2007.

Brown, Preston. *The Kuwait/Iraq Sanctions: U.S. Regulations in an International Setting*. New York, N.Y.: Practising Law Institute, 1991.

Brown-John, and C. Lloyd. *Multilateral Sanctions in International Law: A Comparative Analysis*. New York: Praeger, 1975.

Brownlie, Ian. *International Law at the Fiftieth Anniversary of the United Nations General Course on Public International Law*. Leiden, the Netherlands: Martinus Nijhoff, 1995. http://nijhoffonline.nl/book?id=er255_er255_009–228.

Butler, William E. *International Law in Comparative Perspective*. Alphen aan den Rijn [etc.]: Sijthoff & Noordhoff, 1980.

Cafaggi, Fabrizio, Nicita, Antonio, and Pagano, Ugo. *Legal Ordering and Economic Institutions*. New York: Routledge, 2007.

Calabresi, Guido. *Ideals, Beliefs, Attitudes, and the Law: Private Law Perspectives on a Public Law Problem*. Syracuse, N.Y.: Syracuse University Press, 1985.

Campbell, Barry R., and Newcomb, Danforth, eds. *The Impact of the Freeze of Kuwaiti and Iraqi Assets on Financial Institutions and Financial Transactions*. Dordrecht: Graham & Trotman/Division of Kluwer/International Bar Association, 1990.

Conlon, Paul. *United Nations Sanctions Management: A Case Study of the Iraq Sanctions Committee, 1990–1994*. Ardsley, N.Y.: Transnational Publishers, 2000.

Cortright, David, and Lopez, George A. *Sanctions and the Search for Security: Challenges to UN Action*. Boulder: Lynne Rienner, 2002.

Crasse, Antonio, ed. *Current Problems of International Law*. Pisa, Italy: University of Pisa, 1975.

Dahl, Robert A. *Modern Political Analysis*. Englewood Cliffs, N.J.: Prentice-Hall, 1963.

Deibel, Terry L. *Foreign Affairs Strategy: Logic for American Statecraft*. New York: Cambridge University Press, 2007.

Doxey, Margaret P. *Economic Sanctions and International Enforcement*. New York: Published for the Royal Institute of International Affairs [by] Oxford University Press, 1980.

Doxey, Margaret P. *International Sanctions in Contemporary Perspective*. New York: Macmillan, 1996.

Drezner, Daniel W. *The Sanctions Paradox: Economic Statecraft and International Relations*. Cambridge [England]: Cambridge University Press, 1999.

Farrall, Jeremy Matam. *United Nations Sanctions and the Rule of Law*. Cambridge: Cambridge University Press, 2007.

Ferencz, Benjamin B. *Enforcing International Law: A Way To World Peace*. New York: Oceana, 1983.

Ferencz, Benjamin B. *New Legal Foundations For Global Survival: Security Through the Security Council*. New York: Oceana, 1994.

Forlati, Laura, and Linos-Alexandre Sicilianos. *Les sanctions e´conomiques en droit international*. Leiden: Martinus Nijhoff, 2004.

Franck, Thomas M. *The Power of Legitimacy among Nations*. New York: Oxford University Press, 1990.

Galgano, Salvatore. Legislazione internazionale: leggi, decreti, progetti di legge ...=International legislation . . . =Le´gislation internationale . . . =Internationale Gesetzgebung. Roma: Edizione dell'Istituto di studi legislativi, 1932.

Goubran, Codsi. *Le proble`me des sanctions dans l'e´volution de l'arbitrage international*. Paris: E. Sagot, 1923.

Gowlland-Debbas, Vera, and Djacoba Liva Tehindrazanarivelo. *National Implementation of United Nations Sanctions: A Comparative Study*. Leiden: M. Nijhoff Publishers, 2004.

Gowlland-Debbas, Vera, Mariano Garcia Rubio, and Hassiba Hadj-Sahraoui. *United Nations Sanctions and International Law*. The Hague: Kluwer Law International, 2001.

Haass, Ernst B. *When Knowledge is Power: Three Models of Change in International Organizations*. Berkeley: University of California Press, 1990.

Haass, Richard. *Economic Sanctions and American Diplomacy*. New York: Council on Foreign Relations, 1998.

Harrison, Jeffrey L. *Law and Economics in a Nutshell*. St. Paul, Minn.: West Group, 2000.

Hathaway, Oona Anne, and Harold Hongju Koh. *Foundations of International Law and Politics*. New York, N.Y.: Foundation Press, 2005.

Herczegh, Ge´za. *Development of International Humanitarian Law*. Budapest: Akade´miai Kiado´, 1984.

Hilaire, Max. *United Nations Law and the Security Council*. Aldershot, Hants, England: Ashgate, 2005.

Hufbauer, Gary C. *Economic Sanctions Reconsidered*. Washington, DC: Peterson Institute for International Economics, 1990.

Joyner, Christopher C. *International Law in the 21st Century: Rules for Global Governance*. Lanham, Md: Rowman & Littlefield, 2005.

Kelsen, Hans. *General Theory of Law and State*. Cambridge, Mass: Harvard University Press, 1945.

Kennedy, David. *International Legal Structure*. Baden-Baden: Nomos, 1987.

Klein, Erwin. *Economic Theories and Their Relational Structures*. New York: St. Martin's Press, 1998).

Kuyper, Pieter Jan. *The Implementation of International Sanctions: The Netherlands and Rhodesia*. Alphen aan den Rijn: Sijthoff & Noordhoff International Publishers, 1978.

Legrand, Pierre, and R.J.C. Munday. *Comparative Legal Studies: Traditions and Transitions*. Cambridge, U.K: Cambridge University Press, 2003.

Losman, Donald L. *International Economic Sanctions*. Albuquerque: University of New Mexico Press, 1979.

Mattei, Ugo. *Comparative Law and Economics*. Ann Arbor: University of Michigan Press, 1997.

Mercuro, Nicholas. *Law and Economics*. Boston: Kluwer Academic, 1989.

Milhaupt, Curtis J., ed. *Global Markets, Domestic Institutions: Corporate Law and Governance in a New Era of Cross-Border Deals*. New York: Columbia University Press, 2003.

Mill, John Stuart, and Jonathan Riley. *Principles of Political Economy and Chapters on Socialism*. Oxford [etc.]: Oxford University Press, 1994.

Pheby, John. *Methodology and Economics: A Critical Introduction*. London [etc.]: Macmillan press, 1988.

Posner, Richard A. *Overcoming Law*. Cambridge, Mass.: Harvard University Press, 1995.

Ratner, Steven R., and Anne-Marie Slaughter. *The Methods of International Law*. Washington, D.C.: American Society of International Law, 2004.

Reisman, W. Michael. *Law in Brief Encounters*. New Haven: Yale University Press, 1999.

Royal Institute of International Affairs. *International Sanctions; A Report by a Group of Members of the Royal Institute of International Affairs*. London: Oxford University Press, 1938.

Ruzié, David. *Organisations internationales et Sanctions Internationales*. Paris: Librairie Armand Colin, 1960.

Ruzié, David. *Organisations Internationales et Sanctions Internationales*. Paris: Librairie Armand Colin Paris, 1971.

Sands, Philippe, Pierre Klein, and D. W. Bowett. *Bowett's Law of International Institutions*. London: Sweet & Maxwell, 2001.

Segal Ronald, ed., International Conference on Economic Sanctions against South Africa, and Ronald Segal. *Sanctions against South Africa*. Baltimore: Penguin Books, 1964.

Schachter, Oscar. *International Law in Theory and Practice*. Dordrecht, The Netherlands: M. Nijhoff Publishers, 1991.

Simons, G.L. *The Scourging of Iraq Sanctions, Law, and Natural Justice*. New York: St. Martin's Press, 1998.

Stewart, Ian M.T. *Reasoning and Method in Economics: An Introduction to Economic Methodology*. London: McGraw-Hill Book Co, 1979.

Stowell, Ellery C. Intervention in International Law. Washington: John Byrne, 1921.

Tesón, Fernando R. *Humanitarian Intervention: An Inquiry into Law and Morality*. Ardsley, N.Y.: Transnational Publishers, 2005.

Thomas, A.J., and Joseph Jude Norton. *Public International Law and the Future World Order: Liber Amicorum in Honor of A.J. Thomas, Jr.* Littleton, Colo.: F.B. Rothman, 1987.

Trubek, David M., and Santos, Alvaro, eds. *The New Law and Economic Development: A Critical Appraisal*. New York: Cambridge University Press, 2006.

Tsagourias, Nikolaos K. *Jurisprudence of International Law: The Humanitarian Dimension*. Manchester: Manchester University Press, 2000.

Василенко В.А., Международно-Правовые Санкции (Киев: Вища школа, 1982) [*transl.*, V.A. Vasilenko, *Sanctions Under International Law* (Kiev: Higher School 1982)]

Wallensteen, Peter, and Carina Staibano. *International Sanctions: Between Words and Wars in the Global System*. London: Frank Cass, 2005.

Wallensteen, Peter. *International Sanctions: Theory and Practice: Proceedings of the Nordic Conference on Sanction Research,* Sigtuna, Sweden, April 27–28, 1968. 1969.

Weiss, Thomas G. *Political Gain and Civilian Pain: Humanitarian Impacts of Economic Sanctions*. Lanham, Md.: Rowman & Littlefield, 1997.

Williamson, Roger. *Some Corner of a Foreign Field: Intervention and World Order*. Basingstoke [u.a.]: Macmillan [u.a.], 1998.

Yamamura, Kozo. *A Vision of a New Liberalism?: Critical Essays on Murakami's Anticlassical Analysis*. Stanford, Calif: Stanford University Press, 1997.

SANCTIONS IMPLEMENTATION

Cioffi-Revilla, Claudio A. *Formal International Relations Theory: An Inventory, Review, and Integration*. Thesis—State University of New York at Buffalo, 1978.

Daoudi, M.S., and M.S. Dajani. *Economic Sanctions, Ideals and Experience*. London: Routledge & Kegan Paul, 1983.

Doxey, Margaret P. *Economic Sanctions and International Enforcement*. London: published for the Royal Institute of International Affairs, by Oxford University Press, 1971.

Doxey, Margaret P. *International Sanctions in Contemporary Perspective*. New York: St. Martin's Press, 1987.

Fisher, Roger. *Points of Choice*. Oxford: Oxford University Press, 1978.

Harrison, Horace V. *The Role of Theory in International Relations*. Princeton, N.J. [u.a.]: Van Nostrand, 1964.

Renwick, Robin. *Economic Sanctions*. Cambridge, Mass: Center for International Affairs, Harvard University, 1981.

Rothstein, Robert L. *Planning, Prediction, and Policymaking in Foreign Affairs; Theory and Practice*. Boston: Little, Brown, 1972.

Wright, Philip Quincy. *The Enforcement of International Law Through Municipal Law in the United States*. New York: Johnson reprint corporation, 1967.

THE UN AND PEACEKEEPING

Baldwin, David A. *Economic Statecraft*. Princeton, N.J.: Princeton University Press, 1985.

Clark, Grenville, Elisabeth Mann Borgese, Louis B. Sohn, Elisabeth Mann Borgese, and Elisabeth Mann Borgese. *Introduction to World Peace Through World Law*. Chicago, Illinois: World without War Publications, 1973.

Dorsey, Gray L. *Beyond the United Nations: Changing Discourse in International Politics and Law*. Lanham, Maryland: University Press of America, 1986.

Kasme, Badr. *La capacite´ de l'Organisation des Nations Unies de conclure des traite´s*. Paris: Librairie ge´ne´rale de droit et de jurisprudence, 1960.

Kelsen, Hans, and Hans Kelsen. *The Law of the United Nations: A Critical Analysis of Its Fundamental Problems: with Supplement*. New York: F.A. Praeger, 1951.

Matheson, Michael John. *Council Unbound: The Growth of UN Decision Making on Conflict and Postconflict Issues After the Cold War*. Washington, D.C.: United States Institute of Peace Press, 2006.

McWhinney, Edward. *United Nations Law Making: Cultural and Ideological Relativism and International Law Making for a Era of Transition*. New York: Holmes & Meier, 1984.

Rikhye, Indar Jit, and Kjell Skjelsbaek. *The United Nations and Peacekeeping: Results, Limitations, and Prospects: the Lessons of 40 Years of Experience*. New York: St. Martin's Press, 1991.

Rikhye, Indar Jit. *The Theory & Practice of Peacekeeping*. New York: Published for the International Peace Academy by St. Martin's Press, 1984.

Schachter, Oscar, and Christopher C. Joyner. *United Nations Legal Order*. Cambridge: Cambridge University Press, 1995.

Vincent, Jack E. *Testing Some Hypotheses About Delegate Attitudes at the United Nations and Some Implications for Theory Building*. University of Hawaii, 1971.

Vincent, Jack Ernest. *Testing Some Hypotheses About Delegate Attitudes at the United Nations and Some Implications for Theory Building*. Honolulu: University of Hawaii, Department of Political Science, 1971.

Wiltse, Charles M. *Thomas Jefferson; A Study in the Philosophy of the State*. Ithaca, New York: Cornell University Press, 1932.

Wolfrum, Rüdiger, and Volker Röben. *Legitimacy in International Law*. Berlin: Springer, 2008.

SECURITY COUNCIL

Bailey, Sydney D. *The Procedure of the UN Security Council*. Oxford: Clarendon, 1975.

Bailey, Sydney D., and Sam Daws. *The Procedure of the UN Security Council*. Oxford: Clarendon Press, 1998.

Blokker, Niels, and Nico Schrijver. *The Security Council and the Use of Force: Theory and Reality—a Need for Change?* Leiden: Martinus Nijhoff Publishers, 2005.

De Wet, Erika. *The Chapter VII Powers of the United Nations Security Council*. Portland: Hart Publishing, 2004.

Hiscocks, Richard. *The Security Council: A Study in Adolescence*. New York: Free Press, 1973.

Malone, David. *The UN Security Council: From the Cold War to the 21st Century*. Boulder, Colo.: Lynne Rienner, 2004.

Nicholas, H.G. *The United Nations as a Political* Institution. N.Y.: Oxford University Press, 1965.

Österdahl, Inger. *Threat to the Peace: The Interpretation by the Security Council of Article 39 of the UN Charter*. Uppsala: Iustus Förlag, 1998.

Schweigman, David. *The Authority of the Security Council Under Chapter VII of the UN Charter Legal Limits and the Role of the International Court of Justice*. The Hague: Kluwer Law International, 2001.

Yemin, Edward. Legislative Powers in the United Nations and Specialized Agencies. Leyden: A.W. Sijthoff, 1969.

ARTICLES

Abbott, Daniel W. "The United Nations and Intrastate Conflict: A Legislative History of the United Nations Charter," *U.C. Davis JournalofInternational Law and Policy* 275, no. 8 (2002)

Abbott, Kenneth W. "International Relations Theory, International Law, and the Regime Governing Atrocities in Internal Conflicts." *American Journal of International Law* 93, no. 2 (1999): 361–378.

Abbott, Kenneth W. "Modern International Relations Theory: A Prospectus for International Lawyers," *Yale Journal of International Law* 14, no. 2 (1989): 335–411.

Abbott, Kenneth W., and Duncan Snidal. "Why States Act Through Formal International Organizations." *Journal of Conflict Resolution* 42, no. 1 (1998): 3–32.

Akin-Olugbade, Adesegun A. “Legal Aspects of the Cancellation of Sovereign Debt Obligations by Selected Multilateral Financial Institutions.” *Banking and Finance Law Review*, 23, no. 2 (2008): 275–92.

August, Reinisch 2001. “Note and Comment: Developing Human Rights and Humanitarian Law Accountability of the Security Council for the Imposition of Economic Sanctions.” *The American Society of International Law, American Journal of International Law* 851, no. 92 (2001)

Baldwin, David. “The Sanctions Debate and the Logic of Choice.” *International Security* 24, no. 3 (1999): 80–107.

Belendro, Natasha “Defining Armed Conflict”, 29 Cardozo Law Review 2461, no. 29 (2008)

Benforado, Adam Jon Hanson, “The Costs of Dispositionism: The Premature Demise of Situationist Law and Economics”, *Maryland Law Review* 24, no.64 (2005)

Blum, Yehuda Z. “Proposals for UN Security Council Reform.” *American Journal of International Law* 99, no. 3(2005): 632–49.

Boon, Kristen E. “Coining a New Jurisdiction: The Security Council as Economic Peacekeeper.” *Vanderbilt Journal of Transnational Law* 41, no. 4 (2008): 991–1042.

Bourantonis, Dimitris. “Reform of the UN Security Council and the Non-Aligned States.” *International Peacekeeping London* 5, no. 1 (1998): 89–109.

Brand, Oliver. “Conceptual Comparisons: Towards a Coherent Methodology of Comparative Legal Studies.” *Brooklyn Journal of International Law* 32, no. 2(2007): 405–66.

Christians, Alison D. “Tax Treaties for Investment and Aid to Sub-Saharan Africa: A Case Study.” *Brooklyn Law Review* 71, no. 2 (2005): 639–713.

Crook, John R. “International Economic Law: United States Imposes New Economic Sanctions on Several Countries.” *American Journal of International Law* 174, no.102 (2008)

Dantiki, Sumon. “Power through Process: An Administrative Law Framework for United Nations Legislative Resolutions.” *Georgetown Journal of International Law* 40, no. 2 (2009): 655–702.

de Chazournes, Laurence Boisson. “Collective Security and the Economic Interventionism of the UN: The Need for a Coherent and Integrated Approach.” *Journal of International Economic Law* 10, no. 1 (2007): 51–86.

Drezner, Daniel W. On the Balance Between International Law and Democratic Sovereignty, *Chicago Journal of International Law 321,* no.2, (2001)

Fausey, Joy K. “Does the United Nations’ Use of Collective Sanctions to Protect Human Rights Violate its own Human Rights Standards?” *Connecticut Journal of International Law* 10, no.1 (1994): 193–218.

Haake, Sabrina, “U.N. Dues: Default Ruse.” *Tulane Journal of International and Comparative Law* 39, no. 17 (2008)

Higley, John, and Michael G. Burton. “The Elite Variable in Democratic Transitions and Breakdowns.” *American Sociological Review* 54, no. 1 (1989): 17–32.

Hufbauer, Gary C., and Barbara Oegg, “Economic Sanctions: Public Goals and Private Compensation.” *Chicago Journal of InternationalLaw*. 305, no. 4 (2003)

Hufbauer, Gary C., and Barbara Oegg. “Targeted Sanctions: A Policy Alternative?” *Law and Policy in International Business: the International Journal of Georgetown University Law Center* 32, no. 1 (2000): 11–20.

Joyner, Christopher C. “United Nations Sanctions After Iraq: Looking Back to See Ahead.” *Chicago Journal of International Law* 4 (2003): 329–332.

Kaempfer, William H., and Anton D. Lowenberg. “Unilateral Versus Multilateral International Sanctions: A Public Choice Perspective.” *International Studies Quarterly* 43, no. 1 (1999): 37–58.

Kalmthout, Anton M. van. *Sanctions Systems in the Member States of the Council of Europe 1, Deprivation of Liberty, Community Service and Other Substitutes.* Deventer: Kluwer, 1988.

Kingsbury, Benedict., & Weiler, J.H.H. "Studying the Armed Activities Decision." *New York University Journal of International Law and Politics* 40 (2008): 1–12.

Kirshner, Jonathan."The Microfoundations of Economic Sanctions." *Security Studies* 6, no. 3 (1997): 32–64.

Kittrie, Orde F. "Averting Catastrophe: Why the Nuclear Nonproliferation Treaty is Losing Its Deterrence Capacity and How to Restore It." *Michigan Journal of International Law* 28, no.2 (2007): 337–430.

Koskenniemi, Martti *Letter to the Editors of the Symposium, in* Ratner & Slaughter, *eds.*, The Methods of International Law 114 (2004)

LaRae-Perez, Cassandra. "Economic sanctions as a use of force: Reevaluating the legality of sanctions from an effects-based perspective." *Boston University International Law Journal* 20, no. 1 (2002): 161–88.

MacGillivray, Fiona, and Allan C. Stam. "Political Institutions, Coercive Diplomacy, and the Duration of Economic Sanctions." *The Journal of Conflict Resolution: a Quarterly for Research Related to War and Peace* 48, no. 2 (2004): 154–72.

Major, Solomon, and Anthony J. MacGann "Caught in the Crossfire: "Innocent Bystanders" As Optimal Targets of Economic Sanctions." *The Journal of Conflict Resolution: a Quarterly for Research Related to War and Peace* 49, no. 3 (2005): 337–59.

Mattei, Ugo. "Efficiency in legal transplants: An Essay in Comparative Law and Economics." *International Review of Law and Economics* 14, no. 1 (1994): 3–19.

Mattoo, Aaditya, and Arvind Subramanian. "From Doha to the Next Bretton Woods: a New Multilateral Trade Agenda." *Foreign Affairs* 88, no. 1 (2009): (1): 15–26.

Mayall, James. "To Sanction or Not to Sanction? Rationality and Realism in South African Politics." 4 *LSE Quarterly* 371–94 (1987)

McDougal, Myres S. "Some Basic Theoretical Concepts About International Law: A Policy-oriented Framework of Inquiry," *Journal of Conflict Resolution* 4, no. 3 (1960): 337–54.

Morgenthau, Hans J. "Positivism, Functionalism, and International Law." *American Journal of International Law* 34, no. 2 (1940): 260–84.

Nyun, Thihan Myo. "Feeling Good or Doing Good: Inefficacy of the U.S. Unilateral Sanctions Against the Military." *Washington University Global Studies Law Review* 455, no.55 (2008): 458

Patomaki, Heikki. "Rethinking Global Parliament: Beyond the Indeterminacy of International Law." *Widener Law Review* 369, no.13 (2007)

Pickard, Daniel. "When Does Crime Become a Threat to International Peace and Security?" *Florida Journal of International Law* 12, no. 1 (1998): 1–21.

Reeves, Anthony R. "Sexual Identity as a Fundamental Human Right." *Buffalo Human Rights Law Review* 15 (2009): 215.

Reisman, W. Michael. "Institutions and Practices for Restoring and Maintaining Public Order." *Duke Journal of Comparative & International Law* 6, no. 1 (1995): 175–186.

Schachter, Oscar. "United Nations Law." *American Journal of International Law*1, no.88 (1994): 1–23.

Spencer, David. "The U.N.-A Forum for Global Tax Issues?" *The Journal of International Taxation* 17, no. 1 (2006): 42–54.

Stenzel, Paulette L. "Why and How the World Trade Organization Must Promote Environmental Protectio." *Duke Environmental Law and Policy* 1, no 13 (2002)

Swaine, Edward T. "The Constitutionality of International Delegations." *Columbia Law Review* 104, no. 6 (2004): 1492–1614.

Van Bergeijk, P. A. G., and C. Van Marrewijk. "Why Do Sanctions Need Time to Work? Adjustment, Learning and Anticipation." *Economic Modelling* 12, no. 2 (1995): 75–86.

Weiss, Thomas G. "Sanctions as a Foreign Policy Tool: Weighing Humanitarian Impulses." *Journal of Peace Research* 36, no. 5 (1999): 499–510.

Wellens, Karel. "The UN Security Council and New Threats to the Peace: Back to the Future." *Journal of Conflict & Security Law* 8, no. 1 (2003): 15–70.

Williams, Cynthia A. "Corporate Social Responsibility in an Era of Economic Globalization." *University of California Davis Law Review* 35, no. 3 (2002): 705–78.

SELECTED CASES

Military and Paramilitary Activities (*Nicaragua v. U.S.*), 1986 I.C.J. 14 (June 27, 1986).

Nicole v. United Nations Mission in Liberia (2009 WL 2370179, 2 E.D.Pa.).

Emmanuel v. United States, 253 F.3d 755, 756 (1st Cir. 2001).

Belgium v. Spain (1962–1970).

Democratic Republic of the Congo v. Rwanda 2002 I.C.J. 219, 294 (Jul. 10, 2002).

Karim v. AWB Ltd. 2008 WL 4450265, 1 (S.D.N.Y.) (S.D.N.Y., 2008).

UN DOCUMENTS

Declaration on Essentials of Peace, G.A. Res. 290 (IV), at 10, U.N. GAOR, 4th Sess., 261st plen. Mtg., U.N. Doc A/Res/4/290 (Dec. 1, 1949).

U.N. GAOR, 18th Sess., Res. 1990, Annexes ¶1, U.N. Doc A/5497 (Dec. 17, 1963).

S.C.O.R., The *Situation between Iraq and Kuwait: Report of the Secretary General on the implementation of Paragraph 5 of Security Council Resolution 687* (1991), U.N. Doc. S/22454 (April 3, 1991).

Letter from the Permanent Representative of Canada to the United Nations, to the Secretary General, ¶ 14, 24 (May 26, 1992).

U.N. GAOR, 46th Sess., U.N. SCOR, 47th yr. 47, U.N. Doc. S/24011, A/47/929 (May 27, 1992).

General Assembly, 46th Sess. *Review of the Implementation of the Declaration of the Strengthening of International Security*, U.N. Doc. A/46/936, S/24074 (June 6, 1992).

Security Council, *Letter Dated 19 June 1992 from the Minister for Foreign Affairs of the Republic of Slovenia Addressed to the Secretary General*, U.N. Doc. S/24120 (June 19, 1992).

Security Council, *Letter Dated 22 June 1992 From the Minister for Foreign Affairs of the Republic of Bosnia and Herzegovina addressed to the President of the Security Council*, U.N. Doc. S/24137 (June 22, 1992).

Implementation of provisions of the Charter related to assistance to third States affected by the application of sanctions, Report of the Secretary General, A/53/312 fs (27 August 1998).

Report of the Sub-Commission on the Promotion and Protection of Human Rights; The Adverse Consequences of Economic Sanctions on the Enjoyment of Human Rights, U.N. Doc. E/CN.41/Sub.2/2000/33, at 19–20 (1999).

S.C. Res. 1452, ¶ 1(a), U.N. Doc. SC/RES/1452 (Dec. 20, 2002).

S.C.O.R., Security Council Resolutions, U.N. Doc. S/RES/1493 (July 28, 2003).

U.N. Doc. E/CN.4/Sub.2/2003/12/Rev.2 (2003).

A More Secure World: Our Shared Responsibility, Report of the High-Level Panel on Threats, Challenges and Change, UN Doc. A/59/565, at 8 (2004).

Report from Yoweri Kaguta Museveni President of Uganda, S/2005/770 (Jan. 26, 2006), letter was dated December 7, 2005, Distributed on 26 January 2006 in regards to Uganda observations of November 4–11 (2005).

The Secretary General, *Report of the Secretary General follow up to the outcome of the Millennium Summit titles In Larger freedom: towards development, security and human rights for all*, 59th Sess., U.N. Doc. A/59/2005 (Mar. 21, 2005).

The Secretary General, *Report of the Secretary General on the Question of Uganda, delivered to the Security Council and the General Assembly*, U.N. Doc. S/2005/770 (Jan. 26, 2006)

United Nations Population Fund, *Draft Country Programme Document for Somalia (2008–2009)*, U.N. Doc. DP/DCP/SOM/1/Rev.1 (July 2, 2007).

SELECT REPORTS AND OFFICIAL PUBLICATIONS

A More Secure World: Our Shared Responsibility, Report of the High-Level Panel on Threats, Challenges and Change, UN Doc. A/59/565, 8 (2004), *available at*, http://www.un.org/secureworld/report.pdf

Associated Press, *U.S. Upbeat on NKorea Sanctions Enforcement*, NY Times (July 30, 2009), *available at* http://www.nytimes.com/aponline/2009/07/30/world/AP-UN.

Clinton Warns Eritrea Against Meddling in Somalia, CNN International (August 6, 2009), available at http://cnnwire.blogs.cnn.com/2009/08/06/clinton-warns-eritrea-against-meddling-in-somalia/

David E. Sanger, *U.S. Weighs Iran Sanctions if Talks Are Rejected*, NY Times (August 2, 2009), *available at:* http://www.nytimes.com/2009/08/03/world/middleeast/03nuke.html?_r=1&scp=1&sq=sanctions&st=cse.

OECD Guidelines for Multinational Enterprises (2008), *available at*, http://www.oecd.org/document/28/0,2340,en_2649_34889_2397532_1_1_1_1,00.html

Sharon Otterman, *U.S. Opens Way to Ease Sanctions Against Syria*, NY Times (July 28, 2009), *available at* http://www.nytimes.com/2009/07/29/world/middleeast/29syria.html?scp=3&sq=sanctions&st=cse

Shao Jie, *Washington Expected to Shift Policies Toward Sudan*, Xinhua (August 27, 2009), *available at* http://news.xinhuanet.com/english/2009–08/27/content_11955484.htm

Thomas Erdbrink, *Iran's Ahmadinejad to Address U.N. as Pressure Builds for Sanctions: Nation Must Respond to International Concerns* Washington Post (August 31, 2009), available at http://www.washingtonpost.com/wp-dyn/content/article/2009/08/31/AR2009083102865.html?hpid=topnews

United Nations News, *UN-backed Corporate Responsibility Initiiative Reaches Milestone of 100 Schools*, April 7, 2008. http://www.un.org/apps/news/story.asp?NewsID=26229&Cr=global&Cr1=compact

UN Sanctions after Oil-for-food: *Still a Viable Diplomatic Tool? Hearing, Subcommittee on National Security, Emerging Threats, and International Relations of the Committee on Government Reform, House of Representatives* one hundred ninth congress, May 2, 2006, Serial No. 109–75 *available at* http://www.globalpolicy.org/finance/tables/special/finorgan.htm (UN Expenditures)

U.S. Government policies regarding enforcement of sanctions and related penal programs concerning terrorist acts and states supporting terrorist organizations, *available at* http://www.treas.gov/offices/enforcement/ofac/programs/terror/terror.shtml

U.S. Threatens Eritrea With Sanctions, Al Jazeera (July 29, 2009), *available at* http://english.aljazeera.net//news/americas/2009/07/200972917382499232 4.html.

UN News Center, *Secretary-General Ban Ki-moon UN Headquarters, Speech to the Symposium on Enhancing the Implementation of Security Council Sanctions*, ¶ 14, (April 30, 2007) *available at*, http://www.un.org/apps/news/infocus/sgspeeches/search_full.asp?statID=81

VOA News, *North Korea Threatens to Retaliate Against UN Sanctions*, VOA News (July 26, 2009), *available at* http://www.voanews.com/english/archive/2009–07/2009–07–26-voa7.cfm?CFID=279305498&CFTOKEN=92164657&jsessionid=8830b223298a9324638333163d67a131f463

World Bank Sanctions Committee, *available at* http://web.worldbank.org/WBSITE/EXTERNAL/PROJECTS/PROCUREMENT/0,,contentMDK:50002288~pagePK:84271~piPK:84287~theSitePK:84266,00.html.

Index

Please note: page numbers in italics indicate figures and tables